Defeating the Japanese Zeros

Defeating the Japanese Zeros

Lieutenant Commander John S. 'Jimmie' Thach: One U.S. Navy Pilot and his Part in the Victory in the Pacific

R.J. Gorman

AIR WORLD

First published in Great Britain in 2025 by
Air World Books
An imprint of
Pen & Sword Books Ltd
Yorkshire - Philadelphia

ISBN: 978 1 03613 759 5

A CIP catalogue record for this book is available from the British Library

Typeset in INDIA by IMPEC eSolutions
Printed and bound in England by CPI Group (UK) Ltd, Croydon, CRO 4YY

The Publisher's authorised representative in the EU for product safety is Authorised Rep Compliance Ltd., Ground Floor, 71 Lower Baggot Street, Dublin D02 P593, Ireland.
www.arccompliance.com

For a complete list of Pen & Sword titles please contact:

PEN & SWORD BOOKS LTD
47 Church Street, Barnsley, South Yorkshire, S70 2AS, UK.
E-mail: enquiries@pen-and-sword.co.uk
Website: www.pen-and-sword.co.uk

or

PEN AND SWORD BOOKS,
1950 Lawrence Road, Havertown, PA 19083, USA
E-mail: Uspen-and-sword@casematepublishers.com
Website: www.penandswordbooks.com

MIX
Paper | Supporting responsible forestry
FSC® C013604

Contents

Preface

Six months after the devastating, surprise attack on Pearl Harbor, four of the six great aircraft carriers of Japan's *Kido Butai*, the 'Mobile Striking Force', returned to Hawaiian waters. This time their target was the strategic US base on tiny Midway atoll about 1,000 miles north of Honolulu. Their mission was to attack and occupy Midway and, hopefully, draw out and destroy the US aircraft carriers that had not been in port during Japan's initial surprise attack. After winning victories over the Americans and their British allies in the Philippines; Malaya; Singapore; Burma; the Java Sea, and Wake Island, the Japanese were now poised to wipe out the last important units that the US Navy had left in the Pacific. As the most powerful ships in the Imperial Japanese Navy (IJN) prepared to head towards Midway, one US Navy fighter squadron leader was diligently training his pilots to use a revolutionary new 'weaving' tactic that he had developed. Lieutenant Commander John S. 'Jimmie' Thach hoped that it would help offset the superior performance of the vaunted Japanese Zero fighter. Up until that time, the fabled Mitsubishi Zero had never been beaten in air-to-air combat. When first used against the Zero, Thach's tactical innovation proved a spectacular success. It allowed him and a handful of his pilots to do a lot more than just even up the odds. Either by sheer luck, or by the hand of fate, Thach and a few of his pilots were about to become the right men, at exactly the right place, during the most critical moments of a great battle. The stage was now set for a terrific, no-holds-barred fight over Midway. It would be the turning point of World War Two in the Pacific.

Introduction

On 4 June 1942, Lieutenant Commander John S. 'Jimmie' Thach led six Wildcat fighters escorting a squadron of twelve old, slow TBD Devastator torpedo planes against the four Japanese aircraft carriers that had attacked Midway. As Thach's pilots approached the enemy fleet, twenty high-performance Mitsubishi 'Zero' fighters came screaming down from above. The diving Zeros were faster than the stubby Wildcats, and they were engineered to be far lighter so they could accelerate much faster. They were also vastly more maneuverable than the heavier US planes. The Japanese opened fire on Lieutenant Edgar Bassett's Wildcat before any of the Americans spotted them. Thach saw Bassett's fighter burst into flames and drop down towards the sea. Ed Bassett was gone in seconds. Twenty more Zeros came diving in. They shot down all but two or three of the old, poorly designed, TBDs. The Devastator was the only front-line US warplane that lacked fire-retarding, self-sealing gas tanks. In seconds the sky filled with burning US torpedo planes. Two men likely burned to death inside each one before they crashed into the sea. At Midway, the Navy learned TBDs were unacceptably fragile. They often erupted into huge fireballs once they were hit by heavy machine gun fire. The Americans never used Devastators in combat again.

So right off the bat, Jimmie Thach failed in his primary mission of protecting the torpedo squadron. Desperate to find something that would work, Thach and his wingman, Ensign 'Ram' Dibb, began using a radical new tactic that Thach had been experimenting with since before Pearl Harbor. It was designed to defeat a faster, more maneuverable opponent. Thach and his wingman had already been flying widely spread out and on parallel headings. As a result, both pilots could see any attack coming in from behind the other, i.e., on his 'six'. Now when a Zero dove in to begin an attack, both of the US pilots immediately turned inward. They first flew directly at each other, and then swept past each other. Next, Thach and his wingman would reverse their turns. Their well-timed, almost choreographed turns literally forced a Zero pilot attacking one of the Americans from behind to fly directly under the other US pilot's guns, if only for a split second. And Thach had drilled his men relentlessly until they were all experts at making such quick, split-second shots. A terrific air-to-air shoot-out erupted, and it went on for an incredible fifteen long minutes – an eternity in aerial combat. Firing deadly accurate, short bursts, Thach shot down at least three of the deadly Zeros, possibly four or five. His wingman, Ensign Dibb, got one more.[1] Two other Wildcat pilots, Tom Cheek and Dan Sheedy, shot down at least one Zero apiece, and the few surviving gunners in the torpedo squadron somehow managed to knock down a Zero.[2] Nothing like these shocking losses had ever been inflicted on Zero pilots before. After Midway, this new, winning tactic was taught to thousands of US Navy and Marine Corps fighter pilots before they shipped out to the Pacific.[3] It is called the Thach Weave.

Suddenly, most of the remaining Zeros vanished. They must have been recalled to defend their carriers, but the recall order came too late. Far overhead, Thach glimpsed something flashing in the sunlight. Next, he saw a 'beautiful silver waterfall' as three squadrons of US Navy Dauntless dive bombers – nearly fifty planes – came hurtling down on the Japanese carriers, and now there were no Zeros in position to intercept them.[4] Dozens and dozens of top-notch, Navy dive bomber pilots were about to get an unimpeded, 'free shot' at many of the very same ships that had participated in the surprise attack on Pearl Harbor.

Astonishingly, after six months of bloody American defeat and against overwhelming odds, Jimmie Thach and his pilots had cleared the way for the most decisive dive-bombing attack of the Pacific War. After this day, Imperial Japan would never win another major battle, and the Americans would never lose one. So began the stunning six minutes that one writer has dubbed the 'Miracle at Midway'.[5]

Chapter 1

When War Came to Paradise

As every American high school student should know, on 7 December 1941, Imperial Japan launched a devastating surprise attack on the US Navy's base at Pearl Harbor in Hawaii. On what had been a quiet, peaceful Sunday morning on the beautiful tropical island of Oahu, hundreds of Japanese warplanes suddenly appeared overhead, apparently coming from out of nowhere. The Japanese attacked dozens of different installations all at once. They dropped bombs and launched torpedoes at the ships in Pearl Harbor. They machine gunned trucks, docks, warehouses, troop barracks, and anything that moved. They sank or damaged eight huge battleships; many other smaller vessels, and shot up hundreds of Navy, Marine Corps, and Army Air Corps planes. Many of the Army planes were easy targets – sitting ducks, lined up in nice, straight rows on the neatly trimmed grass that substituted for tarmac on nearby Wheeler Field. In one horrific morning, the Japanese killed over 2,400 Americans; virtually wiped out American airpower in the Hawaiian Islands, and crippled the US Pacific Fleet.

Of course, the Japanese warplanes did not simply appear out of thin air. They were launched from six immensely powerful, fleet aircraft carriers. In late 1941, Imperial Japan's big force of fleet aircraft carriers was by far the most powerful offensive naval fighting force that had ever put to sea. The Japanese caught the overconfident Admiral Husband Kimmel and the rest of the lackluster US military leadership at Pearl Harbor completely asleep at the switch. They scored what, at first, appeared to be a knock-out, sucker punch against the US Navy. Being caught totally by surprise at Pearl Harbor was clearly the greatest intelligence failure (up to that point) in American history, but things could have been worse. By sheer, dumb luck the Americans had many of their older battleships but none of their far more important aircraft carriers anchored in Pearl Harbor on that terrible Sunday morning. Not one US carrier received so much as a scratch during the otherwise highly successful surprise attack, because there were no US carriers there for the Japanese to strike. The incomprehensible failure of the Japanese to attack Pearl Harbor when the American carriers were in port, or to track the carriers down and attack them wherever they happened to be, ultimately led Japan straight to catastrophic defeat at the Battle of Midway.

During the six months immediately following Pearl Harbor, Japanese forces invaded the soon-to-be-independent Territory of the Philippines, and a host of European colonies throughout the Pacific and East Asia. The Imperial Navy's amazing Mitsubishi Zero fighter dominated the skies wherever it was deployed. The legendary Zero could accelerate very quickly due to its incredibly light weight, and it had an excellent top speed of roughly 340mph.[6] More importantly, the remarkable Zero was magically, opponents would say almost diabolically, agile. A good Zero pilot could easily outmaneuver any fighter that he encountered anywhere in the Indo-Pacific region during the first months of the war. In fighter pilot parlance, a Zero could always 'turn inside' any enemy plane that it faced. A Western pilot engaging in a traditional, World War One-style dogfight with the fabled Japanese fighter was almost asking to get shot down.

This is an account of the critical role that US Navy fighter ace Lieutenant Commander (later, four-star Admiral) John S. 'Jimmie' Thach, and a small handful of pilots from his squadron ('Fighting Three'), played in winning what has been called the 'incredible victory' at Midway. Thach and his pilots were clearly the right men; in the right place at *exactly* the right time. They shot down at least half a dozen Zero fighters, probably more, as three squadrons of US dive bombers approached the Japanese fleet. They completely disrupted the strong combat air patrol (CAP) of some forty Zeros defending the enemy carriers. The few remaining gunners in the shattered torpedo squadron that Thach had been trying to protect also managed to knock down one more Zero. All this cleared the way for the amazing dive-bombing attacks that began minutes later, wrecked the Japanese fleet and turned the tide of the war against the all-conquering Empire of Japan.[7]

Thach's victory was a very small one. So small, that it has usually been ignored. Still, it was the first time that the fabled Mitsubishi Zero had been beaten in combat.[8] Arguably, it was the precise moment when the Americans stopped losing, and began winning World War Two in the Pacific.[9] The popular media has never given Thach, or his pilots, much credit for the critical role that they played at Midway. They simply suggest that all the Zeros were out of position, down near the water, attacking the low-flying torpedo planes when the high-altitude dive bombers 'pushed over' into their dives. All the motion pictures and all but one of the dozens of books about the famous battle focus pretty much exclusively on these spectacular US dive-bombing strikes that destroyed the Japanese fleet.[10] So there has been little mention in the print or electronic media of the ferocious air-to-air combat between the Zeros and a handful of pilots from Fighting Three that took place just minutes before the remarkably successful dive bombing began.

The typical account of Midway only tells part of a much more exciting, but a bit more complicated story. Almost no writer has even tried to explain adequately how three squadrons of US dive bombers could get close enough to the most important vessels in the Imperial Japanese Navy to begin dropping bombs without a single shot having been fired at them.[11] Simply put, the Zeros certainly were out of position, but they were also getting the hell shot out of them by opposing enemy fighters for the very first time.

Admiral John Smith 'Jimmie' Thach has long been recognized and honored within the naval service as one of the leading innovators in US Navy aviation history. After Midway, Thach was promoted, and promoted again. As a captain, he served as Operations Officer for the dozens of carriers in the immense, Fast Carrier Task Force. In the last year of the war he came up with two ingenious tactics that helped defeat the horrific threat that *kamikaze* suicide pilots posed to the US fleet. Thach commanded the aircraft carrier *Sicily* that supported the First Marine Division during its epic breakout at the Chosin Reservoir during the Korean War. He led the charge in developing innovative ways to track submerged Soviet nuclear submarines during the 1950s. He became Deputy Chief of Naval Operations (for Air) in 1960. Later, Thach was promoted to four-star rank. He served as Commander-in-Chief of US Naval forces in Europe at the height of the Cold War. After he died, the Navy christened the guided missile frigate *Thach* (FFG-43) in his honor.

Still, only one fine, but twenty-year-old biography, of Jimmie Thach has ever been written, and it covers his entire, eventful, forty-year-long career.[12] No book focuses specifically on Thach's early days as a fighter pilot and his outstanding service to his country during World War Two. In the 1970s Admiral Thach's personal reminiscences about his fabulous career and the Pacific War were recorded and published by the US Naval Institute at Annapolis. His colorful oral history is one of the primary sources for this account, as is the official squadron report that he wrote a few days after the Battle of Midway. This report was apparently filed, or misfiled, with reports from the carrier *Hornet* after Fighting Three's ship, the *Yorktown*, was sunk. This may help explain why writers outside the naval service have never really appreciated the contribution that Thach and his men made to winning the great victory at Midway. In his reminiscences, Jimmie Thach describes in his own words the fierce air-to-air combat between Fighting Three and the Zeros at Midway; his work in Southern California producing animated training films with Walt Disney, and what it was really like being aboard an American aircraft carrier under threat of *kamikaze* suicide attack. Admiral Thach also gives us his personal, eyewitness account of the closing act of World War Two: Imperial Japan's formal surrender aboard USS *Missouri* in Tokyo Bay.

Mr Midshipman Thach at Annapolis and Flight Training at Pensacola

Midshipman John Thach was a tough-as-nails kid from Pine Bluff, Arkansas. He was lean, friendly, and easy-going, especially where academia was concerned. Thach spent far too much time on the Naval Academy's athletic fields and not nearly enough time in the library. He was a remarkable athlete; he could run like the wind. Thach stood 6ft tall but only weighed 135lb. Always the lightest man on the field, he still made second-string quarterback on one of the Navy's better football teams. His main role on the squad was to run practice plays over and over again against the first string. The plays were designed to replicate those used by powerhouse opponents like Michigan and Notre Dame. In the last year of World War Two, Thach almost reverted to his days as a practice team quarterback when he was the Operations Officer of the immense Fast Carrier Task Force. One of his responsibilities was to design tactics for the entire fleet to counter the threat from Japanese *kamikaze* suicide pilots. Thach routinely used football terminology in memos to explain his tactics to the captains of Task Force carriers. A dozen giant aircraft carriers and a thousand Navy pilots would rehearse Jimmie Thach's anti-*kamikaze* 'plays' over and over again, just like his second-string players had done back at the Naval Academy.[13] After a lot of fleet-wide 'practices' it became very unusual for a suicide pilot to get anywhere near an American aircraft carrier. Thach's bigger teammates on the Navy football team – and that was every man on the squad – cruelly nicknamed him 'little Jimmie'.

Thach really hated that, but the second half of his academy moniker stuck with him throughout his career. He eventually came to like it. Even Maddie, his good-looking, socialite wife, usually called him Jimmie.[14]

Midshipman Thach soon learned the hard way that his high school teachers back in Arkansas had probably been giving him better grades than he deserved because of his success in sports. Thach was sinking, academically speaking. Then he got lucky. Thach dislocated the same shoulder twice during football practice. The school doctor told him that he was through playing football; he had to find something else to do. So Jimmie Thach threw himself into his studies. He did manage to graduate from Annapolis, but he only ranked 494 in an Academy class of 579. Thach did not know it at the time, but class ranking can have a profound influence on a young naval officer's career. It can even affect such mundane things like who gets the best living quarters. His relatively poor academic performance at the Naval Academy plagued Jimmie Thach until his outstanding record of active duty success caught the eyes of commanding officers right up to the top of the chain of command.

In those long ago, pre-World War Two days, the Naval Academy actually graduated more new ensigns than the Navy's budget authorized. So Academy leadership went to considerable lengths to pare down the size of the graduating class, and math requirements were greatly expanded. Thach always suspected that they also tried to pare down the number of graduates in other, less straightforward, ways. Decades later, when he was a famous, retired admiral living in pricey Coronado, California, Thach was still irked about this. He complained that right in the middle of the Great Depression cash-strapped midshipmen, like himself, were required to purchase expensive new 'regulation' raincoats just to stay in school.

Immediately after graduating from Annapolis, Thach signed up for his mandatory two years of shipboard service. Ironically, the Navy assigned a future pioneering innovator of naval aviation to what had been the traditional pride of navies for centuries, battleships. The success of the Japanese attack on Pearl Harbor would soon render the old-time battleship nearly obsolete, except in the limited role of bombarding landing beaches. So Jimmie Thach spent his first two humdrum years of active duty learning communication skills aboard the World War One-era battlewagons USS *Mississippi* and *California*.

Ensign Thach then made a life-changing move when *Mississippi* docked in San Diego. He signed up for flight training. His first flight instructor had an odd, incredibly misleading nickname, 'Bubbles' Fisher. Whoever planted that nickname on Fisher had a wicked sense of humor. 'Bubbles' was bigger and tougher-looking than your typical pro-football linebacker. He was a mountain of muscle – a giant, King Kong kind of man with huge shoulders and a chest that almost busted out of his flight suit. He had big, powerful biceps, and strong, steel-hard forearms. Still, to Jimmie Thach, Lieutenant Fisher seemed to be the quiet, studious type of Navy officer – the kind of fellow you would expect to find reading up on nautical protocol, rather than slugging it out in a saloon with some half-drunk Marines. After giving Thach just five and a half hours of hands on flight instruction, Fisher swung down out of the cockpit with a grace and agility that seemed almost unnatural in such a big man. Then he told a shocked and nervous Jimmie Thach, 'Taxi out and take it around the field and land it.'[15] Fisher knew right away, that this wannabe naval aviator had the innate talent and quick reflexes to become an outstanding carrier pilot. Thach was a natural. Full of the jitters, Ensign Thach gingerly pushed the throttle forward; accelerated down the runway, and took off. He circled the field just once, and made a bumpy, but safe, landing. Fisher seemed satisfied. The Navy immediately ordered Thach to report for flight training at Pensacola, Florida.

'Bubbles' Fisher was something of a Navy legend. Although Thach saw Fisher as a quiet and introspective fellow, and maybe he was when he was on duty or teaching people how to fly, but after he had downed a few beers it was a different story. American sailors from Norfolk to Manila Bay admired the strapping 'Bubbles' as a heroic, larger-than-life figure. Fisher was renowned as a great, undefeated champion. He had beaten challenger after challenger in dozens of bar fights in every port where Navy ships dropped anchor. He was big, fierce, and tenacious in a brawl, and for a man his size, Fisher was lightning fast. He would slip punches that even experienced boxers could not avoid. Thach thought that Fisher looked a bit like a gorilla. He certainly had gorilla-like strength. Fisher was the kind of brawler who never stopped coming at his opponent. He always got up off the barroom floor no matter how badly his nose was broken and no matter how many times the other guy had knocked him down. Fisher's barroom challengers had to knock him cold in order to beat him, but nobody ever could.

A famous Navy legend about Fisher tells of him flying 10 or 15 miles off the Southern California coast and ditching in the water when his plane developed engine trouble.[16] Hours passed and the search planes did not find him, so Bubbles decided to swim for it. The next day he finally made it to the surf near La Jolla, practically comatose. Fisher lay flat on his back in the small breakers for over an hour. He was practically naked and covered with long strands of brownish green kelp, the giant seaweed that grows everywhere along the California coast. The sun had almost set and it was getting dark when Fisher finally got to his feet and trudged ashore. Panic! The few beachgoers still around ran for their lives. A horrible new kind of sea creature had emerged from the surf, and it was stalking the night-time beach! Then somebody called the cops. The police arrested Bubbles for disorderly conduct. The half-naked Fisher had a devil of a time convincing anybody that he really was a downed Navy pilot. After they let Fisher make his one phone call, an officer from Air Station North Island drove down with a dry uniform and picked up the worn out, totally exhausted Bubbles.

Thach and 'Bubbles' eventually became squadron mates and good buddies. Fisher never saw action in World War Two as he was killed before the attack on Pearl Harbor in a crash while practicing dive bombing off the Southern California coast.

***

Jimmie Thach arrived at the train station in Pensacola in near agony – with an extremely severe case of appendicitis.[17] Sharp abdominal pains had been shooting through his sore, swollen belly every minute of the long, bumpy, cross-country train ride from San Diego. Chronic abdominal pain was something that would plague Thach for the rest of his life. Although he was in horrendous pain throughout the trip, Thach had refused to stop and get treatment at a civilian hospital. An operation would cost too much money. He was a cash-strapped young ensign, and his parents back in Arkansas were experiencing severe financial problems. His dad had left a secure job as an elementary school principal and had gone into business for himself. Almost immediately, his dad's new business failed. So Ensign Thach just endured the burning pain and treated his tender belly with ice packs. Young and tough, he gutted out his pre-flight physical at Pensacola. He never even mentioned his terrible abdominal pain to the Navy doctors. Thach passed the physical with flying colors. Then he nonchalantly prepared to check himself into sick bay, where operations were free of charge. Luckily, after that his belly pain quickly subsided. However, somehow Thach's superiors at Pensacola got wind of what had happened. The air station's commanding officer viewed Thach's attitude about his physical condition as reckless and irresponsible. He almost kicked this future air admiral out of flight school before he even got started. Luckily, the C.O. changed his mind. By the end of his time at Pensacola Ensign John Thach had rocketed to the top of his class. Remarkably,

Thach finished number one in both flight (pilot) training and in ground (classroom) school.

The 'High Hat' Squadron and Hollywood

In the 1930s, most government leaders, including army generals, and the admirals who ran traditional navies built around the striking power of the battleship, had little appreciation for the tremendous oncoming promise of aviation. The development of powerful, long-range, warplanes like the Zero, Hellcat, and B-29 altered the face of warfare faster in the twentieth century, and just as dramatically, as the development of gunpowder did in the thirteenth. There were a few far-seeing visionaries like Admiral Moffett in Washington, and Isoroku Yamamoto in Tokyo, but most political and military leaders in the 1930s had no inkling of the revolutionary changes in the ways that wars are fought that were just a decade away. So when Jimmie Thach left Pensacola the opportunities for new naval aviators were pretty limited. Still, there were always a few choice spots open for those really gifted individuals who had graduated at the very top of their classes at Pensacola.

Ensign Thach decided that he wanted to be a fighter pilot. There was no better place to learn that particular trade than where he first ended up. Thach joined the elite pilots of 'Fighting One', officially Squadron VF-1, the Navy's original fighter squadron.[18] People christened them the 'High Hatters' because of the top hat insignia emblazoned on the sides of their planes. Navy legend recounts that the insignia originated when one of VF-1's first skippers landed on a carrier while wearing a top hat and tipping his fancy headgear to the American flag. When Jimmie Thach joined VF-1 it was officially a regular squadron assigned to the carrier *Saratoga* based in San Diego. Unofficially, it was very much like today's Blue Angels Navy display team. The High Hat pilots would put on spectacular flying exhibitions for the general public. Their most thrilling routine featured nine planes tethered together wing tip to wing tip with ropes. The ropes made their stunts look a lot more dangerous than they really were. The stunts were simply 'routine' close formation flying with a bit of fancy maneuvering thrown in to impress the audience. The very obvious visual aide of the ropes linking the wings together focused the crowd's attention on the great skill of the pilots. Nine daredevil pilots, including Thach, would push over into dives; soar up into loops, and perform all manner of knuckle-biting stunts. The crowds just loved it. At the same time an Army Lieutenant, James H. 'Jimmy' Doolittle, was putting on similar aerial exhibitions promoting the Army Air Corps.

The High Hat pilots were very popular in San Diego, close to being local celebrities. While he certainly was a 'dashing' fighter pilot, it would be a lie to say that Jimmie Thach was handsome. In fact, he was a pretty homely guy. Still, his intelligence, lively sense of humor and friendly country charm always made 'Jimmie' popular with the ladies. In San Diego, Jimmie Thach met his beautiful, curvaceous, socialite wife to be, Madalyn Jones or 'Maddie'.

The Navy 'lent' the carrier *Saratoga* to MGM Studios when it was shooting the movie *Helldivers of the Navy.* The Navy also lent Jimmie Thach and a few other top pilots to MGM to do stunt flying for the picture.[19] In one scene Thach 'accidentally' skids his plane into a violent ground loop. He was simulating an emergency, forced landing on a rocky beach. The apparent danger of the stunt really shook up the cameramen and the crew; especially the film's director, George Hill. Thach knew that his 'near accident' looked a lot more risky than it really was. Still, director Hill, notorious for shooting multiple takes of the same scene, uncharacteristically only shot one of Thach's forced landing.

Helldivers starred an up and coming young actor who became the biggest movie star of his generation, Clark Gable. To his credit, Gable asked Thach to show him what it was really like to dive in a fighter-bomber. Thach did just what Gable asked, diving almost vertically and stressing his plane's airframe to the limit. After Thach pulled out of the dive and landed, a dizzy, punch-drunk Gable crawled out of the plane's cockpit. Then the great film-star-to-be 'tossed his cookies' right in front of half a dozen bystanders. The other MGM actors, probably jealous of Gable's rising popularity, hooted and laughed. None of the hard-nosed Navy pilots standing around laughed at Gable. They had all been there before.

Test Pilot

After he had finished flying stunts for *Helldivers*, Thach's two-year tour of duty with the High Hat squadron came to an end. The Bureau of Navigation sent him to Norfolk, Virginia, as a test pilot.[20] After a whirlwind courtship, Thach married his pretty society girl, and Maddie and Jimmie packed up their car and headed east.

Amazingly, in those early days the established airplane manufacturers did not have to show the Navy that their newest models met even minimal specifications and safety standards. The test pilots would try to fly just about anything that the aircraft makers dragged through the door. Thach knew that flying some of these odd-looking contraptions would be dangerous. Of course, just being at test pilot itself is an inherently dangerous occupation. Some of the tested planes had unusual control systems that were not particularly user friendly. They did not automatically become 'second nature' for a pilot to operate in a tight spot – as all modern control systems are designed to be. A few were not easy for even the most experienced pilot to figure out. Still, Thach thought that this was a good system for sharpening his flying skills. He looked forward to flying many different kinds of airplanes, and thought it would be great fun.

Thach definitely did not think of his first flight as a test pilot as fun. It turned out to be a dangerous, stupid, practical joke that wrecked a plane and almost got him killed. Minutes after Thach first officially reported for duty at Norfolk, several other test pilots pulled him aside. They told him he was urgently needed to perform a 'hard landing' test on a new plane that had some bugs that needed to be worked out. The plane was then being flown by another test pilot named Ed 'Country' Moore. Edward Peerman Moore was as sharp as they come academically, and a first-rate pilot. But people often underestimated him because he was also a slow-talking, drawling, farm boy. As Thach looked up, Moore was overhead circling the field. He did seem to be having some trouble keeping the plane in straight and level flight, but Moore managed to glide down and land safely enough. Thach's new colleagues quickly ushered him into the cockpit. They told him to simulate the kind of hard landing one makes landing on an aircraft carrier. Some people describe it as a 'controlled crash'. Thach did glimpse what looked like a lopsided grin on Moore's face, but he did try to do what the other test pilots were asking. Like any competent pilot, Moore had already carefully inspected the plane's undercarriage, and suspected that it was poorly engineered and that it would never withstand even one hard landing. Country Moore and the boys were about to have some fun welcoming a newcomer to the realities of life as a test pilot.

Thach roared down the runway and took off. Next, he executed a tight turn near the end of the strip. It was painted to look just like the flight deck of an aircraft carrier. Thach came in for a hard, carrier-style landing. As Moore had guessed, the plane that Thach's new 'friends' had given him had not been engineered for such landings. When Thach touched down both of the main tires blew. Then the entire landing gear disintegrated into shards of sharp, broken steel. Metal fragments shot past the cockpit. When the crumpled pile of sheet metal that had once been his airplane skidded to a halt, Thach saw the other test pilots, including Country Moore, rolling on the grass. They were all laughing their heads off. Jimmie Thach had never cracked up an airplane before in his entire life. He silently fumed, but said nothing.

Those were simpler, more innocent times. Today, of course, Moore and his jokester friends would likely be court-martialed. Thach did not hold grudges. He and Country Moore eventually became squadron mates and pretty good friends. Admiral Thach never even mentioned the incident until long after Moore had retired.

The Aleutian Adventure and 'St Elmo's Fire'

When Thach finished his two-year stint as a test pilot he asked to be assigned to another fighter squadron. The Navy's leadership had other ideas. The top brass were already starting to think of Thach as someone who would be getting important commands a few years down the road. His superiors apparently wanted to give him a wide range of experience in all areas of naval aviation. That is how Thach ended up flying seaplanes on reconnaissance missions off the steaming tropical coast of Central America and then in the freezing ice storms of the Aleutian Islands.[21] Thach first joined Patrol Squadron Nine based in Panama. The Navy's number one priority south of the Mexican border was protecting the Panama Canal. President Teddy Roosevelt had built the canal and the US owned it until Jimmy Carter turned it over to Panama in the 1970s. The canal was the only practical way for the United States to quickly shift naval forces between the Atlantic and Pacific in the event of a 'two-ocean war' with both Germany and Japan. When Thach was well into his first tour of duty as a seaplane pilot, he received priority orders to immediately return to the United States. The Navy needed an experienced test pilot who was also familiar with seaplanes. The Bureau of Aeronautics ordered Thach to check out the long-range capabilities of an experimental amphibious bomber. The test flight would be a near-record, non-stop, twenty-five-hour flight from Virginia to the US base at Coco Solo in Panama. Then Thach was ordered to report back to his squadron for more regular patrol plane duty. The most difficult part of the test flight would be just staying awake while flying the new bomber all day and all night. Surprisingly, the irascible Admiral Ernest King, Chief of Naval Operations, *i.e.*, the leader of the Navy during World War Two, flew down from Washington D.C just to watch Jimmie Thach take off. This is one example of how the Navy's upper echelons were starting to show a close interest in Thach's many talents.[22] Uncharacteristically, the hard-nosed King patted Thach on the shoulder and told him not to take any 'unnecessary chances' during the long test flight. Ernie King was rarely known to give his officers such sympathetic advice. Thach completed the exhausting test flight and reported that the amphibious bomber was not rugged enough for use by the Navy.

When Thach returned to Panama, Squadron Nine had received orders to scout the frigid Aleutian Islands of Alaska. Geographically, and in terms of different weather, the Aleutians are about as far from Panama as you can get and still be on planet Earth. Thach and his colleagues wisely arrived in Alaska at the beginning of July. When they flew to the Aleutians they still ran into monumental seas and horrendous storms. The islands themselves are basically the peaks of high undersea mountains poking up above the surface of the Northern Pacific. Thach and the other pilots had equipped themselves with thick bearskin coats that kept them reasonably warm. Unfortunately, the bearskins stunk to high heaven when they got wet, and it always seemed to be raining in the Aleutians. So after a day or two the seaplane cockpits got pretty rank.

The squadron's maps and charts did not show the exact locations of the islands' shorelines. They just showed dotted-line 'approximations' of where the shorelines were thought to be. In the fogs and vicious currents of the Aleutians, the pilots needed to find the rocky beaches where they could securely anchor their seaplanes. The hair-raising technique that they adopted was to fly just feet above the sea while trying to spot breakers in the surf.

Squadron Nine's seaplanes fought the legendary 'williwaw' winds. Williwaws occur when cold, dense air rushes down from the high mountains to the coast at hurricane-force velocities. Thach flew into one vicious storm and hardly made any progress over the ground at all. Alaskan bush pilots routinely tell of flying into williwaws for half an hour or so; turning around, and being back where they started from in five minutes. Visibility was often zero. Temperatures were usually far below zero, and the wind never stopped howling. Native people working in the isolated salmon canneries along the coast warned the pilots that if they did not get out of the Aleutians by the end of August, they would probably be stuck there all winter.[23] Thach and his companions got out of Alaska just in time, and not one member of the squadron even caught a cold!

After returning to Panama, Thach transferred to Patrol Squadron Five based on the Pacific Coast. This led to the weirdest, most 'otherworldly' experience of Jimmie Thach's flying career. Consolidated Aircraft in San Diego had just built the first PBY Catalina patrol planes. Workhorse PBYs served throughout World War Two and played a pivotal role at the Battle of Midway searching for the Japanese fleet. Some late-model PBYs were still being used to drop retardant on California forest fires as late as the 1970s. Thach, his ten-man crew, and thirteen other aircrews, went to San Diego to pick up the new PBYs and planned to fly them back to Panama. Until they were off the Mexican Coast near Acapulco, Squadron Five followed the safe, traditional route used by the famed Manila Galleons of the old Spanish Empire. As night fell, Thach's squadron flew over the wild, storm-tossed waters of the Gulf of Tehuantepec. It is a strange corner of the Pacific, notorious for incredibly violent tornadic winds called *tehuanos*. These tremendous wind gusts funnel down into the Gulf from Chivela Pass high up in the sierras of southern Mexico. When it was pitch black, clouds engulfed Thach's plane. Visibility was zero. Then the rotational turbulence of what was apparently a tornadic super cell clamped its icy grip on the PBY. It was almost as rough as flying in the Aleutians. Dark columns of something strange started growing on the struts. The PBY was struggling; losing altitude.

A close look revealed that dangerous, lift-destroying black ice was rapidly forming on both wings. Giant lightning bolts blazed all across the dark sky. Thunder crashes rocked the airplane and shook every member of the crew. Then two powerful lightning bolts slammed directly into the plane's fuselage, causing the PBY's airframe to begin creaking. Sparks burned the radio operator's hands and charred his fingertips black. Fantastic, blue-violet balls of light materialized inside Jimmie Thach's plane. The fiery objects were about the size of baseballs.[24] One glowing fireball floated right up to the cockpit. Thach tried to swat it with his hand. He missed. The strange ball of light did not budge. The shimmering globe just hung in the air motionless. It seemed to be looking at him. Thach was plenty puzzled and plenty scared. What the hell were these crazy things? Then he remembered the old Navy tales about the blue lights called Saint Elmo's fire, a kind of ball lightning that sometimes appears right after multiple lightning strikes on ships at sea. Superstitious sailors have considered the lights of Saint Elmo's fire to be a good omen for centuries. Thach dropped the PBY down a few thousand feet into warmer air. The heavy ice fell off the PBY's wings. At dawn the *tehuanos* winds petered out and the great storm subsided. The strange blue lights dimmed and then faded away altogether. Squadron Five ran into another big thunderstorm off Nicaragua, but it was much less powerful than the first storm. Nothing odd happened. Squadron Five made it back to Panama in one piece.

The Navy then ordered Thach to join Fighting Three, the famed 'Felix the Cat' fighter squadron, in San Diego.[25] He was originally slated to become the squadron's new gunnery office, a job Thach would have relished. However, unexpectedly the squadron's commander had a heart attack while playing handball and died. Still only a lieutenant, Thach replaced him instead.[26] As old-timers would say, Thach had 'fleeted up'; he became Fighting Three's new skipper. Despite his mediocre academic record, Thach became the first member of his Annapolis class to command a fighter squadron. Soon Fighting Three was winning award after award for excellence, especially for excellence in aerial gunnery. Thach loved gunnery, and he had always scored 'expert'. Like his mom and dad, Jimmie Thach also loved to teach. He coached his men patiently until most of them were experts too. Shortly before the attack on Pearl Harbor, Fighting Three won the 'All Navy' gunnery championship. Jimmie Thach now commanded what was probably the finest fighter squadron in the Navy. To put icing on the cake, Butch O'Hare, who would become the most celebrated US fighter ace of World War Two, was about to join them.

Butch O'Hare Joins Fighting Squadron Three

Midshipman Edward 'Butch' O'Hare graduated from Annapolis ranked 255 in a class of 323.[27] So, in the sense that he was an indifferent scholar, O'Hare was very much like Jimmie Thach. Also, like Thach, O'Hare's father had taught him how to hunt upland game for dinner during family vacations. This early training obviously helped both men become two of the most outstanding aerial marksmen of the World War Two Navy. Both were masters of deflection shooting, the advanced form of aerial gunnery emphasized by the US Navy and by almost no other fighting service. Both men were natural teachers, and both really enjoyed training new pilots. Both were popular with the other members of their squadron, officers and enlisted men alike. Everybody who met them really liked Butch and Jimmie. So even though Jimmie Thach was O'Hare's commanding officer, they became close personal friends.

In many ways Thach was something of a wise older brother to O'Hare. Still, there were some big differences between them. Thach was thin, hawk-like, and homely. O'Hare was a well-built, bear of a man, and he had movie star good looks. He was the very epitome of the handsome, heroic fighter pilot. O'Hare's good looks, and those of Rita, his beautiful, blonde wife, certainly contributed to the Navy's publicity people sending the couple on a seemingly endless series of war bond drives after he won the Medal of Honor. O'Hare, generally speaking, was a likeable, easy going kind of guy. He was very camera shy. He hated the limelight and all the attention that he received after becoming a famous war hero. Thach was detail oriented and low-key, but an articulate, almost eloquent, public speaker.[28]

Still the biggest difference between Thach and O'Hare was in their family backgrounds. Thach was raised by two traditional, small town elementary school teachers. However, nobody, but nobody in the entire United States Navy had a family background quite as 'colorful' as Butch O'Hare. None of the following reflects on O'Hare personally. He was a normal, unassuming guy from the Midwest. O'Hare fully merited his war hero status and his immense popularity with the American people.

Butch O'Hare and his sisters, Marilyn and Patsy, grew up in the St Louis area. They loved and deeply respected their father, Edgar 'E.J.' O'Hare. 'E.J.' was a politically connected attorney; a successful dog track owner, and a business associate of gang leader Al Capone from Chicago. Characteristically, E.J. was known as 'Easy Eddie' to Capone and other Chicago mobsters. Butch's mom, Selma, moved out of the house and got a divorce when her husband became deeply involved in the rackets. E.J. was not greatly put out when Selma left him. Wealthy and good-looking himself, he had plenty of girlfriends. So Butch and his two sisters spent their formative years in an atmosphere heavy with the gambling industry and mob influence. E.J. sent Butch to an exclusive military school when he was in his teens. He also paid for Butch to take some very expensive and very effective, flying lessons. Butch finished military school and got an appointment to Annapolis. After graduating from the Naval Academy, he went straight on to flight training at Pensacola. E.J. O'Hare eventually turned on Al Capone. He handed over some of Capone's 'books' to federal investigators.

Capone went to prison for income tax evasion. Shortly before Capone was released, E.J. was murdered as he drove away from one of his dog tracks. It was a classic gangland-style 'hit'.[29] Two non-descript men driving a non-descript car shot E.J. twice in the back of the head with a shotgun. Obvious professionals, they drove away normally, never speeding or running a red light. The Navy had another pilot fly the deeply distraught Butch back home to St Louis for the funeral.

After completing flight training at Pensacola, O'Hare put in for assignment to a fighter squadron, and he got it! Butch O'Hare was going to San Diego to join Jimmie Thach's Fighting Three, the famous 'Felix the Cat' squadron. O'Hare and his two sisters packed their bags; left the Midwest permanently, and drove into the scenic desert southwest. They stopped in Arizona and really liked the area. Butch dropped both of his sisters off in Phoenix, where the whole family had decided to live. His sister, Marilyn, had a recurring cough and their doctor thought that Arizona's dry climate might help. Anyway, nobody wanted to stay in the Midwest where all the newspapers had sensationalized their father's gangland-style murder. Butch headed across Arizona's panoramic Sonoran Desert on his way to Southern California and his new squadron. At San Diego, Ensign O'Hare drove through the main gate at North Island Naval Air Station, and parked his brand-new Buick (the family always seemed to have plenty of money) right in front of Fighting Three's small waterfront hangars. There were the squadron's fighters with the famous 'Felix the Cat' insignia. Half the planes in the squadron also had 'E' for marksmanship excellence stenciled on their sides. Ensign Edward 'Butch' O'Hare knew that he was exactly where he wanted to be!

In the US Navy's training system the squadrons finished the final job of preparing new pilots for combat. Squadron veterans taught rookies some advanced but necessary skills, like how to actually hit fast-moving aerial targets with fixed machine guns. Jimmie Thach's use of what he called the 'humiliation team' was probably a big reason for his outstanding success in developing new fighter pilots.[30] The purpose of the team was not to humiliate anyone. It was simply to take overconfident rookie pilots down a peg or two. Newly minted fighter jocks tended to be extremely self-confident individuals. They had to be. Otherwise, they would have gone into a less hazardous line of work. They also tended to think that they had learned everything about flying that was worth knowing at flight school in Pensacola. Such highly self-confident young men could be difficult to teach. Thach also found that most rookie pilots were very poor shots. Jimmie Thach, his executive officer Don Lovelace, future ace Noel Gayler, and future Air Group Commander Rolla Lemmon, made up Fighting Three's 'humiliation team'.

Years ago, in his days with the High Hat squadron, Thach had learned some of the basic rules of flying fighters. One important rule is that, to a fighter pilot, an altitude advantage is like money in the bank. In encounters between pilots of equal ability; flying comparable planes, the pilot with the initial altitude advantage will almost always win. He will win unless he makes a serious mistake. The humiliation team veterans knew a lot more about aerial maneuvering than any of the newcomers. So in mock air battles, called Individual Battle Practice (IBP), the veteran would give the rookie whatever altitude advantage he wanted. Without exception the more experienced man would trick the overconfident rookie into making a 'fatal' mistake. He would then get on the rookie's tail, where he could easily shoot the new man down. Once in a good firing position the veteran would just stay there, riding the new man's tail. The desperate rookies would twist and turn trying to get away. They never could. Jimmie Thach would ostentatiously munch on an apple while showing the now-deflated rookies that they were not the 'hot shot' fighter jocks that they had thought they were. Any overconfident rookie pilot assigned to Fighting Squadron Three quickly discovered that he had a lot to learn.

The humiliation team ran like clockwork until Jimmie Thach ran into Butch O'Hare. Thach took O'Hare up for mock aerial combat.

As usual, he gave O'Hare the altitude advantage. O'Hare turned out to be unique. Thach threw every trick in the book at him, but O'Hare stayed right on Jimmie Thach's tail. He never made a mistake, like all the other rookies did. O'Hare could have shot his commanding officer down any time that he wanted to. Upon landing the mischievous Thach hurried straight to the other veterans on the humiliation team. He bragged about the wonderful new rookie pilot that he had 'discovered'. Lovelace, Lemmon and Gayler laughed and laughed, just as Thach had hoped they would. Then Thach laid some bets. He bet each of the experienced men that they could not handle his new protégé, rookie fighter pilot O'Hare. A smug Thach soon collected from all three. Ensign Edward 'Butch' O'Hare became the one and only rookie pilot to ever make it onto Thach's humiliation team.[31]

Chapter 2

Inventing the Zero Fighter

In 1853 when American Commodore Mathew Perry anchored his flagship in Edo (now Tokyo) Bay, Japan was a very unusual place. It was a 'Sokaku', a place of isolation, or as Westerners would say a, 'Hermit Kingdom'. It shunned contact with the outside world. Japanese society was like some kind of exotic creature afraid of the daylight; hiding away in its den. It had been this way for centuries. A series of military dictators, called shoguns, had usurped the traditional powers of the Japanese emperors. The later shoguns of the Tokugawa clan strove mightily to keep Japan isolated and free from any foreign influence, especially Christianity. Strict adherents to the warrior code of Bushido, the Tokugawas were literally appalled by such alien concepts as 'Love thy neighbor'. They severely limited trade with the outside world, and most foreign traders were restricted to tiny outposts, like the Portuguese on Dejima Island near Nagasaki. Japanese commoners were forbidden to visit other countries. Certain favored nobles, called daimyos, were allowed to trade with the Westerners. The daimyos and the Tokugawa clan became very, very wealthy. On the positive side, the shoguns did bring tranquility and order to a land that had been rocked by decades of local warfare and domestic strife. They punished anyone who violated their rules harshly. A wealthy and prosperous merchant class also arose during the peaceful Tokugawa era, but Japanese society generally became increasingly backward and rigid.

In 1868 supporters of the Imperial family staged a coup. They overthrew the last of the Tokugawa shoguns. The young, dynamic, and forward-looking Emperor Meiji came to power. He started what is now called the Meiji Restoration. Largely unnoticed in the West, Emperor Meiji began to transform feudal Japan rapidly into what has now become a modern, industrial nation. Japan advanced faster economically and grew much more powerful militarily than any other Asian country. At first, the Imperial Government sent young Japanese students to America and Europe to learn how modern, industrialized societies functioned. These students purchased all sorts of Western products, and sent them back to Japan, where they were disassembled, studied, and often copied exactly. After the Wright brothers flew the first airplane at Kitty Hawk, both the Imperial Navy and Army sent young officers to America and Europe. They learned how to fly. The Imperial Government also supplied these officers with the funds needed to purchase Western warplanes and ship them back to Japan. Surprisingly, the famed American aviation pioneer and partner of Orville Wright, Glenn Curtiss, opened up a winter flying school in Southern California. It was not far from what would become Jimmie Thach's home turf, Naval Air Station North Island in San Diego. Curtiss taught several of the visiting Japanese officers how to fly.

The first airplane flight flown over Japan itself was apparently made in 1912 by an Imperial Army Captain named Yoshitoshi Tokugawa. He piloted a biplane that he had purchased in France. Shortly thereafter, Tokugawa flew over metropolitan Tokyo taking pictures of the city to prove to Japan's military leaders the value of aerial reconnaissance.

Both France and Britain dispatched 'goodwill' missions to Japan to help improve Japanese military aviation! In light of subsequent events, sending these missions was at best very shortsighted. In 1919, France sent a team of experts under a Colonel Jean Faure to bolster aviation in the Japanese Army. In late 1921, Britain foolishly sent a team of thirty hand-picked experts under Baron Sempill, a former RAF officer.[32] Sempill helped Japan kick-start its naval aviation program. Only the British Admiralty objected to the obvious danger of the Sempill mission. The British Government vastly underestimated, or more likely, never even seriously considered, the ominous potential threat that a modern, militarized Japan might pose to Hong Kong, Singapore, Malaya and other British interests in the Far East. The Sempill delegation remained in Japan for a year. It provided the Imperial Navy with virtually unlimited access to British aviation technology. The British and French apparently believed that Japan was such a backward country that it could never produce home-grown warplanes that would outclass their own. In less than two decades industrial powerhouses like Mitsubishi and Nakajima (today, Subaru) proved them both to be sadly mistaken.

On the morning of 6 October 1937, Jiro Horikoshi, the Chief Design Engineer of Mitsubishi Heavy Industries, walked into his aeronautical design department. Several engineers stood around, apparently in a heated discussion with their supervisor, a Mr Hattori. Hattori handed Horikoshi some papers. The papers were the cause of the commotion. They were the Imperial Navy's proposed specifications for a new carrier fighter. The new plane was temporarily dubbed 'Prototype 12'.[33] It would become the legendary Zero. At first, Horikoshi was dismayed by what the proposed specifications required. He secretly thought that they must be some crazy admiral's ultimate wish list. The specs described a carrier-based fighter that was far more advanced than any other plane then in service anywhere in the world. The Imperial Navy wanted an escort fighter with dogfighting performance superior to all potential opponents. 'Prototype 12' also had to be a great interceptor, capable of destroying incoming enemy bombers. Horikoshi knew that these two requirements described very different kinds of aircraft with very different characteristics. An escort fighter needs to have very long range and the speed and maneuverability to defeat enemy fighters. A great interceptor has to have a terrific climb rate and the heavy guns needed to knock down incoming bombers. The proposed specifications also included a long list of many other cutting edge requirements. Some seemed mutually exclusive. For example, 'Prototype 12' was supposed to carry very heavy direction-finding equipment, but still have a longer range than all other fighter aircraft then in service.

Horikoshi privately believed that building such an advanced, multi-role fighter was next to impossible given the technology of the day. He also feared that such a daunting task was beyond his personal capabilities. Then he sat down at his desk and addressed the problem. Horikoshi's incredible work designing the Zero fighter would prove him the equal of the greatest aeronautical engineers in aviation history, men like the Leroy Grumman, Kelly Johnson and Werner von Braun.[34] To meet the Imperial Navy's new specifications, Horikoshi's only option was to carefully engineer every individual part in the new plane. Even the smallest rivet would have to be strong, but also extremely light. Every part needed to be just strong enough to withstand the stresses of high-speed maneuvering and hard carrier landings, but not one bit stronger. There could be no margin for error. The new fighter would either be the finest one that ever took off from a flight deck, or it would be too fragile for service aboard an aircraft carrier.

Many Japanese today rightly look on Jiro Horikoshi as a leading pioneer in their country's quest for industrial excellence. Jiro had spent most of his childhood dreaming about flying and building futuristic aircraft. Oddly enough, he was born in 1903, the year of the Wright Brothers' first flight at Kitty Hawk. Horikoshi was deeply in love, almost obsessed, with every aspect of aviation. After visiting a Japanese Navy base and riding along on a demonstration flight, Horikoshi knew that he had found his life's work. He would design world-class aircraft for the Imperial Navy. Horikoshi graduated from Tokyo University's new aeronautical science program, and immediately went to work for Mitsubishi Heavy Industries. Mitsubishi was one of Japan's two big aircraft manufacturers. A top man in his field, Horikoshi was a welcome guest at aircraft manufacturing facilities in countries all over the world, including Europe and the United States.

Under Horikoshi's magical drafting pen 'Prototype 12' slowly began to morph into a widely feared, incredibly maneuverable, and apparently invincible fighter. The Imperial Navy christened the type Zero because it first accepted it for service in 1940, the year 2600 in Japan's traditional calendar. In its early days the Zero easily triumphed wherever it was deployed, first in China against the Nationalist Chinese. The Japanese invasion of China is officially known as the Second Sino-Japanese War. The small Chinese Nationalist Air Force flew a mixed bag of Soviet aircraft, including front-line fighters and outmoded biplanes. A classic example of just how overmatched the Nationalist Air Force was comes from the great Japanese fighter ace, Saburo Sakai. Sakai tells of his first pathetic kill in a Zero. He shot down a brightly colored but doomed Chinese biplane. It was something that you might have expected to find the Red Baron flying over the trenches of France in 1917. The biplane's pilot desperately maneuvered to get away, but he never had a chance. Sakai knocked him down after a wild chase.

Japanese fighters (Navy Zeros and Army Oscars) easily brushed aside the Chinese Air Force. Then Japanese bombers and ground troops mercilessly attacked Chinese cities.[35] It was murder on a vast scale, with the Japanese killing untold numbers of helpless civilians. The 'Rape of Nanking' was one of the most terrible bloodbaths of the bloody twentieth century. Accurate numbers are hard to come by, but the present-day Chinese Communist Party says that between 1937 and 1945 the Japanese invaders killed about 30 million Chinese. The actual number is probably lower, but it is still unimaginably horrific.

The most serious aerial opposition that the Japanese ever faced in China came from the American Volunteer Group (AVG), the 'Flying Tigers'. They were a group of about a hundred US Army Air Corps, Navy and Marine pilots that General Claire Chennault had recruited as volunteers to help the Chinese fight the Japanese invasion of their homeland. Later in the war, the AVG became part of the US Fourteenth Air Force, and most of the volunteers returned to their original branches in the US armed services. Defending cities and airfields deep in the interior of China gave Chennault one great advantage that nobody else then fighting the Japanese had: a peasant-based 'early warning system'. The Americans had distributed two-way radios to friendly Chinese throughout the Chinese hinterland. Hundreds of Chinese peasants risked capture, torture and the most gruesome kind of death to spot and report on Japanese aerial activity to the Americans. They told Chennault where and when Japanese planes were about to attack. Chennault's Chinese observers did not need to identify the specific types of Japanese planes they saw. They were just told to report the number observed, and their direction of travel. Once warned, the Flying Tigers would do the rest.

The Imperial Army used a fine fighter, the Nakajima Ki-47 Oscar. It was nearly a clone of the Zero, and to a casual observer the two planes looked almost identical. They both used similar Sakae engines, and they were both highly maneuverable. In fact, American pilots sometimes referred to the Oscar as the 'Army Zero'. Surprisingly, the larger, heavier Zero was still a bit faster.[36] Simply put, the Oscar was not a true Mitsubishi Zero.

Chennault quickly realized that getting into a traditional 'turning' dogfight with any of the highly maneuverable Japanese fighters was a losing proposition. Alerted by his peasant-based early warning system, Chennault would scramble his P-40 fighters to high altitude when the attacking Japanese planes were still about 50 miles away from the suspected target. It was usually a Chinese city or a Nationalist airfield. The Americans would typically dive on and shoot up incoming Japanese formations. Then they would use the momentum from their dives to pull up and out of range.

The Tigers were very successful. Twenty-two of them became fighter 'aces' with five or more documented kills. Navy pilot Robert Neale was the AVG's top ace with thirteen victories. David Lee 'Tex'

Hill was also a leading ace, credited with twelve and a quarter kills with the Tigers and six more after he returned to the US Army Air Corps. Medal of Honor winner Greg 'Pappy' Boyington was officially credited with shooting down two Japanese planes while he was with the AVG. Boyington returned to the Marine Corps and shot down an incredible twenty-six enemy aircraft when he commanded the famed 'Black Sheep' squadron in the Solomon Islands. The AVG probably would have defeated any enemy they faced; they were terrific fighter pilots. Unfortunately, the Flying Tigers almost certainly never actually went up against the true Mitsubishi A6M Zero.[37] The Flying Tigers did not deploy to China until after the attack on Pearl Harbor. In late 1941, the Imperial Navy had already withdrawn its Zeros from China in order to prepare for all-out war in the Pacific against the United States.

Inventing the 'Thach Weave'

The big Officers' Club at the main Navy base in San Diego is easily the grandest saloon on the West Coast. Maybe it's the finest watering hole in the entire country. The highly polished mahogany bar seems like it's half the length of a football field, and there are about two hundred tables scattered around with plush red leather cushions on the chairs. They say you can order any wine, beer or whiskey from anywhere in the world. Of course, Bourbon on the rocks and an ice-cold beer are still the two most popular drinks among the ensigns, captains, and even admirals who frequent the place.

In the spring of 1941 Jimmie Thach was reading an intelligence report that really caught his eye. It described a new Japanese fighter that had just been deployed in China. The plane had a terrific climb rate and was incredibly maneuverable. If the report was accurate, the Japanese had built a fighter that was faster and clearly superior to anything in the US Navy's arsenal.[38] In the months before the attack on Pearl Harbor, US intelligence analysts summarily dismissed such reports as wild exaggerations. The 'experts' grossly underrated the intelligence and work ethic of the Japanese people. They thought of Japan as a semi-feudal, partially industrialized country. They thought that the Japanese could not possibly have the kind of scientific and engineering know-how needed to build such an advanced aircraft. Thach completely disagreed with all the so-called experts in intelligence. He had the distinct impression that the report he saw had been written by an experienced military pilot. He surmised that the author had actually seen the plane in action. The report Thach saw turned out to be right on the money. The fighter in question was, of course, the Mitsubishi Zero.

It is the source of the information in the report that remains a bit of a mystery to this day. If the report did originate with a military pilot, it almost certainly came from one of two likely observers. Both men were American military pilots, and both had considerable experience in the Far East. Thach's information may have come from General Claire Chennault, the leader of the Flying Tigers. No less an authority than Jiro Horikoshi, the primary designer of the Zero, attested to the accuracy of Chennault's reporting. General Chennault's long-time associate and biographer, Jack Sampson, believed that Chennault had turned over information on early models of the Zero and the Oscar to Army intelligence, but, somehow, his full dossier on Japanese fighters never made it to the front-line squadrons.[39] So the intelligence report that Thach saw may have originated with Claire Chennault, but that seems unlikely.

The second, very likely source of the Thach's information, was the US assistant Naval Attaché in Tokyo. He was an officer whose contribution to the war effort is almost completely unknown outside of the US Navy. Stephen Jurika was the son of a wealthy American family that owned a plantation in the Philippines.[40] He spent much of his youth knocking around China, Japan, and other parts of East Asia. Jurika could speak four different Asian languages, and he was a serious student of Far Eastern culture. He would teach some of

Jimmy Doolittle's pilots simple Chinese words and phrases before they embarked on the famous raid over Tokyo. After growing up in Asia, Jurika came home to the US and got an appointment to the Naval Academy. After he graduated from Annapolis he took flight training at Pensacola, and then spent the next three years flying various types of aircraft off of carriers. In 1939, someone in the State Department had great foresight to get him appointed as the assistant naval attaché in Japan. So the first American naval attaché with a strong aviation background was posted to Japan at just the right moment in history.

Assistant Attaché Jurika simply lucked out one day and scored a magnificent intelligence coup. On a routine visit to a Japanese air show none of the usual 'minders' from the *Kempeitai* secret police seemed to be following him. The air show was probably the one put on annually in connection with Japan's Army-Navy aircraft competition. In 1941, it was held in January at what is now Haneda International Airport. Zero fighters dominated the event. Other Zeros were parked nearby. Surprisingly, they had been put on public display with no guards nearby. Any ordinary Japanese citizen could just walk right up to one of the Zeros and touch it if they wanted to. So Jurika took a huge chance. He boldly climbed into the cockpit of one of the parked Japanese fighters, and jotted down what he saw. One has to wonder if Jurika's diplomatic immunity would have meant anything to the secret police if they had caught him inside that cockpit. Amazingly, there was a placard on the instrument panel that listed all the fighter's stunning specifications. Alarmed by what he had discovered, assistant Attaché Jurika immediately fired off a warning dispatch to the Office of Naval Intelligence (ONI) in Washington. Jurika waited months and months for a reply. When he got a response it was irresponsible; totally unprofessional, and just plain dumb. US Naval intelligence analysts had decided that Jurika's alleged specifications for the Zero had to be gross exaggerations because no American fighter's specs could match the speed and climb rate claimed for the Zero! ONI had committed the cardinal sin for any intelligence agency: it had seriously underestimated the capabilities of a potential enemy. Army intelligence was apparently just as incompetent. No wonder the attack on Pearl Harbor came as such a big surprise.

Wherever Thach's information came from, he discussed it with pilots in his squadron. Future 'ace' Noel Gayler really liked the way that Thach used a blackboard to draw formations of planes and explain the reasons for the tactics that he wanted them to practice. Gayler thought that Thach taught just like a head football coach diagramming new plays for his players.[41] Thach told his pilots that he thought that the Zero's climb rate and high speed were its biggest advantages. There were ways that they could deal with a more maneuverable opponent. Like ONI, some of the pilots in his squadron thought that the intelligence on the Zero was probably exaggerated. There was certainly some reason for the skeptics' point of view in 1941. Japan's industrial infrastructure in those days was a crazy-quilt jigsaw combination of the very advanced, the contemporary, and some almost medieval components. The Zero fighter itself is the classic example of this startling unevenness. No one doubts that the Zero's designer, Jiro Horikoshi, was a world-class aeronautical engineer. No one doubts that the carrier fighter that he designed was also world class. In fact, it was probably the best fighter aircraft in the world in 1941. The Zero was certainly superior to the US Navy's Grumman Wildcats and Brewster Buffalos. Nevertheless, the Mitsubishi Corporation hired a company that used oxcarts to transport the first Zero prototype to Kagamigahara Airfield for flight testing.[42]

Despite the complacency of the skeptics in the intelligence community, Thach immediately got to work trying to find a solution to what he saw as the 'Zero vs Wildcat' problem. Thach and his wife, Maddie, then lived in a small rental cottage near San Diego's North Island Naval Air Station. Every night after dinner Thach broke out a box of wooden matches, and arranged them on their kitchen table. Each match represented a fighter plane. Thach arranged his matchstick fighters into various 'formations'. He hoped to find a way to give a slower, poorer-climbing plane, like the Wildcat, a real chance to defeat a faster, more nimble opponent. He never assumed that the Zero was superior to the Wildcat in all respects. An aerial gunnery expert himself, Thach thought that well-trained American pilots would be better marksmen than the Japanese. Wildcats carried powerful Browning M2 50-caliber machine guns. They could destroy a Zero with a single burst. This weapon is so outstanding that it is still being used with only minor modifications by US ground troops today. The Zero carried two powerful 20mm cannon and two 7.7mm light machine guns, but the big cannons had ridiculously small magazines. So Japanese pilots would fire their cannon sparingly or they would quickly find themselves out of ammo. As the war went on the Americans hardened their already stoutly built fighters. For example, the Grumman F6F Hellcat was not only much faster than the Wildcat, it also carried much more pilot protective armor. A Zero pilot firing just his light machine guns often had to hit one of the later American fighters many times in order to bring it down. Japanese fighter pilots were 'offense minded' to a startling degree. Many Zero pilots opposed adding armor or self-sealing fuel tanks to their planes. They feared that the added weight would only reduce their fighters' fantastic maneuverability.

The US Navy also placed great emphasis on deflection shooting. A well-trained naval aviator was expected to be able hit aerial targets from all sorts of angles, and not just get on an opponent's tail for a direct shot from behind the enemy plane. Deflection shooting is a bit akin to a quarterback throwing a pass to a receiver running from the sidelines towards the center of a football field. The quarterback must 'lead' the receiver. He aims for the spot on the field where the receiver will be when the football actually arrives. The analogy breaks down because the receiver wants to be hit by the ball. He will speed up if the quarterback throws the ball too far in front of him. He will slow down if it is thrown short. A skeet shooter trying to hit a clay target crossing in front of him also learns to lead his target. Deflection shooting from fighter aircraft is analogous to skeet shooting in theory but far more difficult in practice. For one thing, the skeet shooter stands still. In air-to-air combat both targets and shooters are probably moving in different directions at a couple of hundred miles per hour. No World War Two air force emphasized the importance of deflection shooting as much as the US Navy. Pilots firing from 60 to 90 degrees to the side of a target were trying a difficult 'full-deflection' shot. A pilot trying to hit an opponent at 30 degrees had an easier problem. A fighter pilot right on his adversary's tail (what most tried for) had a straightforward 'no-deflection' shot. Major Greg 'Pappy' Boyington, the commander of the famous Marine 'Black Sheep' squadron had no faith in deflection shooting. Boyington, a Medal of Honor winner, always tried for a no-deflection shot. However, when Thach addressed the challenge posed by the Zero he assumed that most US Navy pilots were competent deflection shots. All the experienced pilots in Fighting Squadron Three were certainly far better than just competent. They were outstanding marksmen.

Early in his 'matchstick research' Thach jettisoned the Navy's basic three-plane combat formation. It consisted of a section leader and two wingmen. In this basic set up one wingman flew on each side of the section leader's plane. Thach thought this was far too complicated for combat. When the section leader made the sudden, violent maneuvers that combat required, his two wingmen would have their hands full. Much of their attention would be focused on just avoiding colliding with each other. A simple two-plane section of one leader and one wingman solved that problem. Other Navy squadron commanders were also beginning to doubt the wisdom of the three-plane section, but Thach's ideas were groundbreaking at the time. The British, German and Japanese air forces all flew three-plane sections at the time.

Thach reworked his tabletop formations night after night. He tried a two-plane formation with both the leader and wingman flying close to and parallel with each other. This did not help much. The wingman had little room to maneuver to protect the leader from an attack coming in from behind. In fact, flying close together almost made matters worse. It gave an enemy pilot what amounted to one big target to shoot at. Then Thach tried spreading out his matchstick fighters. He immediately saw that when two Wildcats flew parallel to each other but spread farther apart things got much better. Each pilot would have an excellent view of any plane attacking the other American from above or behind. If both US planes were separated by the right distance one pilot could turn and shoot down a fighter attacking the other. He would turn towards his partner – who would be turning towards him – and usually have a difficult, but makeable, split-second shot at the incoming enemy plane.

The 'right distance' separating the US fighters varied with the speed that they were flying at. Pilots got a pretty good feel for how far apart they needed to fly after they had practiced Thach's maneuver a couple of times.[43] The optimum separation in theoretical terms seemed to be approximately half the diameter that a fighter needed to make a complete, 180-degree turn. This is called a plane's turn radius.[44] However, as Thach said, when pilots were preparing for actual combat this was something that they needed to work out and get a feel for by repeated practice. Thach's proposed new tactic worked this way: Two Wildcats would fly spread out and parallel to each other. Each pilot could easily see what was happening above and behind the other. When one pilot, say the 'leader', saw that his wingman was about to be attacked he would instantly turn towards the wingman. The leader's turn immediately alerted the wingman that he was under attack. The wingman would then turn towards the leader. Both Americans were now 'weaving'. They flew almost directly at each other. This maneuver did two things at once. It gave the leader a difficult but manageable shot at the attacking Zero. It also gave the wingman instant warning that an enemy fighter was behind him. So he had an excellent chance of quickly getting out of the line of fire. No precious seconds were wasted calling out warnings over the radio. The Americans would often weave back and forth continuously. That seemed to confuse the Japanese even more. During the great aerial shootout over the Japanese fleet at Midway, Thach and his wingman, Ram Dibb, weaved almost continuously for about fifteen minutes. This constant weaving by a pair of American fighters is what the top-scoring Japanese fighter ace Saburo Sakai called the 'famous' US 'double team'.[45] Thach's idea seemed workable as long as the Americans flew in small formations that were multiples of two. They could fly in two-plane 'sections' or four-plane 'divisions'.

Thach thought that he may have solved the 'Zero vs Wildcat' problem. It was a way to virtually force Japanese pilots to make their attacks under waiting American guns. Thach put his matches away and got his first full night's sleep in months. Thach originally called his new tactical set-up the 'beam defense' position. Lieutenant Commander Jimmie Flatley, the *Enterprise* fighter ace, later christened it the 'Thach Weave'. That is the name that it has been known by ever since.

Fighting 'pretend air battles' with matches on his kitchen table was one thing. Thach still had to convince himself that his brainchild would actually work in the air. There was only one way to find that out. To really test out his new ideas Thach got hold of the best fighter pilot that he knew, Butch O'Hare. Thach explained his new tactics to O'Hare and to six other Fighting Three pilots. Thach had O'Hare take off leading three Wildcats. They would pretend to be Zeros. Then Thach and three more Wildcats took off. They would use his new tactics. Thach simulated the performance advantage of the Zero by marking lines on his group's throttles. His pilots would not use more than half power. O'Hare and his pilots could use any throttle setting that they wanted. Time after time O'Hare and his men maneuvered their 'Zeros' into position to shoot at Thach's 'Wildcats'. Time after time they found themselves looking down the barrels of 'enemy' machine guns. When he landed Butch O'Hare was ecstatic. He yelled, 'Skipper, it really worked. It really works. I couldn't make any attack without seeing the nose of one of your half-throttle airplanes pointed at me!'[46]

Chapter 3

Pearl Harbor: The Shock Felt Around the World

On 21 November 1941, six large aircraft carriers and their support ships quietly slipped unnoticed out of the icy waters of Hitokappu Bay in the remote Kurile Islands. The Imperial Japanese Navy's *Kido Butai* was finally at sea after months and months of monotonous training exercises. Admiral Chuichi Nagumo commanded the big carriers. Nagumo was one of the most experienced officers in the Imperial Navy but, oddly enough, he had no aviation background at all. The Striking Force was the largest collection of aircraft carriers, and by far the most powerful naval force, that the world had yet seen.

Once the carriers were out at sea, all of the pilots and crewmen were fully briefed. Everyone now understood the reason for all that monotonous training. Everyone aboard was jubilant! They were finally on their way to bloody a lot of pompous American noses! They were about to repay the arrogant Americans for all the insults and indignities that despicable US politicians, like President Franklin D. Roosevelt, had been heaping upon their dear Land of the Rising Sun and its divine Emperor. Some of the torpedo plane crews had probably suspected what was going on months ago. They had been practicing launching specially modified shallow-running torpedoes into the waters of Lake Ogawara since late summer. The US Pacific Fleet had recently moved its base from California to Pearl Harbor, and Pearl Harbor was a very shallow anchorage. Now the torpedo crews knew for certain that there was a connection. The Japanese fleet secretly crossed the cold, fog-shrouded wastes of the Northern Pacific. Nobody detected them. Huge waves continuously pummeled the big ships. Mountainous seas tossed the giant carriers around like little rubber life rafts. When the Japanese reached the latitude just east of Hawaii they cranked up their engines to full speed. Then the *Kido Butai* turned south. Six powerful aircraft carriers were now charging directly at the Hawaiian Islands. They headed straight for the US Pacific Fleet's new base at Pearl Harbor.

The *Kido Butai* struck the Americans with enormous, overwhelming force. The concentrated firepower of over 350 Val dive bombers, Kate torpedo planes, and Zero fighters blasted ships, airfields, and anything that moved. The Japanese took the Americans by complete surprise. They were extremely lucky to do so. The American military leaders in Hawaii were shockingly complacent; overconfident, and totally asleep at the switch. They were simply not prepared for the revolutionary kind of carrier warfare that the Japanese unleashed on their ships that terrible Sunday morning. Admiral Nagumo commanded the Japanese carriers, but Admiral Isoroku Yamamoto back in Japan was the mastermind behind the whole operation. Yamamoto commanded the Combined Fleet, the operational, war-fighting, arm of the Imperial Japanese Navy. Admiral Husband Kimmel and General Walter Short were the US commanders at Pearl Harbor. They had been specifically warned that Japan was about to open hostilities somewhere in the Pacific. In fact, they had several warnings that should have alerted any competent leader to the possibility of an imminent attack. Ten days before the Japanese struck the Navy Department in Washington sent Kimmel the following stark message:

> This dispatch is to be considered a war warning. Negotiations with Japan looking toward stabilizing the conditions in the Pacific have ceased and an aggressive move by Japan is expected within the next few days. The number and equipment of Japanese troops and the organization of the naval task forces indicates an amphibious expedition against the Philippines, Thai or Kra

> Peninsula or possibly Borneo. Execute an appropriate defensive deployment preparatory to carrying out the tasks assigned in WPL 46 [the Navy's basic war plan]. Inform district and army authorities. A similar warning is being sent by the War Department.[47]

That even a semi-competent commander could get such a stark warning and still be surprised by an enemy attack less than two weeks later is literally beyond belief. Simply put, if Admiral Kimmel had been a member of Britain's Royal Navy during Nelson's time, he would surely have soon found himself court-martialed, and dangling by the neck at the end of a very uncomfortable rope.

Still, the warnings kept getting louder and louder right up to the last minute. Over an hour before the first Japanese bombs started falling on the Pacific Fleet, the American destroyer *Ward* detected a strange submarine in the restricted zone just outside of Pearl Harbor. The sub was apparently trying to sneak through the entrance of the harbor. The *Ward* immediately opened fire and dropped depth charges on the submarine. Lieutenant William Outerbridge, the *Ward*'s skipper, promptly radioed in a report of the incident. Amazingly, the hapless Admiral Kimmel dismissed the *Ward*'s report as a probable false alarm – because he had gotten several false reports in the last few days! Kimmel never even lifted a finger to warn the thousands of sailors under his command of a potential attack. Well over two thousand of Kimmel's men would die and much of the Pacific Fleet would be sunk in the next couple of hours. Lieutenant Outerbridge's report was not a false alarm. The *Ward* had just sunk a Japanese midget submarine trying to sneak into Pearl Harbor. President Roosevelt fired Kimmel ten days later. He was eventually reduced in rank for dereliction of duty. Admiral Chester Nimitz, a brilliant strategist, would become Kimmel's permanent replacement.

The most well known of the 'last-minute Pearl Harbor warnings' involved two Army privates, Joe Lockhard and George Elliot.[48] That morning they were operating a mobile radar truck on the beautiful North Shore of Oahu. Their watch had started at 0400 and was scheduled to end at 0700. Just as they were about to call it quits, their blank radar screen sparkled to life. It was showing the strongest contact that either man had ever seen. The screen was so bright that Lockhard thought that their equipment was malfunctioning. The screen appeared to be showing more than fifty planes coming straight at them. The planes seemed to be about 130 miles north of Oahu. Elliot insisted that they call in and report a 'possible' contact, even if they were just having an equipment problem. They called headquarters and spoke with a Lieutenant Tyler. He was the assistant controller and pursuit (fighter) officer that morning. It was Tyler's second day on the job. More experienced people had already gone off duty. After all, it was Sunday morning. Nobody could tell if the contacts on the radar screen were 'friendlies' or not. Nobody could tell if they were real aircraft or just an equipment malfunction. Lieutenant Tyler eventually decided that the radar had detected a flight of US B-17 bombers scheduled to fly in from the West Coast that morning. Like Admiral Kimmel, Tyler did nothing. He told Lockhard and Elliot to shut down their radar. The Japanese bombers, for that is what the radar was showing, were now 75 miles north of Oahu. Private Elliot insisted on tracking them until he lost the contact in the mountains of the island.

Thirty minutes later Commander Mitsuo Fuchida, the Japanese air group leader, flew around Barbers Point at the entrance to Pearl Harbor. A jubilant Fuchida was already radioing the flagship *Akagi*. Almost incredibly, the Japanese had caught the Americans by complete surprise. Due to favorable atmospheric conditions, Fuchida's coded broadcast '*Tora, Tora, Tora*' ('*Tiger, Tiger, Tiger*') was heard all the way back in Japan by a delighted Admiral Yamamoto.[49]

All twenty-one sailors from USS *Arizona*'s band were aboard ship that Sunday morning as two squadrons of Japanese planes closed in. The previous evening they had attended a 'battle of the bands' competition in Honolulu. Many had received invitations to spend the night ashore in friends' apartments. None of the invitations were accepted as all the bandsmen had to be on deck the next morning to salute the colors. The versatile Nakajima Type 97'Kate torpedo bombers that attacked *Arizona* that morning were from the aircraft carriers *Hiryu* and *Kaga.* They dropped ten 800kg armor-piercing bombs. The bombs were actually huge, specially modified armor-piercing artillery shells. The last bomb dropped struck the forward part of the ship near the Number II gun turret. It penetrated *Arizona*'s armor and caused the ship's forward powder magazine to detonate. A monumentally powerful explosion blasted through every inch of *Arizona* in less than a second. The blast instantly crushed the life out of over a thousand sailors, and it killed every member of *Arizona*'s band. Over a mile away the great shock wave that blew *Arizona* apart rocked Commander Fuchida's command plane.[50]

In terms of the material damage that they had inflicted, the Japanese attack on Pearl Harbor was a great success. Eight battleships; three light cruisers; three destroyers and three auxiliary vessels were either sunk or badly damaged. The Japanese killed 2,403 Americans, including sixty-eight civilians. The attack virtually wiped out US air power in the Hawaiian Islands. Still, the Pearl Harbor attack turned out to be an unmitigated disaster for Imperial Japan. In the short term the Japanese had failed to hit even one US aircraft carrier. None had been present in port that morning. It was an almost unbelievable intelligence failure on the part of the Japanese, and would lead Japan directly to defeat in the Coral Sea, and to utter, catastrophic disaster at Midway. More importantly, the attack on Pearl Harbor enraged the entire population of the heretofore solidly isolationist United States. People from all walks of life were as mad as hell. Pearl Harbor galvanized the country for total war as nothing else possibly could. The once quaint and faintly exotic Japanese were now deeply hated by every American at least as much as their vile Nazi allies. Simply put, the arrogant, hyper-aggressive, militaristic thugs who ran Imperial Japan had picked a fight, a bloody fight to the death that their country could not possibly win.

So Long, San Diego!

On the morning of 7 December 1941, Jimmie Thach and his wife, Maddie, were driving their two-year old Ford along Orange Avenue in San Diego. They were headed to a Sunday lunch/picnic with other members of his squadron. Thach was passing cars and pushing the speed limit because he and Maddie were running a bit behind schedule. It would just not be right for the squadron commander and his wife to show up late. After all, they were bringing the beer! Thach had several ice chests crammed full sitting in their trunk. Don Lovelace, Thach's best friend and executive officer, was going to be there. So was Lovelace's wife. So were most of the other pilots in the squadron. They would be bringing their wives and sweethearts too. Well over three dozen people would probably be showing up for the get together, and most of them were sailors. So there had to be plenty of beer.

Most of the squadron's personnel found Fighting Three a congenial assignment. Its thirty-six-year old skipper was low key and popular with enlisted men and officers alike. Thach worked his men hard and insisted that they perform at the highest level, but he was widely respected as an effective leader and a patient teacher. He probably inherited this trait from his two elementary school-teaching parents. The Thach family back in Arkansas was still having real financial problems in the wake of the Great Depression. A naval officer's salary was not very large, but it was reliable, so Jimmie was still sending money home every month to help his folks out. This particular squadron picnic was a combination Christmas party and farewell lunch. 'Farewell' because Fighting Three was about transfer to its new duty station at Pearl Harbor, in Hawaii.

Most of the Pacific Fleet had already moved there from the West Coast. The squadron's ship was the aircraft carrier *Saratoga.* She had just returned to San Diego after a six-week long overhaul at the big Bremerton shipyard in Puget Sound. They would all be sailing for Hawaii the next day.[51] Everybody in Fighting Three would be back at the air station later that afternoon. They would have to work like crazy to get all of the squadron's gear stowed aboard the carrier in time for her departure.

Thach was proud of his squadron. They were the champions of the 'All Navy' gunnery competition. Thach himself was an acknowledged leader in aerial gunnery. He had never scored less than 'expert' in gunnery drills during his entire Navy career. Thach had the squadron's famous 'Felix the Cat' cartoon logo painted on the sides of all of their planes. He even ordered it painted on their two waterfront hangars. The many 'Es' for excellence stenciled on their planes told the world that Jimmie Thach's pilots were the Navy's best. The country might well call on Fighting Three to be the first to engage some enemy if the troubled international situation spun further out of control. Still, that seemed highly unlikely. Neither the Nazis nor their Japanese allies would ever dream of pushing the isolationist United States into the war. It was in their interest to leave well enough alone. They would almost be insane not to let the sleeping American giant slumber. Fighting Three's personnel would probably spend a pleasant, peaceful tour of duty training in exotic Hawaii.

One pilot who would not be going to the squadron lunch was the 'shy' and 'retiring' Lieutenant Edward 'Butch' O'Hare. The twenty-eight-year-old O'Hare was on his way to spend his last free time with his gorgeous new wife, Rita. O'Hare had convinced a very reluctant Rita to say 'yes' to his marriage proposal after a whirlwind courtship of just six weeks. She was a beautiful blonde nurse. O'Hare had met her at a hospital in St Louis. He had been ferrying new Wildcat fighters from the East Coast to San Diego. On a whim he stopped in St Louis to spend one last night in his old home town. The hospital visit was supposed to be a quick 'pay-your-respects' kind of thing. He was supposed to be visiting the wife of a friend who just had a baby. Rita was the new mother's nurse. O'Hare ended up getting a lot more out of that hospital visit than he bargained for.

The story of Butch and the lovely Rita says a lot about O'Hare's intense, single-minded determination once he had settled on a goal. O'Hare was usually a casual and easy-going kind of guy. However, he was not that way at all when things that were really important to him were concerned. On their very first date O'Hare informed Rita that he intended to marry her. He told her that there was a war on and they had no time to lose. Rita demurred; she said that she was too young to marry. Anyway, Butch was twenty-eight years old and that was much too old for her. Rita also had other concerns. She was a devout Roman Catholic and would not consider marrying anyone outside of her faith. Nevertheless, after just six weeks Butch and Rita got married. He went after her like she was an enemy bomber in his gunsights. O'Hare would not let anything get between him and the girl of his dreams. He agreed to convert. So Lieutenant O'Hare spent the next six weekends making the long, hot, summertime drive from San Diego to Phoenix to take instruction in Roman Catholicism. He and Rita got married there that September at St Mary's Catholic Church. On the morning of 7 December O'Hare was on his way to help Rita decorate their new apartment. Then he and the rest of the squadron would be off, sailing for Pearl Harbor. Future fighter ace Noel Gayler also decided to skip the squadron lunch. The San Diego weather report that morning had predicted a beautiful, 78-degree day. Gayler and his wife, Caroline, planned to spend their last free time in San Diego relaxing together on the beach.[52]

Nobody attending Fighting Three's lunch/farewell party suspected what was going on that morning 2,600 miles to the west in what was still the pre-dawn darkness of the Central Pacific. Six large Japanese aircraft carriers carrying over 400 warplanes had secretly crossed the lonely waters of the Northern Pacific. They were now less than 200 miles north of Pearl Harbor, and they were preparing to strike. The Gaylers were sunning themselves on the beach when motorists driving along the Coast Highway started honking their horns. A few people stopped. They yelled that the Japanese had just bombed Pearl Harbor. The Gaylers ran to their car. Butch O'Hare heard the news on his car radio. He was just pulling up in front of the new apartment. O'Hare raced inside. He told Rita what had happened; gave her a big goodbye kiss, and ran out the door. Jimmie Thach and Maddie also heard the news on their car radio. He whipped their Ford into a sharp U-turn and sped back to the base on North Island. On that memorable Sunday morning in December 1941, nobody in Fighting Squadron Three ate a decent lunch and nobody got to drink any beer.

Fighting Three Goes to War

Fighting Three's ship, the carrier *Saratoga*, steamed down the West Coast unnoticed and unmolested by the Japanese. After undergoing a total refit in the big Bremerton shipyard in Puget Sound, the 'Sister Sara' was in top fighting shape.[53] The trip to San Diego would be the big carrier's last peacetime cruise for the next four years. Nobody in California knew it then, but the last few hours of peace were ticking off the clock. *Saratoga* was scheduled to take Thach's squadron on board first thing Monday morning. Then they would find themselves heading off to war in the Pacific, first stop Pearl Harbor! The big ship was also taking two other squadrons out to Hawaii: Marine fighter squadron VMF-221, and Lieutenant Commander Max Leslie's Navy dive bomber squadron, VB-3. Rear Admiral Aubrey Fitch was in overall command. Fitch was one of the few American admirals in those early days of the war that had a good deal of experience handling aircraft carriers. He would eventually take command of all Navy aircraft in the South Pacific.

Astonishingly, Fighting Three's Wildcats now carried fully loaded belts of 50-caliber ammunition for the very first time. The immense pressure of total war instantly obliterated the dangerous Depression-era practice of only loading ten or twelve rounds during training in order to save money. Wildcat fighters handled much differently, more slowly, when they were carrying 1,800 rounds of heavy 50-caliber ammo. They could not accelerate nearly as rapidly and their anemic climb rate got even worse. Thach made sure that his Wildcats were hoisted aboard the *Saratoga* first. Then the crew could position them on the flight deck so that they were immediately available to take off on combat missions if the Japanese showed up. Max Leslie's long-range dive bombers would handle reconnaissance and search missions. Four older, World War 1-era destroyers provided the anti-submarine screen. Army fighters flew air cover until the little fleet swung around Point Loma and sailed out of San Diego Bay. For the first time in American history, US sailors ventured out into what had suddenly become a potentially dangerous and hostile Pacific. Even the crews of the transports taking US troops to the Philippines during the Spanish-American war never had to worry about an enemy ship suddenly turning up. On 9 December 1941, an overly pessimistic Admiral Stark, then the short-term Chief of Naval Operations, sent out the following negative assessment of the situation at Pearl Harbor:

> Because of the great success of the Japanese raid on the seventh it is expected to be followed up by additional attacks in order to render Hawaii untenable as naval and air bases, in which eventually it is believed Japanese have suitable forces for initial occupation of islands other than Oahu including Midway, Maui and Hawaii.

Saratoga's crew had their fair share of first week of the war jitters. They intercepted a false report that a Japanese aircraft carrier had been sighted south of San Francisco. This was the cause of San Diego's first-ever air raid warning. The city fathers ordered every fire engine in every fire station in the city to turn on its siren. Pathetically, this was the only way for one of the Navy's most important West Coast bases to alert nearby civilians of a possible enemy attack. Another time one of Max Leslie's dive bomber pilots sighted what he thought was a surfaced Japanese submarine. This 'enemy sub' was about 100 miles west of the *Saratoga*. Admiral Fitch launched more bombers on a 'scout-strike' mission. The 'submarine' turned out to be an American surface vessel. It was desperately 'blinkering' its identity to any plane that happened to be passing by.

Nearer Hawaii, one of Leslie's dive bombers had mechanical problems, and the two-man crew had to ditch about 50 miles out from the ship. The men got into their rubber life raft and waited and waited for hours. Nothing happened. Finally, Lieutenant Commander Leslie found them. Max Leslie stayed overhead circling and circling until he almost ran out of gas. Then an American destroyer appeared on the horizon and picked up the downed flyers.

Jimmie Thach had plenty of time to think things over on the five-day run out to Pearl. He, O'Hare, and the other pilots spent much of each day in 'condition two': sitting on the flight deck in a warmed up Wildcat. Thach had to be wondering about the largely unknown Japanese enemy and its rumored weaponry. That weaponry had just wrecked what most people thought of as the backbone of the United States Navy. Thach hoped that by developing his new tactics he had found a way to defeat what he guessed was Japan's most potent weapon, the Zero fighter. Six months later at Midway, he got his answer. Thach and a few of his pilots, half of them rookies, would prove that he had done just that. Surprisingly, Thach had found a way for pilots flying the slower, less-maneuverable Grumman Wildcat to defeat the 'invincible' Japanese Zero.

The Graveyard Called the USS Arizona

The once beautiful USS *Arizona* died a violent death on the morning of 7 December 1941. A specially modified armor-piercing bomb detonated the Number II magazine. The gigantic explosion instantly crushed the life out of more than a thousand American sailors. Many of their bodies were just pulverized. The remains of those that could still be recognized as human were almost all decapitated. The shattered *Arizon*a broke into three large chunks, and sank to the bottom of the shallow harbor. Only a bit of her topsides remained above water. Torrents of thick, black bunker oil gushed out of the wreck. When it reached the surface, the oil ignited. It burst into a wild inferno of smoke and flame that nobody could put out. *Arizona* burned and burned uncontrollably for over a week. Then the fires slowly died out. Throughout Pearl Harbor thick, dirty oil floated on the top of the water. An ugly 'bathtub ring' of congealed crud coated parts of the shoreline. Arms and legs and other body parts from dead sailors littered the shallow bottom. Soon, the once beautiful harbor began to stink – from the smoke, from the oil, and from the dead.

On several of the wrecked ships men were still alive but trapped underwater in isolated pockets of air. They screamed, and they screamed, and screamed for someone to help them. Many sailors risked their lives trying to rescue the trapped men, but this was a job for trained experts. The Navy quickly flew rescue teams out to Hawaii from various West Coast ports. Typically, they were made up of salvage specialists and experienced hard hat divers. Chief Petty Officer Edward Raymer was a veteran hard hat diver.[54] He led the rescue team that flew to Hawaii from San Diego. On the afternoon of 7 December, CPO

Raymer and his men boarded a big seaplane that was crowded to the rafters with army and navy officers heading out to the war. Raymer's plane was over Pearl Harbor at dawn on 8 December. Everyone on board was shocked by the terrible sight below. Nothing in President Roosevelt's initial announcement of the surprise attack had prepared them for the enormous damage that the Japanese had inflicted on so many Navy ships and on the planes, and on the airfields nearby. Great gushers of black oil spewed out of a dozen bleeding wrecks. Thick oil covered much of Pearl Harbor. It blackened parts of the shoreline. Many of the great ships along 'battleship row' were under water. *Oklahoma* had capsized. Her keel was pointing straight up into the air. The men trapped inside her were in total darkness. Most probably never realized what had happened before they suffocated or drowned. The crippled *California* was half underwater. She was slowly sinking to the bottom. *Nevada* had been deliberately run aground to avoid blocking the main channel. Hundreds of Army Air Corps planes on the nearby airfields were now just smoldering piles of aluminum junk. The clueless General Short had foolishly ordered that entire squadrons be lined up in long, straight rows to prevent sabotage. The strafing Japanese pilots had found those long rows inviting targets.

***

Five days later *Saratoga*, carrying Jimmie Thach and his squadron, rounded Barbers Point and came charging into Pearl Harbor.[55] The *Sara* moored near Ford Island. The topside remains of the sunken *Arizon*a were still burning, but there were also enormous floating cranes hard at work. Navy engineers were already repairing the tremendous damage. By the end of the war the modernized battleships *Californi*a, *Nevad*a, and *West Virginia* were all pounding away at Japanese-held positions in the Western Pacific.

Admiral Fitch hurried off to get his new orders. When Thach went ashore he immediately noticed a look of fear in the eyes of the people. The cowed expressions on their faces was much different than the 'let's go get the bastards who did this' attitude in Fighting Three. All of these were just everyday folks. They had just gone through the terrible shock and violence of a surprise attack made by hundreds of enemy warplanes. And before all of the bombing; all of the explosions, and all of the killing, it had been such a beautiful, peaceful Sunday morning.

Thach had a talk with one of the few Army fighter pilots who had gotten airborne on 7 December. He had actually tangled with a Zero. The Army pilot confirmed the incredible intelligence out of China that Thach had seen concerning the Zero's superiority. Zeros were lightning fast. They had an incredible climb rate, and they were amazingly maneuverable. The Army pilot recounted how he had gotten behind a Zero and was about to open fire. Then the Japanese pilot pulled up effortlessly into a fantastic vertical climb. Next, he flipped his Zero on its back. He smoothly dove back down behind the US fighter. Then he shot the American down. The Army pilot was describing the 'turning in' maneuver. It was invented by the Yokosuka Air Group, and was taught to most Zero pilots early in their careers. Thach would later encounter this same maneuver at Midway.

Fighting Three handled the next morning's patrol duties over Pearl Harbor. It replaced an Army squadron that no doubt had been shot to pieces on 7 December.

***

A month later, Chief Petty Officer Edward Raymer was the first diver to venture inside the wreck of the ruined *Arizona*.[56] Raymer was the salvage expert who had led the rescue team sent to Pearl Harbor from San Diego on 7 December. The *Arizona* had been one of the finest capital ships in the US Navy, a real showpiece. Now she was just a watery burial ground; a dark, grotesque, chamber of horrors. Raymer's first hair-raising job was to locate and deactivate some kind of large

Japanese projectile that had punched a hole in the *Arizona* but had never detonated. The water inside the wreck was putrid and thick with pitch black oil and ooze. Once Raymer got inside the hull he was in total darkness. He could not even see the lining of his own dive helmet. He felt his way past wrecked machinery and shattered bulkheads. He bumped into a large spongy object hovering in the darkness above him. He stepped back. Then he inched closer to the strange thing. It felt like a half-inflated bag. It was about the size of a man, but Raymer could not make out what it was. The object in front of him was not heavy so he just tried to brush it away. His bare hand punched right through to the insides of the thing. Its insides felt like a cold, rotting sponge. As the thing drifted away, boney skeletonized fingers scraped across Raymer's dive suit.[57] CPO Raymer began coughing. Then he retched. The bag-thing was a decapitated corpse! It was the headless body of an American sailor. Scavenger crabs and other sea creatures must have eaten out the man's insides. What had once been a living, breathing, human being was now nothing more than a slowly decaying, fleshy bag. Three strands of thick cable tethered Raymer to a dive boat on the surface: a virtually unbreakable safety line; a telephone line, and an air hose. Because Raymer could see nothing at all inside the hull, a sailor in the dive boat with a copy of the ship's blueprints guided him along via telephone. Raymer did not know it yet, but his air hose was starting to kink up behind him. It was getting tangled up in some wrecked machinery.

Raymer eventually located the unexploded projectile. It was not what anyone was expecting him to find. The Japanese had welded metal fins onto huge armor-piercing artillery shells. They had made about eighty of these 'special anti-battleship weapons' just for the attack on Pearl Harbor. The carrier *Kaga*'s second squadron of Kate torpedo bombers had dropped eight of these giant, modified shells on *Arizona*. The last one had hit the battleship in exactly the right place. Light glimmered from somewhere above Raymer. It pierced through the black oil and muck. Raymer's eyes began to adjust to the darkness. Now he could see that there were more of the hideous bag-corpses hovering in the murk all around him. The unbelievable overpressure from the magazine blast that ripped the *Arizona* apart had also decapitated these sailors and burst the internal organs of every man who had been below deck. Their remains were now unspeakably hideous. Raymer's kinked up air hose finally closed. It shut off his oxygen supply. The air pressure inside his helmet collapsed. Putrid black liquid poured into his helmet. He gagged and reflexively swallowed a mouthful of the horrible stuff. Raymer was drowning inside his own helmet. He pushed his way through the hovering corpses and raced to find the blockage in his air hose. He used his helmet phone to alert the guys upstairs. Miraculously, he found the kink in his air hose and somehow untangled it by feel alone. Then Raymer passed out. He had untangled his air hose just seconds too late. Somehow the alert sailors in the dive boat managed to manhandle Raymer's limp body through 100ft of sharp wreckage. The sailors eventually revived one very lucky hard hat diver.

First Combat

After Fighting Three arrived in Hawaii, Admiral Pye sent *Saratoga* to help relieve the besieged Marine garrison on tiny Wake Island. The entire atoll is comprised of two far away specks of coral and sand in the Western Pacific. It is actually several hundred miles closer to Tokyo than it is to Pearl Harbor. President Roosevelt had removed Admiral Kimmel from command in the Pacific on 17 December. Surprisingly, Roosevelt appointed the highly excitable Vice Admiral William Pye as temporary commander. Although he wore three stars, and had served in World War One, William Pye had never seen combat. He was the ultimate desk jockey. He is said to have boasted that Japan would never dare go to war against the United States – just one week before Pearl Harbor! William Pye was clearly not the right officer to lead the Pacific

Fleet for even a couple of days. Still, Pye had served as Chief of Naval Operations (CNO), so he had many powerful friends in Washington. Unfortunately, Admiral Chester Nimitz, Kimmel's brilliant, permanent replacement would not reach Hawaii until Christmas Day, and the skittish Pye managed to turn his one week of command in the Pacific into a time of disgrace and disaster.

Aside from his other shortcomings, Admiral Pye was appointed as a short-term caretaker. Short term caretakers rarely act boldly. So when *Saratoga* was almost within striking range of Wake Island, Admiral Pye got cold feet. He decided to back off. Pye recalled the *Saratoga* and the escort ships that had been racing to rescue the besieged Marines on Wake. He also recalled *Enterprise* and its Task Force. Jimmie Thach, Admiral Fitch and all the men involved in the rescue mission were stunned and sickened. Thach actually recommended that Fitch disobey Pye's order. He wanted Fitch to pretend that he had never gotten a recall at all, just as the great British Admiral Horatio Nelson had done a century earlier at the Battle of Copenhagen. Thach was desperate to continue on and save the outgunned Marine garrison.[58] Admiral Halsey aboard *Enterprise* was also shocked by the order not to help the Wake Island Marines. Halsey seems to have thought about doing exactly the same thing that Thach was recommending to Fitch. Unbelievably, two career American naval officers in two different carrier groups were seriously considering disobeying the same direct order. A sad Admiral Fitch reluctantly complied with Pye's directive. He turned the *Saratoga* around and headed back towards Pearl. Halsey did likewise aboard *Enterprise.* A sarcastic broadcast by Radio Tokyo ridiculed the American withdrawal: 'Where, oh where, is the United States Navy?'[59]

The Japanese suffered very heavy casualties at Wake Island given the tiny size of the battlefield. The 400-man Marine garrison killed over 700 Japanese troops, even though the Marines were constantly under heavy bombing and strafing attacks from the air. They threw back at least one amphibious landing attempt. Marine artillery sank three small Japanese ships. Then the tiny garrison was finally overwhelmed. The Japanese sent the Marines who had survived the battle to horrific prison camps. Many of them nearly starved or died of disease before the war ended and they were liberated. The Japanese forced about a hundred American civilian construction men who had been working on the island into what amounted to slave labor. They treated these men worse than animals. When their work was completed Japanese soldiers machine-gunned all the construction men, and buried their bodies in a mass grave on the beach. After the war, the Allies tried and hanged the Japanese admiral who had ordered the murders.[60]

A week after the Wake Island fiasco, *Saratoga* was patrolling southwest of Hawaii. Admiral Pye apparently wanted to keep the aircraft carriers out of Pearl Harbor, where they would be sitting ducks. Still, the big carrier was making less than 10 knots in order to conserve fuel. So *Saratoga* was a nice, easy target for any enemy submarine that happened to be around. Thach and his pilots were down in the wardroom eating lunch when a huge explosion rocked the ship.[61] A torpedo from a waiting Japanese submarine tore a gash the size of two trucks in her side. The blast killed six men, but the tough old *Saratoga* hardly slowed down. She did have to return to Puget Sound for repairs though. That is how Thach and his squadron lost their ship. Fighting Three was left stranded 'on the beach' so to speak, in beautiful Hawaii. They had been racing to relieve Wake Island, but had been recalled at the last minute. Their ship had been torpedoed by an enemy submarine, and was forced to head home for repairs. Yet, not one man in the entire squadron had even fired a single shot in anger. This unhappy situation would end soon enough.

The US Navy organized its fighter squadrons with more flexibility in mind than the Japanese did. Each Japanese squadron was almost an organic part of a carrier's regular crew. They were what American sailors would call 'ship's company'. Each American squadron was nominally attached to a specific carrier, but in practice the units actually constituted separate entities. They were almost akin to small naval vessels like PT boats or submarines. The number of American fighters aboard a US carrier was basically limited by aircraft availability. Right after Pearl Harbor, carrier-based fighters were in short supply. When the war began, Fighting Three just had eighteen planes, a couple of spare Wildcats, and eighteen pilots. They were the only fighters available to protect *Saratoga.* As the war went on US aircraft manufacturers built great numbers of much more capable aircraft. After the *kamikaze* attacks began later in the war more and more fighters were needed to protect the carriers, Admiral Halsey ordered that the number of fighter aircraft aboard the American carriers be increased dramatically. By the end of the war, US fleet carriers often carried air groups with seventy or more fighters, and/or fighter-bombers.

The pilots aboard Japanese carriers were essentially crew members of that one particular ship. This difference proved important to the Americans during the dreadful months right after Pearl Harbor when the Japanese were racking up victory after victory. American commanders could easily deploy their squadrons wherever they were needed most. The less-flexible Japanese system aggravated the effects of the shocking overconfidence, the incredible hubris that the Japanese military displayed at the start of the war. When the Japanese were winning pretty much every one-sided battle fairly easily, success went right to their heads. The Japanese themselves called this wild overconfidence 'victory disease'. It eventually hamstrung them, and helped lead to the debacle at Midway. At the Battle of the Coral Sea the large fleet carrier *Zuikaku* (Fortunate Crane) escaped damage, but her air group had been shot to pieces. Her sister ship *Shokaku* (Soaring Crane) had been severely damaged, but her air group was largely intact. The overconfident Admiral Yamamoto could have transferred *Shokaku*'s air group to the undamaged *Zuikaku.* With a little bureaucratic juggling the Imperial Navy could have brought one more fully equipped, powerful fleet carrier to Midway.[62] It may have made a huge difference in the outcome of a battle that changed the course of the war. As far as is known, the cocksure Isoroku Yamamoto never even tried to make such an obvious switch.

Saratoga was heading back to the West Coast for repairs without Fighting Three. So it is no surprise that Admiral Fitch started moving his fighter squadrons around. Fighting Two aboard the *Lexington* needed to come ashore and replace its poorly designed Brewster Buffalo fighters with Grumman Wildcats. When Fighting Three still flew Brewsters, Butch O'Hare tried to diagnose why their engines were stalling out at high altitude. O'Hare and the squadron's mechanics fitted a dozen pressure gauges onto his plane's engine. O'Hare took off and climbed to 20,000ft. His Brewster's engine began misfiring, and then it sputtered to a stop. O'Hare executed a long, steep 'dead stick' landing from 20,000ft. While unusual, a dead stick landing from that altitude was no great feat for a skilled pilot like O'Hare. He probably enjoyed gliding down all those many miles. The squadron mechanics finally traced the engine problem to cheap replacement oil gaskets that deteriorated with heavy use.

After Fighting Three had been ashore in Hawaii for a few weeks, Admiral Fitch notified Jimmie Thach to prepare his squadron for duty aboard *Lexington*. This temporary, bureaucratic move would soon lead Fighting Three into its first combat against the Japanese. It would also make the shy and retiring Butch O'Hare a famous war hero. Newspapers all across the country would run front-page stories extolling his exploits in the Pacific, and O'Hare would become a household name in every town and city in the United States.

Admiral Chester Nimitz relieved Pye at Pearl Harbor on Christmas Day. He immediately ordered a series of hit and run carrier raids on Japanese positions throughout the Pacific. These raids seem to have driven the hyper-arrogant Admiral Yamamoto right up the wall. They were certainly one of the main factors motivating Yamamoto's fatal decision to take a big gamble; attack Midway, and try to destroy the US carrier fleet.

Fighting Three flew out to *Lexington* on 31 January 1942.[63] She was the flagship of Task Force 11. Vice Admiral Wilson Brown was in overall command. Thach was immediately impressed by the quiet professionalism of *Lexington*'s crew. He loved their 'can do' spirit. He also thought that Fred Sherman, *Lexington*'s aggressive captain, had brilliantly organized the carrier's operations to maximize the striking power of the ship's air group. Captain Sherman set aside plenty of time for Thach and his pilots to go aloft to practice aerial gunnery. As always, gunnery was Thach's first love. Admiral Nimitz first ordered *Lexington* to steam south towards lonely Canton Island. That same day *Enterprise* and *Yorktown* kicked off Nimitz' raiding campaign by bombing Japanese bases in the Gilbert and Marshall Islands. Then the Navy's head man got into the act. Admiral Ernest King in Washington ordered Brown to take *Lexington* deep into the remote, rarely traveled waters of the South-west Pacific. The Japanese were already building bases there. Ominously, the victorious Imperial Army seemed to be preparing for an eventual invasion of Australia. The only charts of the South-west Pacific available to Brown were over a century old. They had been drafted in the 1800s for wooden sailing ships by cartographers of Britain's Royal Navy. Admiral Brown had not provisioned *Lexington* for such a long voyage. Thach, his pilots, and apparently *Lexington*'s entire crew, were soon reduced to a diet of nothing but spinach and beans. Thach complained that the beans were not 'tasty pork and beans', just plain, pink beans. Such a diet was unappetizing in the sweltering tropical heat of the South-west Pacific. More importantly, the gas-producing beans tended to give pilots painful attacks of 'the bends' when they were up at high altitude. Thach came to really dislike their taste and never ordered a plate of beans for the rest of his life.

On 13 February, Admiral King ordered Brown to attack the Japanese in the 'area' of the Solomon Islands. Brown decided to launch airstrikes on Rabaul, a very important Japanese base on the island of New Britain just north of the Solomons. Brown hoped to avoid Japanese search planes and take the enemy by surprise. Thach expected to lead the attack on Rabaul at dawn the next day. His Wildcats would go in strafing, and hopefully destroy most of Rabaul's Zeros while they were still sitting on the ground. US dive bombers and torpedo planes would go in next. They would try to sink any Japanese shipping still anchored in nearby Simpson Harbor.

On the day before the scheduled attack, *Lexington* was over 400 miles north of Rabaul.[64] Thach, O'Hare, and Lieutenant Burt Stanley were all aloft leading two-plane sections on combat air patrol (CAP). Thach's wingman was Ensign 'Doc' Sellerstrom. For the first time since the war began, Thach heard somebody with a loud voice break radio silence! That somebody was calling out an emergency alert over the radio. Thach would have jumped right out of his seat if he had not been belted in. Strict radio silence was pretty sacrosanct during World War Two. Enemy direction finders could hone in on a ship's exact location if there was too much 'extracurricular chatter' over the radio. The loud voice on the radio turned out to be *Lexington*'s fighter director. He was excitedly reporting a radar contact 35 miles south-west of the carrier. Thach, Butch O'Hare and their two wingmen raced south-west. Then Thach waved at O'Hare – motioning him to go back. He wanted O'Hare to turn around and head to *Lexington*. Thach was absolutely sure that the contact had to be a long-range patrol plane and not a Zero fighter. Thach was certain that no fighter could possibly have enough range to fly 400 miles out from land and then return safely. Reluctantly, O'Hare turned back. Thach later quipped that the aggressive O'Hare was being a 'good boy'.[65] Thach was right about the contact being a patrol plane and not a Zero, but he was right for the wrong reason. Unknown to the Americans, the amazing Zero did have a remarkable range of over 1,800 miles – when using auxiliary external fuel tanks ('belly tanks'). The arrogant, wildly overconfident Japanese had simply neglected to send Rabaul the auxiliary tanks necessary for long-range fighter missions.

After racing south-west for several minutes, Thach realized that the target that he and Sellerstrom were looking for was probably inside a big thunderstorm just up ahead. A lightning-filled squall line of towering thunderheads was boiling up directly in front of them. *Lexington*'s fighter director confirmed the contact's position. The enemy plane was apparently out of sight inside the big storm, so Jimmie Thach and Doc Sellerstrom plowed right into a solid wall of swirling grey clouds. With visibility near zero, both men flew on instruments. Intense bursts of rain beat down on their windshields. It was dark. They could see nothing at all outside, but occasionally, great bolts of lightning illuminated their cockpits. Thach and Sellerstrom came to a small gap inside the clouds. Thach caught a glimpse of a gigantic, Rising Sun. The red insignia was painted onto the fuselage of a very large airplane. Its big fuselage bristled with machine guns. Thach just glimpsed the Rising Sun, part of a wing, and two big radial engines. Then the big enemy plane vanished into the storm. *Lexington*'s radar seemed to show that the two American fighters had 'merged' with the blip on the radar screen. That was almost exactly what had happened. Thach and Doc Sellerstrom came within 20ft of colliding with a Kawanishi 'Type 2' flying boat (future Allied code name Emily). It was an airplane that American intelligence had never even heard of before, and was huge by the standards of the day. It had four, fourteen-cylinder radial engines and a crew of nine. It wingspan was a gigantic 124ft and it stood 30ft tall. The Emily had a range of almost 4,000 miles. The big seaplane was loaded with guns; it could carry two 20mm cannon and five machine guns. Unlike most Japanese planes, it featured armored protection for the crew. So it was a hard plane to bring down unless you could really shoot. The Americans soon learned that the quickest way to knock down an Emily was to aim for those big radial engines.

After a brief glimpse of what they were up against, Thach and Sellerstrom were right back inside the blinding clouds. Just as quickly, they popped out of the clouds and into the clear. They had flown completely out of the thunderstorm altogether, but no giant flying boat came into view. Thach figured that the Japanese crew must have spotted them, and that they were probably circling around somewhere inside the storm. Thach and Sellerstrom turned back into the storm, and began a careful, hair-raising search. Fortunately, *Lexington*'s fighter director came back on the air. Radar had lost all contact with the Japanese plane. This probably meant that the Emily had dropped down near the ocean's surface.

Thach and Sellerstrom both dove down under the storm clouds. They gunned their engines for all they were worth. There she was! The big Emily was out in the clear bright daylight – down 1,000ft above the water. And she was running. She was running for home! The two Americans tore after the Japanese search plane. Thach remembered thinking to himself that, with all his expensive training, and all his awards for gunnery, he had better hit this, his first real-life target![66] Attacking big airplanes protected by many machine guns was easier and safer for pilots like Thach who had mastered deflection shooting. They could attack from an angle not well covered by all those guns. Thach opted for a high side approach. He ordered Sellerstrom to 'bracket' the enemy plane. Thach wanted his wingman to dive under the Emily and attack from the opposite side. Sellerstrom misunderstood what his leader wanted. He flew around and behind the dangerous tail end of the enemy seaplane. This took time, and it was where one of the big cannon would be, so it gave the Emily's tail gunner a clear shot at Sellerstrom's Wildcat. Big, red 20mm tracer shells burst out of the back of the enemy plane. They missed. Sellerstrom somehow made it across to the other side of the Japanese seaplane without being hit.

Thach dove in, firing burst after burst into those big engines. Due to short-sighted, depression-era budgeting this was the first time that Jimmie Thach had ever fired all his six machine guns at the same time. He poured round after round into the engines and into the starboard wing. Tracers were even passing through the wing and seemed to be striking inside the seaplane's cockpit. Then … nothing happened. *Absolutely … nothing at all was happening!* When Thach stopped firing, the huge Emily just kept lumbering along. It appeared to be completely undamaged. Thach had apparently missed a target that was much larger than the broad side of a barn. It was as if he had been firing blanks.[67] Thach, supposedly one of the US Navy's top gunnery experts, and a squadron commander to boot, had apparently missed his very first target in actual combat! Shamefully, it had been a very large target indeed, and the range had been point blank. Five or six immensely long seconds slowly ticked off the clock. There was not even a wisp of smoke coming from the Japanese seaplane. More time went by. Then two of the Emily's big radial engines exploded. The entire starboard wing burst into flames. Three large bombs dropped out of the bomb bay, and the big flying boat slowly nosed over. It dove and dove, headlong down 1,000ft, plummeting right into the sea. Back aboard *Lexington* the crew cheered. They could see a tall column of thick black smoke rising from the ocean's surface 10 or 12 miles away.

Later in the war, Doc Sellerstrom, Thach's wingman, was transferred to another squadron for the Battle of the Coral Sea. He shot down several Japanese planes, but just being a Navy carrier pilot was a dangerous occupation – even when there is no fighting going on. Sellerstrom was severely burned in the fiery crash of a torpedo plane that he had been 'hitching' a ride in a few weeks after Midway. He lingered on in the hospital suffering terribly for about a week. Then he died.

When Thach and Doc Sellerstrom were almost back over *Lexington*, its radar detected another Japanese search plane. The new contact was a bit farther north than the one Thach had shot down. This time Butch O'Hare was really itching for a fight. Sadly, for the frustrated O'Hare, the ship's fighter director ordered Lieutenant Stanley and Ensign Haynes to go after the new contact. Twenty miles out, Haynes spotted the target. It turned out to be another big Emily. Its crew also spotted Haynes. The Japanese jettisoned their bombs just like the crew that Thach had shot down. They apparently hoped that by lightening their load they would increase their speed and help them outrun the Americans. Stanley was shocked by the Emily's great size; it was the largest airplane that he had ever seen in his life.

Both US pilots gunned their engines and pulled up into steep climbs. They would try to dive in for a 'high side' attacks, just as Thach had done. Nervous, Stanley flipped the wrong switch and his guns would not fire. Ensign Haynes' guns worked just fine. He apparently killed the Japanese tail gunner. At least, no more fire came from the big cannon in the seaplane's tail. On their second pass both men poured round after round into the Emily's wings and into its engines. The Japanese plane's wings caught fire, then it nosed down towards the sea and crashed.

The appearance of another Japanese search plane so near *Lexington* convinced Admiral Brown that his plan for a surprise attack on Rabaul had failed. He decided to hit the Japanese somewhere else. Captain Sherman strongly disagreed. He thought that they should just fight their way in and destroy Rabaul. Rabaul was a very important Japanese base. It was on the direct route to Imperial Japan's prime target in the South Pacific, Australia. Admiral King, the Navy's commander-in-chief, also disagreed with Brown. Surprisingly, Wilson Brown stuck to his guns. He quite reasonably thought that attacking a major enemy base when it was already on high alert was just a foolish thing to do. He made the correct decision in the face of strong opposition from the 'higher ups'. After his run in with Admiral King, Brown never commanded a carrier task force again. Still, he had some pretty important friends high up in the government in Washington. Wilson Brown spent the rest of the war serving as President Franklin D. Roosevelt's, and later President Harry S. Truman's, personal naval advisor.

Lexington's radar soon detected more Japanese aircraft. This time they turned out to be bombers, not search planes. At long last the eager Lieutenant Edward 'Butch' O'Hare would finally get his chance to fight. O'Hare was about to single-handedly save *Lexington* and her two-thousand-man crew from almost certain destruction. He would win the Medal of Honor and become one of the most beloved American heroes of World War Two. O'Hare did all this, incredibly, in one near-miraculous shoot-out with half a squadron of enemy aircraft.

Butch O'Hare Gets His Chance

By mid-afternoon Thach, Sellerstrom, Burt Stanley and Butch O'Hare were all back aboard *Lexington*. The entire crew was wildly excited. All of his pilots crowded around Thach. They all had the same questions for him: had their training really prepared them for actual air-to-air combat? Would they be able to hit a live enemy who would certainly be shooting back at them? Thach assured his men that their training had been excellent, far more than adequate for what they were about to face. Shooting at towed aerial practice sleeves off the California coast was pretty good preparation for the real thing. He told them that if they just kept their cool and did what they had been taught to do, everything would work out just fine. They would hit what they shot at. O'Hare was quiet, but he seemed unhappy and agitated. He had missed out on his first chance for combat. Thach had waved him back when he was searching for that first patrol plane. The fighter director had selected Burt Stanley to go after the second one. O'Hare need not have worried. He would get his chance to fight soon enough, but just not right away.

Admiral Aritomo Goto on Rabaul had no intention of letting the Americans shoot down two of his finest patrol planes and just go sailing merrily away. In fact, he was expecting an airstrike on Rabaul the next morning. Goto was determined to hit the Americans first, and he would hit them with everything he had. While Thach and his men were eating their 'gourmet' chow of spinach and pink beans, Goto was ordering eighteen twin-engine bombers ('land attack planes') to locate and destroy *Lexington*. The Mitsubishi G4M1 bomber (Allied code name Betty) was powered by two 1,530hp radial engines, had a range of 1,500 miles, and a top speed of 266mph. It typically carried an 1,800lb load of bombs and torpedoes, and bristled with four 7.7mm machine guns and had a 20mm cannon in the tail.

Lieutenant Commander Takuzo Ito's squadron left Vunakanau airfield at 1420. One bomber had engine trouble and never got off the ground. Ito divided his force into two divisions. He probably did so in order to search a larger area. Big thunderstorms were already boiling up all over the Bismarck Sea, and reconnaissance typically became more difficult as the afternoon wore on. Ito led the eight bombers of the First division (*chutai*), while Lieutenant Nakagawa commanded the Second *chutai*. He had nine bombers. All told the seventeen Bettys had a total crew of 119 pilots, radiomen, and gunners. Only twenty of these men would make it back to Rabaul alive.

Noel Gayler's division of six Wildcat fighters was up above *Lexington* on CAP when the first large contact appeared on the carrier's radar. Many planes were approaching from the south-west. They were about 75 miles away. Then the contact faded out. Ten minutes later it reappeared on the radar screen. Lightning strikes and heavy thunderstorms all around the area were apparently interfering with the ship's electronics. The bogeys were now 47 miles away. At 1630 they were only 24 miles out, and they were coming in fast. The radar was showing Lieutenant Nakagawa's nine-plane *chutai*. They were up at 11,000ft. Gayler's pilots scrambled for altitude, but the Wildcat's slow climb rate was a big problem. Gayler barely had any altitude advantage at all when the nine *Bettys* came into sight. They were barreling straight for the carrier.

Gayler and his wingman, Dale Peterson, dove on a bomber at the tail end of the formation. Both men blasted away with their big 50-caliber machine guns, and the Betty's left wing burst into flames. Then it spun out of control, and began spiraling towards the sea. The two US pilots used the momentum from their dives to climb up above the rest of the Japanese bombers. Now all six Wildcats from Gayler's section were with him. All six dove on the bombers. One Wildcat was hit by machine gun fire and the pilot bailed out. The American destroyer *Patterson* charged in and sailors on the destroyer pulled him out of the water. Dale Peterson knocked one of the leading planes out of formation, and Rolla Lemon shot down two more *Bettys*.

Jimmie Thach was sprinting across the flight deck to his plane. He took off. As he climbed towards the air battle overhead, Thach had a panoramic view of a fantastic sight.[68] Four of the big Japanese bombers were engulfed in dark red flames and were spewing out long trails of dirty brown smoke. Three *Bettys* were spiraling down completely out of control. All four hit the water with a great white splash. In true samurai fashion, Nakagawa tried to crash his damaged bomber into *Lexington*. Every US ship opened fire. Ships were blazing away at the burning Mitsubishi from half a dozen different directions. The bomber started gyrating, and then it spun down towards the sea. At the end Nakagawa's right wing was pointing straight up into the air, as his left wing dug into the water. The bomber cartwheeled over and its nose smashed into the ocean. The impact sent up another enormous white splash. Lieutenant Nakagawa crashed about 75 yards short of the carrier. It had been a tremendous effort. His failed attempt to destroy *Lexington* would not be the only *kamikaze*-style attack on the carrier that day.

Surprisingly, Lieutenant Nakagawa's remaining pilots seem to have lost their nerve. They dropped their bombs over 1,000 yards astern of *Lexington*. These men were definitely not samurai! They shamefully turned tail and ran for home. Thach and the rest of his flyers chased after them in hot pursuit for miles and miles. One Wildcat pilot was killed when he got too close to the big cannon in one bomber's tail. Thach shot that bomber down. Then he shot down another one. Thach let the last two enemy planes go. Without their heavy bomb loads, the Bettys were very fast, and it was hard to catch up with them in a Wildcat. Unfortunately for the retreating Japanese, they ran into two US dive bomber pilots who probably should have been flying fighters. Lieutenants Edward Allen and Walter Henry knocked down the last two of the retreating Mitsubishis. The Americans shot down all nine of the bombers in Nakagawa's *chutai.* All sixty-two of the brave lieutenant's men were dead, and they had not even scratched the paint on one of the American ships.

Fighting Three had done a magnificent job protecting the *Lexington.* Still, Jimmie Thach had made a serious mistake. It was a mistake that he would never repeat. Thach and all the pilots with him had chased after the retreating bombers far to the south-west. Now they were out of position to defend *Lexington* from any attack coming at the carrier from the north or east, and just such an attack was about to get under way. Lieutenant Commander Ito's *chutai* of bombers was north-east of *Lexington* when he heard Nakagawa's initial contact report. Then Ito heard nothing but static. Twenty minutes after sighting the American ships, Nakagawa and all his men were dead. Ito's bombers now turned to the south-west and came barreling in, charging straight for *Lexington.* Lieutenant Commander Ito could not have timed his attack more perfectly. *Lexington*'s fighter director only had two fighter pilots in reserve, Butch O'Hare and his wingman, Duff Dufilho.[69] Now O'Hare would finally get his chance to fight. When O'Hare and Dufilho got the call to intercept Ito's planes, the Japanese bombers were only 12 miles out from *Lexington.* This meant that the enemy bombers were only three minutes away. Both American pilots turned on their fragile illuminated gunsights and test fired their machine guns. O'Hare's guns worked fine. Dufilho's would not fire at all. He had a jam or a short circuit. O'Hare waved at his wingman to go back to *Lexington.* To his everlasting credit, Dufilho decided to stick around. He would try to draw the fire from the Japanese gunners away from O'Hare and towards himself.[70] Eight big cannon and thirty-two machine guns would soon be shooting at both of them. O'Hare had less than three minutes to stop Ito's eight fast-moving *Bettys.* In three minutes they would be directly over the carrier, dumping tons of high explosive right onto *Lexington*'s flight deck. It seemed almost impossible for one fighter pilot to stop all those planes in just three minutes. Then Butch O'Hare did what seemed impossible. Several hundred very interested sailors were closely watching what happened next.

O'Hare already had the altitude advantage, so he let the first V-shaped group of Bettys pass beneath him. Then he dove on the trailing planes on the right side of the Japanese formation. He fired short, amazingly accurate bursts. Incredibly, he knocked two bombers out of formation on that first pass. It took him less than ten seconds. Even with Dufilho playing decoy, most of the Japanese gunners were blazing away at O'Hare. O'Hare pulled up and passed over to the left side of the Japanese formation. An incredible marksman, O'Hare aimed for the bombers' engines, not just at their wings. He dove again and fired another burst. O'Hare shot up Petty Officer Uchiyama's left engine. It conked out. Uchiyama's plane fell away to the left. Incredibly, on that same pass O'Hare hit Petty Officer Mori's right engine and put a gaping hole in his fuel tank. A silver jet of gasoline began streaming out behind Mori's bomber. Mori could still fly, but he fell behind the others.

The fight was getting close to the *Lexington* now. Anti-aircraft shells from the US ships were exploding all around him, but that did not stop O'Hare. He simply ignored the 'friendly fire'. He made one more pass and fired again. Using up the last of his ammo, O'Hare shot down Lieutenant Mitani and blew the left engine completely off of Lieutenant Commander Ito's command plane. Out of ammo, O'Hare pulled away. Amazingly, O'Hare had shot down or fatally damaged six Japanese bombers in less than three minutes. Officially, he was only given credit for five 'kills' because Petty Officer Mori was able to fly off. Leaking gas behind him, Mori finally had to ditch after nearly making it all the way back to Rabaul. Forty plus enemy gunners had been shooting at him, but Butch O'Hare completely wrecked Lieutenant Commander Ito's First *chutai.* It had been a magnificent performance, but would it be enough?

Three of the Japanese bombers had survived O'Hare's onslaught. Their crews stoically flew on towards the carrier, braving heavy anti-aircraft fire from *Lexington* and from the ships in the screen. One of their bombs missed *Lexington* by only 30 yards, and the explosion sprayed shrapnel along the flight deck. Then the last three bombers turned away and flew off towards Rabaul. With the last three Bettys limping towards home, all danger seemed to have passed. Then, from out of nowhere, Lieutenant Commander Ito's command plane came hurtling down at *Lexington.* Flames and brown smoke poured out of the huge hole in the wing where O'Hare had shot away an engine. Ito and his crew were trying for another *kamikaze*-style suicide attack. They fought desperately to control their burning bomber. Then the Betty veered wildly off to the left and was suddenly flying parallel to *Lexington.* Captain Sherman turned *Lexington* away. Finally, Ito's plane careened down and crashed about 100 yards off of the carrier's port bow. Again, white seawater splashed 100ft up into the air. Ito and his crew had died as true samurai were expected to die.

Still, Butch O'Hare had saved *Lexington* from near certain destruction. Hundreds of sailors aboard the carrier and the ships in the screen had witnessed his spectacular performance. Captain Sherman and Admiral Brown had front-row seats. The entire crew could finally relax; the knuckle-biting minutes were over. One incredibly talented fighter pilot had just saved the lives of more than two thousand grateful sailors. Everyone on board was laughing and cheering. It was like they were all spectators at a championship football game, and O'Hare had just scored the winning touchdown.

O'Hare was just lowering his plane's landing gear when a jumpy teenage sailor manning one of *Lexington*'s anti-aircraft guns completely lost his mind. Dozens of 50-caliber bullets began zinging past O'Hare's cockpit. The hysterical young man almost killed O'Hare before his buddies pulled him away from the gun. O'Hare then landed safely enough. Backslapping sailors almost carried the sweat-soaked O'Hare out of his cockpit. Then he slowly sauntered down the flight deck towards the trigger-happy youngster manning the machine gun. O'Hare did not lose his temper. He did not yell, or make a fuss, or swear. O'Hare calmly told the hysterical young boy, 'If you keep shooting at me when I've got my wheels down I'll have to report you to the gunnery officer.'[71]

The few Japanese flyers that made it back to Rabaul that day were pretty hysterical themselves. Only two bullet-riddled bombers actually landed at the Vunakanau airstrip. As noted, Petty Officer Mori almost made it back, but his leaking bomber ran out of gas and he had to ditch in Simpson Harbor. The surviving Japanese were not just hysterical, they were full of themselves. They claimed that they had shot down eight Wildcats. They claimed that they had sunk a cruiser or a destroyer. They also claimed that Lieutenant Commander Ito had successfully crashed his bomber into an American aircraft carrier, and set it ablaze. A few days later newspapers in Tokyo proudly reported the same story: Japanese pilots had left a *Lexington*-class carrier in flames. Not a word of it was true.

Jimmie Thach gathered his pilots together in the wardroom later that evening. Thach's main take away was that their deflection-shooting technique had been spectacularly successful. They had made mistakes, but they had proven that their tactics worked, and that their training had prepared them to win in combat. Big planes like bombers with half a dozen machine guns were no match for a well-trained fighter pilot who really knew how to shoot. Thach wanted to go over in detail what they had done wrong and what they had done right while it was still fresh in everyone's mind. He recorded each pilot's recollections. Unfortunately, the recording was lost weeks later when *Lexington* was sunk at the Battle of the Coral Sea, so we have no actual record of what

Butch O'Hare or anyone else really said right after his magnificent performance. We do know that both Thach and O'Hare were pretty keyed up. Neither man got a wink of sleep that night. Later, O'Hare always tried to downplay the significance of what he had done. He said that he had just been in the right place at the right time, and that any other pilot in the squadron could have done just as well. Neither his squadron buddies, nor the American press, nor President Franklin D. Roosevelt, nor an admiring American public, would ever let Butch O'Hare get away with that kind of nonsense.

New Guinea: The Raid on Lae and Salamaua

With the Japanese at Rabaul on full alert and aware of *Lexington*'s presence off the coast of New Britain, Admiral Brown was now absolutely convinced that he should strike somewhere else. Brown was adamant and stood by his decision, even though Admiral King and Captain Sherman strongly disagreed. Brown and King both really wanted to hit Rabaul, arguably the key Japanese base in the South-west Pacific. King even sent Brown the carrier *Yorktown* to reinforce *Lexington.* Still, Admiral Brown stuck to his guns, and he was right to do so. The Americans would soon find a new target, a very lucrative one. The next raid would take the Japanese completely by surprise and do the kind of damage that really gave Admiral Yamamoto heartburn.

Lexington refueled in the New Hebrides (today Vanuatu), a small group of islands about 1,000 miles east and a bit north of Australia. Here, Butch O'Hare first learned that newspapers all across the United States had run front-page stories trumpeting his single-handed defense of *Lexington.*[72] He was now a national hero. The publicity shy O'Hare was appalled. All the pilots in Fighting Three jokingly lined up to ask him for his autograph. Admiral Brown and Captain Sherman were both eyewitnesses to O'Hare's spectacular defense of their ship. They both recommended that he be awarded the Navy Cross. O'Hare complained vociferously about all this unwanted attention to Jimmie Thach. He did not want a medal. He certainly did not want any publicity. After what all the newspapers had written about Al Capone and his father, he never wanted to see the O'Hare name in print again. O'Hare continued to make the almost ludicrous claim that any other pilot in the squadron could have done what he had done. He continually claimed that he had just been in the right place at the right time. O'Hare really pressured his commanding officer to do something! Thach just sat back and smiled; he was not the least bit sympathetic to his friend's plight. Thach knew that O'Hare richly deserved the recognition. Anyway, Thach told O'Hare that the matter was completely out of his hands. He was right about that. Admiral King in Washington was already thinking about awarding O'Hare the Medal of Honor. So was President Roosevelt.

Admiral Brown was still looking around for a suitable target to attack with his enlarged task force. He now commanded a powerful array of two carriers; eight cruisers, and fourteen destroyers.[73] On 7 March an Australian Hudson bomber on a reconnaissance mission over the Solomon Sea spotted a Japanese convoy headed for Lae and Salamaua. Both places were tiny Australian mining outposts on the northern shore of rugged, unexplored Papua New Guinea. New Guinea was the last land barrier between the Japanese military juggernaut and an invasion of northern Australia. The Japanese convoy included a cruiser, a couple of destroyers, and a number of troop transports. The transports carried about three thousand Imperial troops. The Japanese landed on New Guinea's north shore and began to rather leisurely unload both troops and supplies. They apparently had no idea that they had been spotted. The Japanese were unready; out in the open, and vulnerable to attack. This was exactly the kind of soft, lucrative target that Admiral Brown had been hoping to find.

In 1942, few places on earth were as out of the way and as primitive as Papua New Guinea. Wild headhunting tribes warred against each other deep inside the jungles of the mountainous interior. Some scattered gold mines, mainly operated by Australians, supported what little modern economy there was. The dirt airstrips that the Australian companies had built at Lae and Salamaua were probably what had first attracted the attention of Japanese war planners. Admiral Frank 'Black Jack' Fletcher was in command of the newly arrived *Yorktown*, and he came aboard *Lexington* to plan the Lae-Salamaua attack with Admiral Brown. Because Brown had unsuccessfully tried to evade Japanese search planes by approaching Rabaul from the north-east, he and Fletcher decided to try and stay beyond the reach of enemy searches by approaching Lae and Salamaua from the south. Both carriers would be operating in the Coral Sea about 45 miles off New Guinea's southern coast. This meant that the attacking American planes would have to fly all the way across the big island in order to reach the target area. It also meant flying over the 13,000ft-high Owen Stanley Mountain Range.[74] These mountains form the rugged 'backbone' of eastern New Guinea. The Owen Stanley Mountains are notorious for heavy mists and fogs, and for poor visibility generally.

The route that Brown and Fletcher chose posed little difficulty for the long-range SBD dive bombers, while Thach worked out the fuel consumption problem for his shorter-range fighters. He figured that they could reach the Lae area and still have at least ten minutes of fighting time over the target. It would be close-run thing, but his Wildcats should have no problems. Ten minutes would be enough. The older TBD torpedo planes posed a huge problem for Brown and Fletcher. The underpowered TBDs would never get over those 13,000ft peaks lugging 2,000lb torpedoes. Brown and Fletcher needed more detailed information about those mountains, so Admiral Brown had his Air Group Leader, Commander Ault, fly to Townsville, Australia. There Ault talked with a mining company pilot who knew that part of New Guinea like the back of his hand. The Australian pilot spoke of a low, 7,500ft pass in the mountains that the torpedo planes might just be able to get through.

Lexington and *Yorktown* launched their planes from the Coral Sea at 0810 on 10 March 1942. Thach's division of eight Wildcats led the way. He kept Butch O'Hare in reserve flying 'high cover' because he was his best pilot. As usual, O'Hare just saluted and said nothing about being held back again, but he did not seem to be very happy about it. A powerful force of ten more fighters, sixty dive bombers, and twenty-five torpedo planes followed Thach's eight lead Wildcats. As the large American formation passed over New Guinea's southern shoreline, Lieutenant Commander James Brett's thirteen TBD Devastator torpedo planes were already straining for altitude. Brett found the low pass in the Owen Stanley Mountains that the mining company pilot had spoken about. It was just as the Aussie flyer had said. Thach's fighters easily zipped over the final mountain ridge and flew down into the valley beyond. Thach stayed behind. He hovered over Brett's squadron of old torpedo planes hoping to see if they could clear that last ridge. It began to look like the old TBDs did not have enough power to make it over the mountains after all. Each torpedo pilot would push his plane right to the limit as they flew dangerously close to that last summit. None of them could get over it. They all turned back. Brett radioed Thach to go on the raid without them. Thach replied that he still had plenty of gas, so he would stay with them a while longer. Then Jim Brett had a bright idea. Years before Brett had trained as a glider pilot. Experienced glider pilots are adept at searching out thermals. These are updrafts of warmer air created by the sun's rays heating the earth's surface unevenly. A strong thermal can send a well-designed glider soaring up and up for thousands of feet. Of course, the old TBD torpedo planes were heavy and awkward in the air; nobody would ever mistake one for a sleek glider. Brett flew parallel to the ridgeline hoping to find a thermal powerful enough to help his squadron get over that last ridge. Thach and the rest of Brett's squadron watched closely as he stopped and began circling over a brightly lit patch of jungle. That patch of jungle was getting hit by a lot of direct sunlight. Almost magically, Brett's heavy torpedo plane began rising. It was lifted up higher and higher. Brett stopped circling. He turned his plane north and swept over that last ridge. Brett came up on the radio calling out: 'Halfway House!'[75] Every Navy pilot who had ever trained at Pensacola knew exactly what that meant. The Halfway House was a small, home-style restaurant halfway between the city of Pensacola and the naval air station. The food was terrific. Everybody, but everybody, stopped at the Halfway House for a snack or some ice cream before going on to flight training. Soon all of Brett's pilots were circling the bright patch of jungle. They all rode what must have been an unusually powerful thermal up and over the ridge. For a few it was a close call. Some just cleared the treetops on the ridgeline by less than 100ft. None of Brett's pilots would have any trouble getting back over the mountains on the return trip home. The Devastators would all be 2,000lb lighter after launching their torpedoes at the Japanese. Thach was astonished by the skill and determination displayed by Brett and his pilots. Brett's masterful use of the thermal to sweep everyone over that last ridge really did seem like magic.

Thach banked his Wildcat and turned north. He tore over the mountains and raced to catch up with his division. When Thach and his pilots arrived over the target area they scanned the sky for enemy fighters. However, this time the Americans had caught the Japanese napping. There were no dangerous Zeros anywhere in the area. Lae and Salamaua are roughly 20 miles apart on Huon Gulf. In 1942, they were separated by a lot of dense jungle. Today, they are part of the same metropolitan area. Both places can easily be seen from the air at the same time. When Thach's fighters arrived, the airstrips at both outposts were empty. The overconfident Japanese were planning to deploy Zero fighters to the area in a few days. Now it was too late. There were also sixteen Japanese ships out in Huon Gulf: a cruiser, two destroyers, a mine layer, and about a dozen vulnerable troop transports. Astonishingly, some of the transports were still landing troops and equipment. Most of the Japanese soldiers that had already come ashore were in the process of setting up anti-aircraft guns near the beach. With no fighter opposition in sight, Thach's Wildcats tore into the Japanese. They relentlessly strafed the vulnerable troops again and again. They fired thousands of big 50-caliber rounds into the anti-aircraft positions, which were probably not as well dug in as they would have been a day or two later. Flying high overhead, Butch O'Hare could see that there were no Zeros around, so he came diving in to help out his buddies. The ill-prepared Japanese soldiers were pretty much sitting ducks out in the open and proved to be very easy targets. One big 50-caliber slug can tear a man's arm off. Thach, O'Hare, and the rest of Fighting Three's pilots mowed down dozens of the hapless enemy soldiers. After eliminating the anti-aircraft threat, Thach and his men began methodically shooting up the buildings near the airstrip. Then sixty US Dauntless dive bombers came screaming down on the ships offshore. They sank three of them and seriously damaged five more. All told, at least eight Japanese ships were put out of action. Some of the transports were still full of soldiers. The losses at Lae and Salamaua were the Imperial Navy's biggest of the war to date. The only aerial opposition that Fighting Three faced that day came from an odd 'amphibian-fighter'. It looked like a Zero riding on an outsized pontoon landing float. The strange plane appeared from out of nowhere, but it was no match for a Wildcat as it was slow and ungainly. Noel Gayler quickly shot the strange airplane to pieces. Then the Wildcats machine gunned the ships still out in the bay.

When Fighting Three had done about all the damage that it could do, Lieutenant Commander Brett showed up leading his thirteen old, slow torpedo planes. Brett and his pilots went right after the cruiser *Yubari*. They executed a beautiful, well-timed 'anvil' attack. Attacking a ship from both port and starboard sides makes it difficult for its captain to dodge torpedoes. However, after all the trouble that Brett had getting his squadron over the Owen Stanley Range, the results of the torpedo attack were infuriating.[76] Thach saw two torpedoes go right under *Yubari*. Both harmlessly buried themselves in the sand along the shore. Two other torpedoes were direct hits, but both warheads were duds. They failed to explode, and the torpedoes just sank to the bottom. Due to foolish Depression-era budget constraints, early American torpedoes had poor warheads and unreliable depth controls. During that first hard year of the war many turned out to be defective.

After the success of the raid on Lae and Salamaua, *Lexington* returned home to Pearl Harbor. It was time for her to reprovision and refit – no more pink beans and spinach. *Lexington* needed to pick up her original fighter squadron, Fighting Two. Thach and Fighting Three would now be based at Kaneohe Naval Air Station about 30 miles from Honolulu. Butch O'Hare soon found himself in a most uncomfortable position. For O'Hare it was probably more nerve wracking than shooting it out with the Japanese. He was the center of attention at a news conference at the Royal Hawaiian Hotel in Honolulu.[77] The handsome, but painfully shy airman was reluctantly becoming a famous celebrity. He was immensely popular with the American people – a beloved national hero. Nosey reporters crowded around asking him all sorts of prying questions. Fortunately for O'Hare, Jimmie Thach was also at that first press conference. To O'Hare's great relief, Thach handled most of the reporters' questions. It would not be that way at his next press conference – in Washington, D.C. While he was still in Hawaii Navy public relations officials arranged for O'Hare and Thach to have a photo shoot. Two obviously staged and unrealistic photos show them flying along in their Wildcats posing for the cameras with canopies wide open. Two months later O'Hare, and his beautiful wife, Rita, were at the White House meeting President Roosevelt. O'Hare was now in front of a much larger crowd of reporters than there had been at the Royal Hawaiian. Flashbulbs were going off left and right. The camera-shy O'Hare could not stop nervously blinking and blinking while President Roosevelt promoted him to lieutenant commander.

O'Hare and the President shook hands, and Rita proudly placed the blue Medal of Honor ribbon around her husband's neck. When the official medal ceremony was over, President Roosevelt took O'Hare aside. He asked him if the Navy needed a new fighter plane. O'Hare enthusiastically nodded yes. He famously quipped, 'Something that can go upstairs faster!'[78] A prototype of the F6F Hellcat, a fighter that could really 'go upstairs', was already being prepared for flight testing at the Grumman factory in Bethpage, New York.

The hit and run carrier raids that Admiral Nimitz ordered had done their job. The missions had seriously disrupted the Japanese timetable for conquest in the Pacific. They had also given the American defense industry some breathing space and time to ramp up weapons production. The raids had also infuriated the arrogant, out-of-touch, Isoroku Yamamoto back at Combined Fleet headquarters. They helped convince Yamamoto to foolishly stick the Imperial Navy's neck way out and attack Midway. Still, the most daring and most unusual carrier raid of all was still in the planning stages. It would be launched against the Japanese home islands themselves.

Chapter 4

Admiral Yamamoto's Plan to Attack Midway

The idea of attacking Midway was the brainchild of Admiral Isoroku Yamamoto.[79] He was the commander of Japan's Combined Fleet,[80] the operational arm, the war-fighting part of the Imperial Japanese Navy. Yamamoto wanted to draw out and destroy the remnants of the US Pacific Fleet that had been missed at Pearl Harbor. Most of all he wanted to get rid of the US aircraft carriers. American carriers had been raiding Japanese bases all over the Pacific and they were driving Yamamoto crazy. For decades Japanese war planners had envisioned fighting the Americans in an entirely different way than the one Yamamoto had decided on. They never dreamed of opening hostilities with a surprise attack on Hawaii. In fact, until mid-1941 the US Pacific Fleet had been based on the West Coast, where a surprise attack would have been almost impossible to pull off. President Roosevelt had ordered the Fleet moved to Pearl Harbor in a long-shot effort to pressure the Japanese into calling off their bloody invasion of China. To put it mildly, Roosevelt's gamble did not succeed. Prior to Yamamoto's time, Japanese war planners had envisioned whittling down the US Fleet in a series of small-scale battles as the Americans crossed the Pacific. Then a 'decisive battle' (*Kantai Kessen*) would be fought in waters closer to Japan. Yamamoto's daring plan to reach out across the Pacific and strike the Americans at Pearl Harbor was revolutionary. Yamamoto wanted to knock out the US Pacific Fleet before American war production really got going. Then Japan could quickly win the war, or, if not, Japanese troops would dig in on their island conquests. They would fight to the death defending every inch of coral and sand, and eventually force the weak-kneed Americans into negotiating a settlement that was favorable to Japan. At least, that was what Yamamoto thought would happen.

Yamamoto had lived in the United States. He had taken English classes at Harvard.[81] He had twice served as Japan's naval attaché in Washington. He was deeply interested in North American oil production, and had even visited some important oil fields in Mexico. Isoroku Yamamoto was also a very intelligent man. He had finished second in the highly competitive, nationwide selection process to get into Japan's naval academy at Etajima. So one wonders how a man with that kind of experience and intellect could make the colossal blunder of mounting a surprise attack on the United States. The raid on Pearl Harbor killed well over two thousand Americans. In one morning the Japanese infuriated the entire population of the once deeply isolationist United States, a country with a strong aversion to getting involved in another world war. The US also had vast mineral resources, a huge industrial base, and a large, well- educated population. Yamamoto had to know all of this. He had to know that the US had the industrial and military potential to crush Japan. Still, it is almost impossible to overstate how blindly arrogant and out of touch with reality the otherwise brilliant Yamamoto and other high-ranking officers in the Imperial forces really were. After the successful attack on Pearl Harbor Isoroku Yamamoto became the second most popular man in the Japanese Empire. He was second only to the revered Emperor Michinomiya Hirohito. The Japanese public simply adored Yamamoto. Few Japanese seemed to have seriously considered the possibility that Japan and its Nazi allies might actually lose the war. However, the surprise attack on Pearl Harbor and the great damage that the attack inflicted on the Americans guaranteed, as almost nothing else could, that the people of the US would enter the war completely unified and with a deep determination to win at any cost.

While not an active aviator himself, Yamamoto had taken flying lessons. He strongly promoted building up the Imperial Navy's air arm. He had served as the captain of the aircraft carrier *Akagi*, and he was extremely popular with young Imperial Navy pilots. He knew how aviation was dramatically changing the nature of modern war. So why did Yamamoto do it? Why did he think that a surprise attack on the Americans was a good idea? Sadly, the best answer seems to be a very old and familiar one. Hubris is overwhelming arrogance and pride. It was a vice that infected many of Japan's militarist leaders, especially Yamamoto. They believed that the Japanese 'race' was superior to, and destined to rule over, or at least lead, other Asian peoples. After all, these powerful men, and most everyday Japanese people, really seem to have believed that their somewhat frail, awkward, and downright homely Emperor Hirohito was a divine being. The higher-ranking officers, especially, tended to look down on the Chinese and the Koreans. This becomes obvious when one considers the frequent, wide-scale, and incredibly vicious atrocities that Japanese forces regularly committed against both groups in the 1930s while invading the Asian mainland. After their forces scored victory after victory against the Americans and their British allies at the beginning of the war, many Japanese officers became supremely confident that their armed forces were invincible. Yamamoto was clearly one of these incredibly overbearing individuals. Their great arrogance also made many top Japanese officers congenial partners with their German allies. Important Nazis officials frequently shared the same nasty character trait.

Yamamoto only stood 5ft 3in tall and could not have weighed more than 130lb. In other words, he was about average size for a Japanese man in those days. However, photographs of Yamamoto were usually shot in such a way that he appeared to be an imposing, almost heroic figure. Face to face, Yamamoto appeared to be almost delicate. Japanese sailors meeting him for the first time were often surprised by his slight appearance. Oddly enough, Isoroku Yamamoto is still revered by a few Japanese today. He is honored along with other unsavory characters at the Yasukuni Shrine in Tokyo. There is even a small museum shrine dedicated to Yamamoto in his hometown of Nagaoka.

Throughout the 1930s Yamamoto was reluctant to tangle with the Western powers. Some believe that he opposed war with America as a matter of principle.[82] This was far from the case. Yamamoto simply thought that the Imperial Navy needed time to catch up with the United States technologically. Then he would take on the arrogant Americans who had unjustly stopped selling oil and metal to Japan in order to punish her because of the invasion of China. In private correspondence with another officer in 1934, Yamamoto predicted that the right time to take on the West would come. Then both the United States and Great Britain would be 'kowtowing' to the mighty Japanese Empire.[83] Yamamoto's correspondence shows that he always had contempt for the 'Anglo-Saxon' powers, most especially for Britain.

Yamamoto apparently thought that by late 1941 Japan had caught up with the United States technologically. The obvious aerial superiority of the Mitsubishi Zero very probably contributed to his view. In late 1941, the right time for the Japanese Empire to strike had apparently finally come. After all, Japan's Nazi allies looked like sure winners both in Europe and in Russia. The fascist powers were on the march all around the globe. History seemed to be on their side. The Western democracies appeared to be weak and in decline, and seemed to be on the defensive everywhere. The isolationist people of the USA, the most powerful Western nation, were almost unanimously opposed to getting involved in more foreign entanglements. World War One had taught them the hard way to keep out of other peoples' disputes. Yamamoto obviously thought that Imperial Japan should take advantage of this favorable world situation while it could.

The war that he started at Pearl Harbor did not destroy Japan, as Isoroku Yamamoto had once feared that it would. It did though lead to the death of millions of Japanese civilians, and the post-war American occupation completely remade Japanese society. Japan flowered into a peaceful, functioning democracy and has become a prosperous economic superpower. The aggressive, militarist monarchy that Yamamoto greatly cherished, fought, and died for, is now just a nightmare footnote in history. So, in that sense only, the attack on Pearl Harbor did begin the destruction of the Japan that Yamamoto so dearly loved. In every other way Japan is now a much better place, for the Japanese people and, most especially, for the people who now live peacefully in neighboring countries.

Despite his many faults, Yamamoto was undoubtedly a military visionary. At a time when battleships were the centerpiece of every navy on earth, Yamamoto predicted that ships carrying aircraft would someday dominate the world's oceans.

***

The Japanese failed to find any American aircraft carriers at Pearl Harbor on 7 December. By pure luck, none had been in port that day. After Admiral Nimitz took command in the Pacific, planes from the US carrier *Lexington* destroyed an entire squadron of Japanese bombers defending the important base at Rabaul on New Britain. *Lexington* and *Yorktown* had also severely mauled the fleet landing troops and supplies at Lae and Salamaua in New Guinea. Other carriers had bombed Japanese bases in the Gilbert and Marshall Islands. These bases were critically important to the defense of the Japanese homeland. So Yamamoto became obsessed with tracking down and destroying the American carriers. The raids ordered by Nimitz were not only deeply frustrating to Yamamoto, they were pushing him into taking chances. An inveterate poker player, Yamamoto decided to push his luck and stick the Imperial Navy's neck way out in an attempt to trap, ambush, and destroy the carriers.

Midway is a tiny, two-island atoll a little over 1,000 miles northwest of Honolulu. Geologically speaking, it is the northernmost piece of the Hawaiian Island chain. In early 1942, Midway's Eastern Island housed an air base with three runways. Sand Island was primarily a seaplane base. Yamamoto thought that Midway was an important enough asset that the American Navy would simply have to defend it, or do everything possible to take Midway back if it was captured by the Japanese. He viewed the Americans as gun-shy and timid. Amazingly, he thought that he would have to force them to come out and fight. He had misjudged his American enemy about as badly as he possibly could. Yamamoto named his plan to attack Midway and get the US carriers 'Operation MI'. Yamamoto's general idea was simple, as most good military plans are: Four Japanese aircraft carriers of the *Kido Butai* would launch a surprise morning attack on Midway. They would knock out the US air base there. Amphibious troops would quickly overrun both Sand and Eastern islands. Yamamoto and most of the Combined Fleet would be waiting nearby in ambush. They would pounce on the American carriers when they sortied from Pearl Harbor to take back Midway. Yamamoto also planned to transform Midway into a Japanese air base as soon as it was captured. He would ferry Japanese land-based planes into what had been an important US base only a day or two earlier. Then the Japanese aircraft on Midway would join the ships of the Combined Fleet in attacking the oncoming US carriers. Yamamoto hoped to surprise and overwhelm the Americans just as he had done at Pearl Harbor. The general idea was bold, but pretty simple. Unfortunately for Yamamoto, he left developing the details of the plan up to his eccentric operations officer, Kameto Kuroshima.

Among high-ranking Imperial Navy officers Kuroshima was known as the 'god of operations'. He turned Yamamoto's ambitious, but relatively simple plan into something that was horrendously complicated. Kuroshima had powerful units popping up unexpectedly in isolated spots all over the Central Pacific. The unnecessary complexity of Operation MI contributed mightily to Japan's disastrous loss at Midway. When they still had an overwhelming superiority in naval air power, the Japanese divided their forces and threw away the enormous, almost invincible advantage that would come from concentrating that great power. That is, fundamentally, how the Imperial Japanese Navy lost the most crucial battle that it would ever fight. Kuroshima had two hundred surface ships and submarines at his disposal. He had four big fleet carriers; three light carriers; eleven battleships, including the largest battleship ever built, *Yamato*. He was also deploying twenty-three cruisers and scores of destroyers. The Imperial Navy was flush with a great abundance of naval power. This great abundance probably led both Yamamoto and Kuroshima to squander the services of an entire fleet: two light carriers and a score of cruisers and destroyers. They sent these ships off on a bizarre mission 1,000 miles to the far north. An entire Japanese fleet would be off attacking the frigid Aleutian Islands just when the most critical naval battle of the Pacific War was being fought. Additionally, the Japanese could have easily brought one more large fleet carrier to Midway.[84] *Zuikaku* (Fortunate Crane) had lost most of its aircraft at the Battle of the Coral Sea, but the ship itself was basically unscathed. A sister ship, *Shokaku* (Soaring Crane), had been badly damaged, but her air group was largely intact. Yamamoto could have simply transferred *Shokaku*'s air group to *Zuikaku*. He could then have attacked Midway with five big fleet carriers, instead of four. He apparently chose to avoid the bureaucratic hassle involved in transferring an entire air group to a different carrier. Anyway, the overconfident Yamamoto was certain that he was already bringing more than enough force to Midway to overwhelm the outgunned Americans. The decimated US Pacific Fleet only had three operational aircraft carriers. One of those was the damaged *Yorktown*. The Americans had no battleships at all. They did have eight cruisers, but only fifteen destroyers and a handful of submarines. This was certainly not enough to even slow down the tremendous naval juggernaut that was about to descend on Midway. Or was it? Operation MI spread powerful Japanese fleet units all over the Pacific. Yamamoto and Kuroshima divided their forces in such a way that one unit could not support another if things got out of hand.

The details of Operation MI make dense reading. In summary they looked like this: four big fleet carriers from the *Kido Butai* would secretly cross the lonely reaches of the northern Pacific just as they had done before Pearl Harbor. Vice Admiral Chuichi Nagumo would again be in command. Nagumo's carriers would be screened by two battleships, three cruisers, and eleven destroyers. They would bomb Midway in a surprise morning attack. Yamamoto thought that planes from four big carriers would easily destroy every US plane on Midway in one strike. Two hundred miles behind the *Kido Butai*, Admiral Yamamoto himself would be waiting. He would pounce on the weakened Americans with his Main Force. The Main Force included the superbattleship *Yamato*, two other battleships, the light aircraft carrier *Hosho*, the cruiser *Sendai*, a pair of seaplane tenders, and nine destroyers. Rear Admiral Raizo Tanaka's Transport Force would head for Midway from further south. Tanaka's transports carried 5,000 amphibious shock troops, which would storm the American base. Tanaka commanded twelve troop transports, the light cruiser *Jintsu*, and ten of Japan's most modern destroyers. The destroyers were equipped with the fearsome 'long lance' torpedo. These torpedoes had an incredible range of 24,000 yards and were far superior to anything that the Americans had.

While Tanaka was landing his amphibious troops, Vice Admiral Kurita would bombard anything left standing on Midway. Kurita commanded four heavy cruisers plus a pair of destroyers. Admiral Kondo would stand farther offshore with two more battleships. Kondo also had two cruisers, the light aircraft carrier *Zuiho*, and nine destroyers. Rear Admiral Fujita, with two seaplane tenders, a destroyer, and a patrol boat, would set up a seaplane base on tiny Kure Island, 70 miles north-west of Midway.

Finally, Yamamoto wanted to make absolutely certain that the American carriers would not leave Pearl Harbor before his trap was set. Operation MI called for two different kinds of surveillance missions on Pearl Harbor. Long-range flying boats would refuel from tanker submarines at French Frigate Shoals, a lonely atoll north-west of Hawaii. A cordon of seven Japanese submarines would also be set up between Midway and Hawaii. They would report any American fleet movements towards Midway.

Yamamoto's plan looked like it took all possible eventualities into account. Yet Yamamoto made two big, unwarranted assumptions, and both turned out to be wrong: (1) Yamamoto assumed that the Americans were reluctant to face the Japanese in open battle. He thought that they would meekly hide inside Pearl Harbor until the loss of Midway forced them to come out and fight. (2) He was also certain that he could take the Americans by surprise again, just like he had done at Pearl Harbor. As things turned out, a brilliant but highly unconventional team of Navy cryptanalysts monitoring Japanese radio traffic broke the Imperial Navy's secret operations code and discovered Yamamoto's plans weeks in advance. It would be the Americans who were waiting off Midway to ambush the Japanese, not the other way around. Yamamoto's estimate of American morale and fighting spirit was also dead wrong. It turned out that the Americans were not reluctant to take on the Japanese after all. In fact, they were just itching for a fight.

Yamamoto's actions after the defeat at Midway were reprehensible. In an attempt to cover up its disastrous losses, the Imperial Navy announced to the Japanese public that Midway had been a victory. This was just typical wartime propaganda. The US Navy sometimes withheld the extent of its losses from the American public in order to keep from tipping off the enemy. What is stunning is that Yamamoto also deceived the Japanese Army about the magnitude of the disaster at Midway. Worse still, he locked up many lower-ranking sailors who had been wounded. They were put in 'secure' naval hospitals and had no contact with the outside world. When they recovered many were shipped off to remote island bases in the Pacific. Higher-ranking officers were also warned of dire consequences if they discussed the debacle at Midway with anyone. Even Lieutenant Commander Mitsuo Fuchida, the national hero who led the attack on Pearl Harbor, got such a warning.

Given Yamamoto's widespread popularity and prestige throughout Japan, it is surprising that his plan to attack Midway initially faced stiff internal opposition. The plan was that bad on its face. Throughout the early months of 1942 officers on Japan's Naval General Staff adamantly opposed Yamamoto. They argued that there was not enough shipping to support a base on far off Midway – even if the place could be taken. These General Staff officers also feared a counter-attack from American bases farther north in Alaska. The strange idea of invading the Aleutian Islands had apparently been a concession by Yamamoto to these officers. He probably approved the Aleutian campaign just to get the naysayers on the General Staff to go along with his Midway plan. Then the Japanese Army chimed in, claiming that it could not spare the troops. Clearly, many Japanese war planners saw Operation MI as a very risky gamble. For a time there seemed to be a real chance that the Midway operation would not take place at all. If that had happened, Admiral Yamamoto would surely have resigned, and might even have committed ritual suicide.

Then, on 18 April 1942, a startling event took place in the skies over Tokyo. It shook the collective psyche of Japanese society to the core and instantly silenced all Admiral Yamamoto's critics on the Naval General Staff.[85] It changed everybody's mind about the advisability of attacking Midway and trapping the US carriers. It was the most unusual aircraft carrier raid in history. It was the Doolittle Raid.

The Doolittle Raid

On 18 April 1942 – less than five months after the disaster at Pearl Harbor – sixteen US Army Air Force B-25 Mitchell medium bombers led by Lieutenant Colonel James 'Jimmy' Doolittle swept across Japan's home island of Honshu on the first, daring raid over Tokyo.[86] Doolittle's raiders also hit targets in three other Japanese cities. The Doolittle Raid was the most unusual aircraft carrier raid in history. The big, twin-engined B-25s were land-based aircraft. They were designed to take-off and land on long, paved airbase runways. Instead, Doolittle's pilots took off from the far shorter flight deck of the aircraft carrier *Hornet.* None of Doolittle's men had ever taken off from a carrier before, yet because of their intense training and excellent planning, every one of them took off safely from *Hornet.* The reason for using B-25s for the mission was their very long range; B-25s could fly further than any plane designed to take off and land on an aircraft carrier. The Japanese never suspected that a US carrier would launch bombers at their home islands when the carrier was still many hundreds of miles offshore. Doolittle had planned to take off from *Hornet* when she was about 400 miles from the Japanese coast, but picket boats sighted the American ships when they were still 600 miles out. So Admiral William Halsey, the American fleet commander, decided to launch Doolittle's planes at once.[87]

Everyone aboard the carrier knew that the B-25s would never be returning to *Hornet.* The entire Doolittle mission was strictly a one-way proposition. The plan was to bomb targets in Tokyo and in other Japanese cities. After hitting their targets, Doolittle's B-25s would head southwest and fly across the interior of Japan. Then the Americans would fly across the East China Sea. Doolittle hoped to make it to China and pass over the coastal areas that were occupied by the invading Japanese Army. The raiders would then try to reach airfields deep in the Chinese hinterland that were still in the hands of friendly Chinese Nationalist forces. The Doolittle Raid was an incredibly dangerous, one-of-a-kind mission, and every man was a volunteer. None of Doolittle's planes ever reached those friendly Chinese Nationalist airfields, with all but one plane running out of gas. All the other aircrews either bailed out or had to crash land. Doolittle himself was one of those who had to bail out. He landed safely, but unpleasantly, in a Chinese farmer's rice paddy that had recently been fertilized with human excrement. Luckily, most of Doolittle's men made it on foot to the Chinese Nationalist lines. Many were helped to get there by friendly Chinese peasants. When Japanese Army leaders learned that Chinese civilians had helped the Americans get to safety, their troops went on a horrific, vindictive, rampage, murdering tens of thousands of innocent Chinese peasants. They killed most of the people living in the small city of Nancheng. Then they burned it to the ground. The one aircrew that did not crash or bail out had navigation problems. They ended up landing safely in Siberia, where the Soviets, who were not at war with Japan, interned them before allowing them to return to the United States. Eight raiders were captured by the Japanese, with two executed after a rigged 'trial'. The others were sent to prison camps, where they almost starved to death. One unfortunate man went insane.

Doolittle and his raiders bombed Japanese airplane factories and other industrial facilities. They did relatively little physical damage to Japan's large war machine, but they did enormous harm to the national psyche of Imperial Japan. The Doolittle Raid knocked some sense of reality into a supremely overconfident Japanese public. People throughout Japan were deeply surprised and distressed by the raid. They apparently assumed that their military could bomb Pearl Harbor and invade other countries, but that the Japanese homeland itself would somehow remain immune from retaliation. The Doolittle Raid first showed all of Japan that this blasé attitude towards war with the United States was, obviously, a great mistake. By the fall of 1945, large sections of metropolitan Tokyo had been burned to the ground by US firebomb raids, and over a million Japanese civilians were dead. The Doolittle Raid was just a small foretaste of the terrible destruction that would soon rain down on Japan.

Admiral Yamamoto, in particular, felt profoundly humiliated by the Doolittle Raid. He thought that he had suffered a great loss of 'face', or public respect. The Imperial Navy's most sacred responsibility was to protect the divine person of Emperor Hirohito. While Doolittle and his raiders carefully avoided hitting the Imperial Palace, they most certainly could have plastered the place if they had wanted to. Still, the Emperor no doubt heard the distant rumble of the first bombing of his capital city. Yamamoto did not feel badly enough about putting the Emperor's life in danger though that he felt any need to resign, or to commit ritual suicide.

The Doolittle Raid came about at the personal, constant, and adamant insistence of US President Franklin D. Roosevelt.[88] In late December 1941, Roosevelt convened a meeting of his so-called war cabinet. It included General John Marshall, Admiral Ernest King, and General Hap Arnold, leader of the Army Air Corps. Roosevelt was not known for raising his voice, but all three service chiefs caught hell. Roosevelt was absolutely determined. He demanded that his military chiefs find a way to strike the Japanese home islands. Roosevelt wanted to retaliate for the attack on Pearl Harbor and for the Japanese invasion of the Philippines. Defeat after stunning defeat continued unabated for the United States and its allies during the dark days of December 1941. The humiliating losses continued on into the first months of the following year. The Imperial Navy destroyed a large Allied fleet in the Java Sea. Japan conquered the Dutch East Indies. Japan conquered Hong Kong. The Japanese Army chased US General Douglas MacArthur out of the Philippines, and continued its bloody invasion of China. Roosevelt thought that the need to hit back was urgent, if only to raise the American public's morale. Yet Roosevelt's military leaders were stumped. They could not figure out a practical way to surprise the Japanese and strike at their home islands. The most obvious way to hit the Japanese homeland was a carrier raid, but after Pearl Harbor the Japanese would be ready for something like that. Importantly, all the precious American carriers in the Pacific carried short-range airplanes. So the carriers would have to get dangerously close to the Japanese main islands to strike. Roosevelt kept pressing his war cabinet to find a way to hit back at Japan. When Roosevelt's top generals and admirals caught hell, the people lower down in the pecking order really heard about it!

Then in early January, a naval officer with no aviation experience at all came up with an ingenious idea.[89] Captain Francis 'Frog' Low was a submarine officer working on Admiral King's staff. Low was on an inspection tour of Navy bases along the Virginia coast when he saw Army Air Force bombers practicing attacks on the outline of an aircraft carrier that had been painted onto an airstrip. It was the airstrip at Norfolk, the very same airstrip that Jimmie Thach had cracked up on during his first flight as a test pilot. Captain Low tried to explain what he had in mind to Admiral King. Low wondered if long-range Air Force bombers could be loaded aboard an aircraft carrier. Then the carrier could attack the Japanese mainland from far off. There would be no need to get too close to the dangerous Japanese coast. It seemed like a brilliant idea, but was such a thing even possible?

Impressed, Admiral King sent Low to discuss the idea with his aviation expert, Navy Captain Don 'Wu' Duncan. Captain Low had two strange questions for Duncan. The first was: could long-range Air Force bombers land on an aircraft carrier? Duncan knew the answer to that one right away. The answer was 'No'. All the big Air Force bombers needed long runways to land on. Low's second question was a real puzzler: Could such bombers take off from a carrier? Duncan needed to do some research to answer that one. After a week Duncan had part of the answer. Only the twin-engine B-25 medium bomber had a short enough wingspan to fit on the flight deck of a carrier, and the B-25 had almost enough range for the daring mission that Captain Low had dreamed up. If something could be done to extend the B-25's range, the odd plan just might work. Still, someone would actually have to try taking off from a carrier in a B-25. Only then would anyone really know if Low's ingenious plan was even possible.

Lieutenants John F. Fitzgerald and James F. McCarthy got the job.[90] They were both regular Army Air Force bomber pilots stationed at a base in northern Virginia. They had no advanced warning or a chance to make any special preparations for their strange test flight. They just did what they were ordered to do on a 'normal' training day. Three weeks after Captain Low thought up his brainchild, Fitzgerald and McCarthy flew two B-25 medium bombers off the flight deck of the brand-new carrier *Hornet.* Both pilots gunned their engines, and both bombers almost popped into the air. They landed at nearby Norfolk. *Hornet* had been heading at 25 knots into a headwind of 20 knots. B-25s needed an indicated airspeed of 70mph to take off. This meant that McCarthy and Fitzgerald only needed to be moving down the flight deck at 25mph to get airborne. McCarthy had no problems at all. Fitzgerald almost lost control and nearly crashed into the carrier's island. Nevertheless, the dangerous test was a complete success. The Americans now knew for certain that B-25 bombers could definitely take off from an aircraft carrier. Nobody bothered to tell either Fitzgerald or McCarthy what the purpose of their strange test flight had been. They would figure that out for themselves three months later when every newspaper in the country ran big front-page stories about Jimmy Doolittle's daring raid over Tokyo. Photographs of Jimmy Doolittle's sixteen outsized B-25s jammed on to the same flight deck the following April show just what a daring feat Fitzgerald and McCarthy had pulled off, and they had done it with almost no notice at all. For them it had just been a regular, if somewhat exciting, training day.

Wu Duncan reported back to Captain Low and Admiral King that B-25s really could take off from an aircraft carrier. Fitzgerald and

McCarthy had not been carrying heavy loads, but Duncan calculated that even B-25s heavily laden with bombs could also make it. Duncan's answer to Captain Low's first question was still a resounding 'no'. A carrier flight deck was far too short a platform for a B-25 to land on. Any B-25 pilot taking off from an aircraft carrier to bomb Japan would never return to the ship.

Army Air Force General Hap Arnold began looking around for an expert pilot with some very unusual, technical skills. Arnold wanted a top man to lead an all-volunteer force on what might well be a suicide mission. Arnold made an inspired choice when he selected an officer that he had known for over twenty years. Jimmy Doolittle had proven himself to be a skilled and fearless pilot dozens of times. He had gained an international reputation by flying amazing stunts at air shows and winning international air races all over the world. As an added plus for this technically challenging mission, Doolittle had a doctorate in aeronautical engineering.

Doolittle first signed up to be an Army Air Corps pilot in 1917. He had spent his last summer vacation from UC Berkeley working at a dangerous job as a hard-rock miner in Nevada. When he returned to Berkeley that fall, many of his fellow students had volunteered to serve in World War One. A good friend told him that he was seriously thinking about enlisting too. Intrigued, Doolittle signed up for Army pilot training. Somehow, his paperwork got misplaced and his orders were delayed. Doolittle ran out of money. He could not get a regular job because he was honest enough not to hide the fact that he would soon be going into the Army. Doolittle nearly starved, so he found a little restaurant where soup cost 15 cents, but they placed two big stacks of bread on each table. He ate all the bread. However, after two days of Doolittle devouring all his free bread, the restaurant owner threw him out. Doolittle went back to hard-rock mining, where there were plenty of temporary jobs. Luckily, he soon got his orders to report for Army training.

Doolittle missed seeing combat in World War One and spent the interwar years flying in air shows and promoting Army Air Corps aviation. Orville Wright even came to see one of his flying exhibitions. Doolittle broke speed records; won international air races, and became an international celebrity. He modestly attributed his popularity with everyday Americans to his strange last name. The Army gave Doolittle two years' leave to get a masters degree in aeronautical engineering from the Massachusetts Institute of Technology. Working like mad night and day, Doolittle got a PhD instead. Doolittle always attributed his unbelievably rapid progress at MIT to his very supportive wife, Jo. Every evening she would type up his class notes. Then Jo and Jimmy would sit together and discuss aeronautical theory for much of the night.

In the late 1930s Congressional funding for Army Air Corps aviation dwindled. Promotions were scarce. Doolittle was still a lieutenant, but now he had a wife and two small children to take care of. His Army pay of $200 a month was just not enough to support his larger family. So Doolittle resigned his regular commission and became a major in the reserves. He then went to work for the Shell Oil Company promoting a new kind of high-octane aviation gasoline. A civilian now, Doolittle's salary immediately tripled. On one of his sales trips for Shell Oil, Doolittle visited Nazi Germany and was alarmed by what he saw there. The German aircraft manufacturing industry appeared to be gearing up for war. So Doolittle did his best to sound the alarm. He reported what he had seen in Germany to the US Embassy in London. The Army attaché hardly listened at all to what he had to say, but the Navy attaché was intensely interested.[91]

Doolittle also wrote to General Arnold about the situation. He volunteered to go back on active duty. Shortly after Hitler invaded Poland, Doolittle started working as General Arnold's right-hand man. Arnold gave Doolittle a number of interesting assignments. One assignment was to check out the Martin B-26 Marauder medium bomber. The Marauder was getting a reputation as a dangerous plane to fly; it was said to be a real 'widow maker'. Doolittle went to the Martin factory to check it out. He flew the bomber and really liked it. He did think that the powerful, twin-engine B-26 would be a fairly difficult and unforgiving plane for an inexperienced pilot to handle. He thought that some additional training would be needed for pilots transitioning to the Marauder from planes that were easier to fly. So Doolittle drafted additional lesson plans for pilots new to the B-26. Then he travelled around to various Army Air Corps training facilities, and asked new pilots what they thought was wrong with the plane. Their complaints always concerned rumored problems that they had heard about but had never personally experienced. Many new pilots thought that the B-26 would spin out of control if one of its two engines conked out. Every time Doolittle heard this complaint he would put on a little demonstration. Doolittle would take off in a B-26 and then shut off one of its engines. Then he would circle the training field on only that one engine, and land. His B-26 never went into a dangerous spin. Doolittle never lost control or had any other kind of problem. After seeing these demonstration flights most new pilots immediately lost any fear they had of flying the B-26, but pilots new to the Marauder were still required to take the extra lessons that Doolittle had written up.

Although the B-26 was also medium bomber, it was a completely different airplane from the B-25 medium bombers that Doolittle's men flew on the famous raid over Tokyo. One day General Arnold unexpectedly asked Doolittle what he thought about the idea of flying long-range Army Air Force bombers off an aircraft carrier to strike Japan. Doolittle immediately fell in love with this revolutionary, totally counter-intuitive, idea, and volunteered to lead such a raid himself. He even recommended using the B-25 off the top of his head. After all, he was an aeronautical engineer. Doolittle knew that the standard B-25 did not have quite the range for such a long mission. So he began drawing up specifications for fitting B-25s with additional fuel tanks. General Arnold ordered that eighteen B-25s be modified to meet Doolittle's specifications. Then he put the modified bombers under Doolittle's command. Wu Duncan flew to Hawaii to meet with Admiral Nimitz and arrange for an aircraft carrier. They decided that the brand-new *Hornet* would carry Doolittle's bombers on the raid. After all, Lieutenants Fitzgerald and McCarthy had already flown their B-25s off of *Hornet* with no problem at all. Then Nimitz told Vice Admiral William Halsey about the plan. 'Wild Bill' Halsey instantly 'volunteered' *Enterprise* to go along on the mission as escort. (Newspaper reporters nicknamed this famous carrier admiral 'Bull' Halsey but inside the Navy he was always known as 'Wild Bill'.)

The Navy assigned Lieutenant Hank Miller as an instructor to train the pilots who would go on the raid. Miller would teach Doolittle's men some of the tricks of the carrier pilot's trade, like how to get airborne almost instantly from what seemed an impossibly short flight deck. Doolittle looked around and located some available B-25 crews in Oregon. They were part of the 17th Bombardment Group. All Doolittle told these men was that he was looking for volunteers to go on a very dangerous secret mission. It was so secret that he could not tell them anything about it. Almost everyone in the 17th volunteered to go. Doolittle and his volunteers set up shop at an out-of-the-way Army air strip near Elgin, Florida.

Then Navy instructor pilot Lieutenant Miller showed up and got his first face-to-face look at a B-25. That same day, Miller got one of Doolittle's bombers into the air after an incredibly short ground roll. His bomber was only going 50mph. Then, somehow, Miller's B-25 was airborne.[92] He was actually flying. The Army Air Force pilots were stunned. Nobody could get a B-25 off the ground when it was going so slowly. The plane's specifications clearly stated that its pilot needed to reach a minimum indicated airspeed of 70mph to get off the ground! How the heck had the Navy pilot done it? Then Miller taught the Army Air Force pilots a few of his simple Navy tricks. Soon Doolittle's men were confidently taking off after amazingly short ground rolls, and at impossibly low speeds. A month earlier none of the Army Air Force pilots would ever have dreamed of trying such crazy things in a B-25.

At 0600 on 18 April 1942, *Enterprise* and *Hornet* were plowing through dirty weather 800 miles east of Tokyo. Thirty foot waves rolled both ships back and forth so steeply that even old salts were getting queasy stomachs. Vice Admiral William Halsey commanded both carriers and a dozen cruisers and destroyers screening them. An *Enterprise* pilot who had been scouting out in front of the fleet buzzed the ship and dropped a weighted 'bean bag' message pouch right in the middle of the flight deck. It said that there was a Japanese picket boat up ahead, and that the pilot thought that he had been spotted. Halsey immediately ordered a change of course. The American ships were still over 800 miles from Japan. Then another Japanese picket boat materialized. This one was in front of *Hornet.* The Americans began intercepting radio warnings that the boat was sending back to Tokyo. Halsey ordered a cruiser to sink both picket boats. Amid rain squalls and tossing seas, the picket boats turned out to be hard to hit. It took a while to sink them. The radio warnings continued. *Enterprise* blinkered a coded order for Doolittle's raiders to launch at once. Halsey's message read: 'Launch planes X to Col. Doolittle and his gallant command good luck and god bless you X.'[93]

Jimmy Doolittle took off first. This meant that he had the shortest amount of flight deck in front of him, and the diciest take-off. If he could get off safely, then everyone coming behind him would have a slightly better chance of making it. Doolittle put his plane's nose wheel on a white guideline that the *Hornet*'s crew had painted on the flight deck. If his wheel stayed on the line during take-off, his right wing would just clear the carrier's superstructure. Doolittle stood on his brakes. The wind was howling at 30mph. *Hornet* turned into the gusts doing 20 knots, so Doolittle had a 50mph headwind that would give his big bomber plenty of lift. The carrier was pitching wildly, and timing was critical. *Hornet*'s bow sank down to the trough of a 30ft wave. It slowly began to rise back up. Doolittle shoved his throttles full forward and released his brakes. The big B-25 seemed to almost float off the flight deck. There were no problems at all.[94] Doolittle circled the carrier once so that his navigator could recalibrate their magnetic compass. Then he turned away from *Hornet* and headed towards Tokyo.

***

Jimmy Doolittle apparently thought that he might be court-martialed for losing all of his planes during the raid over Tokyo. Instead, President Roosevelt promoted him to brigadier general and awarded him the Medal of Honor. After he had retired from the service, President Ronald Reagan awarded General Jimmy Doolittle his fourth star.

The Code Breakers

Joseph Rochefort probably did more to win the Battle of Midway than Jimmie Thach, Dick Best or Wade McClusky, even though he never fired a shot. He was an intelligence officer, a cryptanalyst, a code breaker. Commander Rochefort was also a pretty eccentric individual. He was a regular Navy officer, but he is said to have occasionally worked on breaking codes while wearing a smoking jacket and bedroom slippers. This oddball behavior was tolerated apparently because his superiors viewed the brilliant Rochefort an 'indispensible man'. He was the head of the Navy's Combat Intelligence Unit (CIU) at Pearl Harbor. Its code name was Station 'Hypo'. Rochefort commanded a talented but quirky group of hand-picked intelligence specialists. He had ten officers and thirteen enlisted men working for him, and his 'office' was a large area in the basement of the Pearl Harbor Administration Building. Everyone working in the building referred to that basement as the 'dungeon'. Visitors were never very welcome. You had to go down a long narrow stairwell just to get to the entrance, and there was always an armed Marine guard stationed at the door. Once inside, 'by the book' officers were appalled by the clutter and the informal atmosphere. Rochefort's officers called each other by their first names, while enlisted men rarely saluted, or even addressed their superiors as 'sir'. The dungeon was usually filled with a thick, eye-watering haze. The creaky ventilation system never worked very well, and many of Rochefort's intelligence experts were heavy smokers. That included the pipe-chomping Rochefort.

Station Hypo was part of a far-flung radio intelligence network that the Navy had built up across the Pacific. Rochefort and his team did not actually intercept any Japanese transmissions themselves, that work was done by radio operators based at various listening stations north of Pearl Harbor. The Navy had a similar set up in the Philippines called Station Cast. There was also a small listening station on Guam.

Rochefort had lied about his age while still in high school just to get into the Navy. Still, he was such a talented and intelligent fellow that he earned an officer's commission just a few years after enlisting.[95] Rochefort was a 'mustang', a naval officer who had not gone to Annapolis or been through Reserve Officers' Training Corps (ROTC). Because Rochefort joined the Navy right out of high school, he never had a loyal group of academy buddies who would stick up for him through thick and thin. This handicapped Rochefort in the vicious bureaucratic infighting that still characterizes much of the American intelligence community. A climate of jealousy and never-ending turf wars has long permeated virtually all US intelligence agencies. It is a shameful situation that the American public rarely hears anything about. One silly rivalry ended up with his powerful bureaucratic enemies in Washington getting the brilliant Rochefort kicked out of intelligence altogether. This disgusting wrong was partially righted in 1986 when Rochefort was posthumously awarded the Presidential Medal of Freedom. Rochefort had been part of the Navy's first code-breaking team. He spoke fluent Japanese, he was an expert bridge player, and he was fiendishly adept at solving the most difficult kinds of crossword puzzles. In other words, Rochefort was the perfect man for deciphering codes and doing similar kinds of secret intelligence work.

By the spring of 1942, Rochefort and his team in the dungeon were beginning to decipher bits and pieces of 'JN-25', the Japanese Navy's top secret operational code. In April, Station Hypo received a high-priority request for information from Washington DC. Admiral King, the Commander in Chief of the US Fleet, wanted Rochefort's forecast of the Japanese Navy's upcoming moves in the Pacific.[96] At the time the Japanese carrier force had been raiding British possessions in the Indian Ocean. Still winning victory after victory, Japanese planes had just sunk the British aircraft carrier *Hermes* off Ceylon (present-day Sri Lanka). Rochefort came up with the following predictions: Japanese operations in the Indian Ocean were over. The carriers were on their way back to the home islands. The plan to invade Australia had been temporarily postponed. A big fight was brewing deep in the South Pacific, and an even bigger operation was being readied for somewhere in the Central Pacific. This Central Pacific operation turned out to be Admiral Yamamoto's plan to attack Midway, but Rochefort had not identified the target at the time of Admiral King's request. Rochefort's forecast turned out to be stunningly accurate. Rochefort and his team correctly predicted every major move that the Japanese military made during the spring of 1942.

That April, Japanese radio transmissions began referring to a place with the code name 'AF'. Soon many transmissions were talking about AF and it was clearly going to be the target of the big Central Pacific operation, the one that Rochefort had already gotten wind of. Most of the ships in Yamamoto's Combined Fleet would be converging on the place. So the big question was: Where is AF? Then someone on Rochefort's team remembered that months back a Japanese transmission had referred to something in the 'Midway area' as AF. The only thing of importance in the 'Midway area' is Midway itself. So Rochefort concluded that Midway had to be the target of the big Central Pacific operation. Unfortunately, less-knowledgeable analysts high up in the Navy Department bureaucracy in Washington thought that Rochefort was dead wrong. These were the petty men who eventually railroaded Rochefort right out of intelligence. These bureaucrats fought Rochefort tooth and nail. The Army was also rightly worried that the Japanese might be planning to attack Hawaii, or even the West Coast of the United States.

Edward Layton, Admiral Nimitz's lead intelligence officer, also spoke fluent Japanese. In fact, he knew Rochefort well from the days when both men were living in Japan learning the language. Nimitz deeply respected Layton's opinion on such matters, and Layton was sure that Rochefort's quirky, hand-picked team of experts had gotten it right. So Nimitz was sold on Midway being the target right off the bat. Still, the debate and infighting with the bureaucrats in Washington raged on. Was the target Midway or not? Then Jasper Holmes, one of Rochefort's code breakers, came up with an ingenious plan.[97] It would definitively prove whether or not AF was the Japanese code word for Midway. An undersea communications cable still connected Midway with Pearl Harbor. The Americans on Midway were secretly ordered via the cable to broadcast an un-coded 'emergency' radio transmission. The broadcast was to say that Midway's water desalinization equipment had blown up, and that the base was short of water. Sure enough, a few days later an American listening station intercepted a Japanese radio transmission saying that AF was running out of water. Midway definitely had to be the target!

On 25 May, Rochefort's team hit the jackpot. They decoded a long transmission giving the exact times of Japanese ship movements for the Central Pacific operation, and when the Japanese planned to strike specific targets.[98] So now the Americans knew all of the most important details in Admiral Yamamoto's super-secret Operation MI. Rochefort even learned about Yamamoto's plan to reconnoiter Pearl

Harbor with flying boats refueled at French Frigate Shoals. Admiral Nimitz sprung into action. He ordered his three carriers, all three operating deep in the South Pacific, to drop everything and come charging back to Pearl Harbor. They were *Enterprise*, *Hornet*, and the badly damaged *Yorktown*. If the Pearl Harbor Navy Yard could repair *Yorktown* in time, all three carriers would be north-east of Midway waiting to ambush the Japanese. Nimitz also dispatched a seaplane tender to anchor at French Frigate Shoals. This made it impossible for the Japanese to secretly refuel reconnaissance planes there. Nimitz also arranged for US submarines to shadow the oncoming Japanese carriers. Nimitz stuffed the tiny base on Midway with all the military supplies that he could lay his hands on. He sent Midway thousands of yards of barbed wire. A radar installation was set up. Nimitz sent Midway all kinds of aircraft: PBY search planes, B-26 medium bombers, heavy B-17 bombers, half a dozen brand-new TBF torpedo planes, and some Wildcat fighters. Nimitz even reinforced Midway with a Marine raider battalion.

The Americans on Midway were as ready for a Japanese attack as they could possibly be. All this was solely because of the brilliant work done by Rochefort and his intelligence specialists. Rochefort's team accurately predicted every move that the Japanese made at Midway with one notable exception: they never discovered that Yamamoto's 'Main Force' of battleships would be trailing hundreds of miles behind the carriers of the *Kido Butai*.[99] Since these ships were so far behind the carriers that they never came close to seeing any action, this 'mistake' hardly mattered at all.

While he was alive Rochefort never received the official recognition that he so richly deserved. When Admiral Nimitz recommended Rochefort for the Navy Cross, the intransigent, vindictive bureaucrats in Washington opposed it. Incredibly, Nimitz' recommendation was blocked by these small and jealous men. The primary culprits were two brothers who were also both 'political' admirals based in

Washington. Their names are unimportant. Later, Rochefort was moved out of intelligence altogether. When he requested sea duty, Rochefort was assigned to command a 'floating dockyard' in San Francisco Bay.[100] Rochefort did receive some unexpected recognition in 1976 when he was still alive, but already living in a nursing home. The Ohio-born Rochefort served as a coach to actor Hal Holbrook when he was portraying an odd, 'southern-fried' version of Rochefort in Hollywood's inaccurate, highly fictionalized blockbuster *Midway!* President Reagan did his best to right these obvious official wrongs in 1986. Reagan posthumously awarded Rochefort the Distinguished Service Medal and the Presidential Medal of Freedom. Rochefort's Distinguished Service Medal citation reads as follows:[101]

> For exceptionally meritorious service to the Government of the United States in a duty of great responsibility while serving the Commander-in-Chief of the Pacific Fleet as Officer in Charge of the Combat Intelligence Unit (Station Hypo) from March 1942 through June 1942. By virtue of his superb professional knowledge, astute guidance, and personal dedication, Captain (then Commander) Rochefort provided technical expertise and inspiring leadership to discover, analyze, and provide to the Fleet Commander-in-Chief astoundingly timely and accurate intelligence on Japanese naval plans and intentions leading to the Battle of Midway in June 1942. The information provided by Captain Rochefort's Radio Intelligence Unit served as the singular basis for the Fleet Commander-in-Chief to plan his defenses, deploy his limited forces, and devise strategy to ensure US Navy success in engaging the Japanese forces at Midway. His unrelenting efforts in this endeavor and the intelligence information he developed resulted in a Naval engagement with the Japanese fleet that is acknowledged as the turning point of the Pacific War. Captain Rochefort's distinctive accomplishments,

tenacious commitment to excellence, and steadfast devotion to duty reflected great credit upon himself and were in keeping with the highest traditions of the United States Naval Service. For the President,

John Lehman
Secretary of the Navy

Admiral Nimitz Inspects *Yorktown*

Enterprise and *Hornet* charged into Pearl Harbor on 26 May. They had raced up from the South Pacific on the urgent order of Nimitz. Both carriers were ship-shape and ready for anything. The wounded *Yorktown* limped along about a day behind them. She was trailing a mile-long black oil slick behind her. Admiral Bill Halsey, the aggressive commander of *Enterprise*, was in pitiful physical shape.[102] Halsey had developed a painful case of the shingles, and inflamed red skin burned and itched like crazy all over his body. Halsey and the medics desperately resorted to all sorts of remedies, including 'oatmeal baths'. Nothing worked, and the horrible itching got worse and worse. The ship's doctor officially put Halsey on the sick list, but the moment *Enterprise* moored in Pearl Harbor, he hurried off to talk with Admiral Nimitz. He wanted to get the latest skinny on the big operation that he knew was in the works. Nimitz took one look at Halsey and ordered him to check himself into the hospital. Halsey was stunned. He had really been looking forward to a winner-take-all shoot out with the Japanese. Halsey was deeply disappointed, but he immediately recommended that Admiral Raymond Spruance replace him and take command of *Enterprise* and its support ships. Spruance had no carrier experience at all. He had been following Halsey all over the Pacific, commanding the cruisers and destroyers screening the *Enterprise*. Spruance was a 'black shoe' admiral, *i.e.*, a battleship and cruiser man. Naval aviators wore more stylish brown shoes. Still, Halsey deeply respected Spruance's low-key temperament and good judgment. Anyway, Spruance would have Halsey's top-notch aviation staff on hand to advise him.

The bleeding *Yorktown* dragged herself into Pearl Harbor the next day. Dockyard crews had worked hard to fabricate giant blocks to support her great weight. The damaged flattop eased into Dry Dock Number One. Repair crews started working right away. Admiral Nimitz showed up at the dry dock in a pair of chest-high waders to personally inspect the damage. Nimitz saw right away that *Yorktown*'s leaking exterior plates could be repaired fairly easily. The heavy bomb damage deep inside the carrier was another matter altogether. The dockyard chiefs and engineers estimated that they could repair *Yorktown* in about three months. Nimitz turned around and quietly told them, 'We must have this ship back in three days.'[103] From that moment on hundreds of welders, electricians, pipe fitters, and shipwrights of every description swarmed all over every compartment and deck of *Yorktown*. The work went on feverishly, twenty-four hours a day. Some men worked forty-eight hours straight; then they just had to lie down and rest. The din from the jack hammering, welding and drilling was terrific. The tropical air inside the ship grew so hot and stifling that many men, especially the welders in their heavy helmets, began to pass out. Supervisors would give these men something to drink and a sandwich, and send them topside for a breath of fresh air. Then the men would come right back down to work, and the whole process would start all over again. Repairing the *Yorktown* on a crash basis took an enormous amount of electric power. Hawaii Electric, the local utility company, resorted to rolling blackouts throughout Honolulu to handle the extra load. Seawater began flooding into Dry Dock Number One in the early morning hours of 30 May. The yardmen refloated *Yorktown* just in time to meet Admiral Nimitz's seventy-two-hour deadline. The repairs were far from pretty, and they were probably not as strong as they might have been if there had been three months to do the work. Some electricians were still finishing up last-minute jobs when the screws started turning and the big ship got under way. The last of the workmen hurriedly dropped into waiting shore boats. Then the mighty *Yorktown*, like the *Lexington,* sailed out of Pearl Harbor for the last time.

Chapter 5

Thach Loses His Squadron

About the same time that Butch O'Hare was nervously trying to deal with a crowd of reporters during the Medal of Honor ceremony at the White House, Jimmie Thach got word that Admiral Fitch wanted to see him. Thach had been expecting the admiral's call. He was certain that he and his squadron would be back at sea in no time. Fitch told Thach that he was taking *Lexington* back to the South Pacific. That was exactly what Thach had been hoping to hear. Then Admiral Fitch dropped a bombshell. He was taking Thach's pilots with him, but he was not taking Thach! Thach was one of the Navy's top gunnery experts. He had done a magnificent job training Fighting Three's pilots. They were the 'All Navy' gunnery champions. So Admiral Fitch wanted Thach to stay in Hawaii. He was needed there to show all the new rookie pilots flooding into Oahu how to fight, and most particularly how to shoot. Thach was floored. Fitch had hurt his feelings. He actually begged Fitch to take him along, but the final decision had already been made.[104] Thach's veteran pilots would be transferred to *Lexington*'s regular squadron, Fighting Two. Don Lovelace, Thach's exec, was being promoted. Lovelace would now command a fighter squadron of his own. Fitch explained that Thach would soon be getting twenty-seven factory-new Wildcat fighters for Fighting Three. He would also be getting twenty-seven new pilots, many fresh out of flight school. They would need to be trained by an expert in the finer points of aerial combat.

Lexington and her escort of cruisers and destroyers sailed out of Pearl Harbor. The '*Lady Lex*' would never return. The fleet headed south-west to the Coral Sea and the first real 'carrier versus carrier' battle in history. The Battle of the Coral Sea was an important strategic victory for the United States, but it came at a high price. The Americans stopped Japan's drive on Australia, but *Lexington* was sunk. *Yorktown* was badly damaged. A fleet oiler and a destroyer were also lost. Thach's veteran pilots who had been transferred to Fighting Two fought well. Noel Gayler shot down two Japanese bombers. He would become a fighter ace, an admiral, and eventually Commander-in-Chief in the Pacific. Rolla Lemon went on to command an entire carrier air group.

Thach got all of his promised new Wildcat fighters right away. They were the new F4F-4 featuring six 50-caliber machine guns instead of only four in the older, 'dash three' model. His new pilots trickled in slowly over the next month. For a week or so, Fighting Three had twenty-seven brand-new Wildcats fighters but only one pilot who was qualified to fly them. Thach, the former test pilot, dutifully climbed into the cockpits of all twenty-seven of his new planes. He flew careful 'check-out' flights in every single one.[105]

Then Don Lovelace decided to delay going to San Diego to take over his new squadron and unexpectedly told Thach that he would stick around Kaneohe for a while. He wanted to help Thach train all the new rookie pilots that he would be getting. Lovelace's decision to help out a friend in a tough situation was incredibly gracious. Few men in his position would have been thinking about anything other than their new command. It was a gracious decision, but it was one that would end up costing Lovelace his life.

The first new replacement pilot showed up toward the end of April. He was Ensign 'Ram' Dibb, who would be Thach's wingman at the Battle of Midway. They would be flying together when the Thach Weave was first used in combat. Ensign Dibb was already 'famous' throughout the Pacific Fleet. He had somehow managed to walk away unscathed from a spectacular crack-up when he was trying to land on

Hornet. His Wildcat was totally demolished, but Dibb himself did not even get a scratch. Thach had more time to teach Dibb the finer points of tactics and aerial gunnery than any of the other replacements who showed up later. Most especially, he taught his young wingman a lot about a new tactical set-up that eventually came to be known as the Thach Weave.

A large group of new pilots showed up in May. Thach trained these new men relentlessly. He pushed them hard, as if he expected them to be in combat almost immediately, and, of course, he did. Most of their time aloft was spent practicing Thach's favorite subject, aerial gunnery. Thach would fly right alongside a new man and coach him while the rookie tried to hit an aerial target or 'sleeve' being towed by another plane. After weeks of intense gunnery practice, both Thach and Lovelace agreed that all their new rookie pilots could shoot 'pretty well'. More and more new pilots kept flooding in. Thach soon had a full complement of twenty-seven fully qualified fighter pilots.

In late May he got the alert to get his squadron ready to fly out to *Yorktown.* Lovelace volunteered to go along. The battered *Yorktown* was at sea again after its quick, three-day, emergency repair job at Pearl Harbor. Thach was told that a big Japanese push was expected soon and it was supposed to take place somewhere in the Central Pacific. He was told that and nothing more. Thach would not get a full briefing until his entire squadron had landed and was safely tucked in aboard *Yorktown.* Fighting Three and two other squadrons flew out to the carrier on 30 May. She was steaming about 50 miles north of Oahu. Scores of fighters, dive bombers and torpedo planes orbited overhead. Such rare, multi-squadron fly-ins are spectacular sights. The planes started to land, and at first everything ran like clockwork. Then disaster struck. Lovelace had just landed and was taxiing down the flight deck. His rookie wingman came in behind him but lost control when he smacked his landing gear way too hard on *Yorktown*'s flight deck. The rookie's fighter bounced up into the air, sailed forward and crashed right on top of Lovelace's plane. The fighter's spinning propeller hit Lovelace square in the neck and decapitated him.[106] Lovelace was Thach's best friend, and his ugly death was a terrible, totally unexpected blow. The gruesome sight of Lovelace's mangled, headless body and his blood splattered all over the cockpit stunned every one of Thach's young pilots. They had all looked up to Lovelace as a friendly mentor. Technically, Lovelace was not even supposed to be aboard *Yorktown*. He should have been on his way back to San Diego getting ready to take command of his new squadron.

Thach immediately called all of his young fliers together in the wardroom. He told them that what had just happened to Lovelace was a far greater shock to him than it was to any of them. Lovelace was the best friend that he had ever had in his life. Still, there was a big battle coming up. They all had a big job to do. Thach told his men that for the present time he was just going to forget about what had happened to Lovelace. He was just going to completely put it out of his mind, and he expected them to do the same.

Later that night Thach called his pilots back to the wardroom for a briefing by Murr Arnold, *Yorktown*'s air officer. Arnold gave them a detailed rundown of what they were up against: a big Japanese fleet was coming down from the north-west and was going to attack Midway. The Japanese fleet would include four or five aircraft carriers, and the carriers would be screened by dozens of battleships, cruisers, and destroyers. At the same time an invasion force carrying thousands of assault troops would be approaching Midway from the south-west. This invasion force would be backed up by a separate group of battleships and cruisers. At the same time, another Japanese fleet would be attacking US bases in the Aleutian Islands. *Yorktown* was heading out to join up with *Enterprise* and *Hornet*. They were already waiting in ambush north-east of Midway. Arnold had incredibly detailed information about the Japanese plan of attack. He was so specific that it almost seemed like some crafty American spy had been in the room taking notes when Admiral Yamamoto was issuing his orders. The briefings aboard *Enterprise* and *Hornet* had been similarly detailed. Everybody wondered where such fantastic intelligence had come from, but nobody bothered to ask. They all knew that they would never get a straight answer anyway. Of course, very few people even among the Navy's top brass actually knew the great secret that the Japanese Navy's most important operational code had been broken. Dick Best, aboard the *Enterprise*, was still worried about the safety of his wife and baby back in Honolulu. On the *Enterprise* Admiral Spruance did the briefing himself. So Best asked Spruance what would happen if the Japanese bypassed Midway? What would happen if they just went straight for Pearl Harbor? Best was a dive bomber pilot. He was a man who might easily fall into the hands of the Japanese. So Spruance simply said, 'We just hope they will not.'[107]

Opening Moves

Joe Rochefort's Combat Intelligence Unit (CIU) had predicted that the Japanese carriers would strike Midway early on the morning of either 4 or 5 June. As things turned out, they came on the 4th. CIU said that the Japanese would approach the US base from the north-west on a bearing of approximately 320 degrees. So on the night of 3 June all the pilots in Patrol Squadron 23 on Midway were keyed up and ready to go. When Lieutenant Howard Ady saw the next day's assignments on the blackboard at the Bachelors Officers Quarters he knew that he and his crew had hit the jackpot.[108] On the morning of 4 June they would be flying an outbound search on a course of 322½ degrees. That was close enough!

The radio call sign for Lieutenant Ady's PBY was 'Strawberry 5'. In the early morning hours of 4 June, Strawberry 5 was already aloft flying over 100 miles north-west of Midway. Dawn broke on a typically beautiful Central Pacific morning, but there was nothing in sight but a few low-hanging clouds on the distant horizon. Otherwise there was only blue sky and blue water for as far the eye could see. Ady and his crew should have been seeing a huge fleet of warships by now. So where were the Japanese carriers? Where were all the battleships and cruisers that were supposed to be escorting them? Could all that magnificently detailed intelligence have been dead wrong? A minute or two went by and nothing appeared on the horizon. Then it was like the opening scene of some great Broadway play or a Hollywood blockbuster. A small float plane shot right past Ady's PBY. It did not veer left or right. Obviously on important business, the float plane was racing on a direct course for Midway. Then two giant aircraft carriers and dozens of escort ships emerged from beneath the clouds on the horizon.[109] It was an entire fleet! Scores of ships; two aircraft carriers; a battleship, and dozens of cruisers and destroyers were throwing up big white bow waves. They were all racing full speed for Midway. It was just as the intelligence boys had predicted. Lieutenant Ady radioed in a description of the enormous fleet that had just materialized in front of him. However, Ady sent out his message in code. His broadcast would take a few precious minutes for the guys back on Midway to decipher. Ady continued sending out bits of information as he circled the giant Japanese fleet. His warning would not be the first. Flying a few miles away, Lieutenant William Chase spotted over a hundred Japanese warplanes – Zero fighters, Kate torpedo planes, and Val dive bombers – all heading straight for Midway. Chase immediately sent out his broadcast in plain English: 'Many planes headed Midway, bearing three-twenty. Distance one-fifty.' This was the startling broadcast that alerted everyone aboard the three American carriers waiting in ambush. This was the broadcast that put all of the forces that Nimitz had sent to Midway into motion. Later, Admiral Nimitz would jokingly complain that Joe Rochefort's predictions about the Japanese attack on Midway had been off by five minutes and five degrees. Rochefort and his team of intelligence gurus had actually done much better than Nimitz' happy joke implied. Their predictions about the movements of the all-important Japanese aircraft carriers had literally been perfect.[110] They should have been. After all, Rochefort and his team had been reading Admiral Yamamoto's direct orders exactly as they had been issued from Combined Fleet headquarters.

Lieutenant Joichi Tomonaga led that morning strike on Midway. Standing 6ft tall and strikingly handsome, Tomonaga commanded a total of 108 warplanes. His mission was to destroy every American plane on Midway and render its airfields temporarily unusable. Admiral Yamamoto then planned to quickly repair any damage to the runways and use Midway as a Japanese air base. Lieutenant Tomonaga had replaced Mitsuo Fuchida as the Japanese air group leader. Fuchida had led the attack on Pearl Harbor and was a national hero. He was originally picked to lead the attack on Midway, but luckily (for Fuchida) he developed an acute case of appendicitis after the *Kido Butai* had left Japan. Tomonaga's command plane (with distinctive feathered 'leaders insignia' on its tail) was shot down by Jimmie Thach later that afternoon.[111]

Rear Admiral Frank 'Black Jack' Fletcher was in overall command of the US carriers waiting in ambush. When the PBYs began broadcasting contact reports he immediately ordered *Enterprise* and *Hornet* (Task Force 16) to head for the enemy. Fletcher ordered them to attack the Japanese carriers when they were 'definitely located'. Fletcher planned to follow in *Yorktown* (Task Force 17) as soon as he had recovered some search planes. Historians have largely praised Fletcher's aggressive action. He was determined to hit the Japanese before they could locate and hit the American carriers. In this, Fletcher succeeded marvelously. Yet Jimmie Thach always thought that Fletcher's decision to send two carriers ahead was a big mistake. Fletcher was dividing his forces rather than concentrating them. Thach thought that carefully coordinating the search plans of the three US carriers would have eliminated any need to separate them. Two years later, when he was the Operations

Officer of the huge Fast Carrier Task Force, Thach synchronized the movements of up to sixteen carriers and over a thousand planes in just this way. Thach always believed that Fletcher's decision to separate the US carriers at Midway led to the unnecessary loss of *Yorktown*. Decades later, when Thach was a crusty, retired four-star admiral he adamantly maintained that he had not changed his opinion on the subject, 'one damned bit'.[112]

All the US planes based on Midway were ordered to start warming up their engines at 0530. Midway's new radar installation was showing that the incoming Japanese planes were only 90 miles to the north-west, and they were coming in fast. Twenty-six Marine Corps fighters took off first. The Marines flew six relatively new Grumman Wildcats and twenty semi-obsolete Brewster Buffaloes. The Marines turned north-west and climbed as fast as their sluggish fighters could go. Luckily, the slow-climbing American fighters had plenty of warning and plenty of time to gain altitude. Six brand-new TBF torpedo planes were the next to take off from Midway. They were a great improvement over the outmoded TBDs still flown by the torpedo squadrons aboard the carriers. The TBFs too headed north-west. The Japanese carriers were now 150 miles out. Four Army Air Force B-26 bombers launched next. They were led by Captain James Collins. Collins' medium bombers had been 'jury rigged' to carry anti-ship torpedoes. This shows just how desperate the Americans were during the early months of the Pacific War. The B-26s made a beeline to the north-west straight for the enemy fleet. Then the American dive bombers took off. When the last Marine pilot scrambled into the air, the Japanese were still 29 miles away.[113] The only American planes that the Japanese would catch on the ground that morning were a few 'unflyables' that were undergoing major repairs. Lieutenant Tomonaga and his pilots never had a prayer of accomplishing their primary mission and destroying all the US planes on Midway.

The Marine fighter pilots spotted the incoming Japanese first. They surprised Tomonaga. Even the old Brewster Buffaloes got in one good firing pass. The Americans were able to shoot down two enemy bombers before the high-performance Zeroes came screaming down from above. Then it was pretty much a slaughter. The Marine pilots tenaciously fought the Zeroes all the way back to Midway, but there was little that they could do except try to stay alive. The Zeroes were just too fast and too agile. The Zeros shot up the slower American planes like they were practice targets. Occasionally, an American pilot came out on top. Captain Marion Carl spotted a Zero on his tail. It was in perfect position to open fire. The future Medal of Honor winner cut his throttle and slammed down his flaps. The Zero shot past him, and Carl shot it down. Still, the Zeros destroyed fifteen of the twenty American fighters. They badly damaged almost all the rest. Only two of the Marine fighters that made it back to Midway were actually flyable.

With the American fighters knocked out of action so quickly over a hundred Japanese bombers and fighters ominously circled the tiny US base. Then they all came swarming in from the north. The American anti-aircraft fire was much more accurate than the Japanese had expected. The Kate level bombers quickly released their payloads and flew away. They destroyed a seaplane hangar on Sand Island, an anti-aircraft battery, and a mess hall. The dive bombers wrecked the power station on Eastern Island and blew up Midway's big oil storage tanks. They also smashed an important underground gasoline pipeline. Huge columns of thick black smoke billowed up thousands of feet into the air. The entire atoll looked like it was on fire. Next, the Zero fighters dove in shooting up anything that moved. On the surface it looked like the Japanese had thoroughly wrecked the American base. Every inch of Midway seemed to be on fire. In reality, the raid had been an unmitigated failure. It never had a chance to succeed. The Japanese had killed fewer than a dozen Americans, and they had lost a number of their own planes to the unusually accurate US anti-aircraft fire. Most importantly, they had not come close to achieving their main goal of destroying Midway's airpower. The Americans had gotten every flyable plane into the air when the Japanese were still miles away, and Midway's three runways were still very much intact. Lieutenant Tomonaga reluctantly radioed a coded message back to the Japanese flagship, *Akagi*.[114] The American air base on Midway appeared largely undamaged. A second wave attack was needed to neutralize it. Unfortunately for the Japanese, the second attack that Lieutenant Tomonaga requested would never materialize.

Nagumo's Dilemma

Lieutenant Tomonaga's request for a second strike on Midway put Admiral Nagumo on the horns of a dilemma – apparently one that the overconfident admiral never anticipated. Nagumo's short-sighted response to what was an admittedly confusing situation contributed mightily to Japan's disastrous defeat at Midway. To his credit Admiral Yamamoto had prudently instructed Nagumo to keep a strong force of planes in reserve just in case any US carriers showed up unexpectedly. Nagumo dutifully made sure that his reserve planes were loaded with torpedoes and armor-piercing bombs. These were the kinds of weapons used to attack ships. Both Japanese admirals assumed that one surprise attack on Midway would be more than enough to knock out the air base there. This turned out not to be the case after all. Both men had seriously underestimated their American enemy. Somehow, the Americans had managed to get all their planes into the air before the Japanese bombers arrived. There were no long lines of US planes neatly arranged into nice easy targets like there had been at Pearl Harbor, and the American anti-aircraft fire had been much more accurate than the Japanese had expected. Lieutenant Tomonaga's planes were now well on their way back to the *Kido Butai* from the strike on Midway. In a short time they would be preparing to land. No Japanese search plane had spotted any US ships in the area. So what was Nagumo to do? He could prudently keep his reserve aircraft armed with anti-ship weapons in case the

US Navy really did show up, or he could rearm them now with the high-explosive weapons needed for the second attack on Midway that Tomonaga said was needed. As things turned out, almost immediately it became clear to Admiral Nagumo that Lieutenant Tomonaga was right; Midway's air power had not been neutralized at all.

Shortly after 0700 *Akagi*'s bugler began blaring out the ship's old-fashioned air raid warning. A mixed bag of US warplanes from the island began showing up to drop bombs and launch torpedoes at the Japanese ships. The first planes to attack were the six brand-new TBF Avenger torpedo planes. The TBF was a huge improvement over the semi-obsolete TBD, being tougher and faster than the misnamed Devastator. Grumman and General Motors manufactured almost ten thousand Avengers during the course of the war. Still, the TBF pilots attacking Nagumo's ships had no fighter support at all. Dozens of Zeros swarmed them before they could get in position to launch their torpedoes. The TBFs made no hits and the Japanese shot down five of them. Only one made it back to Midway.

Captain Collins' four B-26 medium bombers charged in next. They were in time to see the end of the failed torpedo plane attack. The army bombers had been jury-rigged to launch anti-ship torpedoes, a far from ideal set-up. Additionally, the gun turrets on one of the B-26s lost power and the machine gun in its tail jammed after firing just one burst.[115] Six Zeros made a slashing head-on attack just as the Army Air Force pilots launched their torpedoes. Lieutenant Herbie Mayes apparently tried to crash his damaged bomber into a carrier. It looked like he missed the flight deck by about a foot. Again, the Americans scored no hits, and only two heavily damaged Army bombers made it back to Midway.

These two daring, but ineffective air attacks on his ships were more than enough for Admiral Nagumo to make up his mind. At 0715 Nagumo decided that he would disregard Admiral Yamamoto's careful instructions about keeping planes in reserve. After all, the search planes

A Japanese Zero about to crash into the sea after an unsuccessful Kamikaze attack on USS *Essex* (CV-9), on 15 May 1945. (United States Naval History and Heritage Command; USNHHC)

Fleet Admiral Chester W. Nimitz, USN, signs the Instrument of Surrender as United States Representative, on board USS *Missouri* (BB-63), 2 September 1945. Standing directly behind him are (left-to-right): General of the Army Douglas MacArthur; Admiral William F. Halsey, USN, and Rear Admiral Forrest Sherman, USN. In front row, background, are (left to right): Rear Admiral Frederick C. Sherman, USN; Vice Admiral Charles A. Lockwood, USN; Vice Admiral John S. McCain, USN; Vice Admiral John H. Towers, USN; Admiral Richmond K. Turner, USN; Rear Admiral Robert B. Carney, USN; General Walter C. Krueger, U.S. Army; General Robert L. Eichelberger, U.S. Army and General Carl A. Spaatz, USAAF. Others identified behind the front row include (in no order): Brigadier General Joseph H. Fellows, USMC; Captain Tom B. Hill, USN; Commodore J.C. Cronin, USN; Rear Admiral Ingram C. Sowell, USN; Rear Admiral Richard E. Byrd, USN; Rear Admiral Howard F. Kingman, USN; Rear Admiral Lloyd J. Wiltsie, USN; Rear Admiral J. Cary Jones, USN; Captain John S. Thach, USN and Commodore Joel T. Boone, USN(MC). (NARA)

USS *Arizona* (BB-39) ablaze, just after her forward magazines exploded. At right, shrouded in smoke from the fire, are the main and foremasts of USS *West Virginia*, which is listing sharply to port after she was torpedoed. Upright mast further to the right is the mainmast of USS *Tennessee* (BB-43), moored inboard of *West Virginia*. The bow and foremast of USS *Vestal* (AR-4), moored outboard of *Arizona*, are visible at the left. (National Archives and Records Administration; NARA)

The burned-out, sunken wreck of USS *Arizona* (BB-39), photographed a number of days after the attack. (NARA)

USS *West Virginia* (BB-48) afire forward, immediately after the Japanese air attack. USS *Tennessee* (BB-43) is on the sunken battleship's opposite side. (USNHHC)

An SBD Dauntless scout-bomber and five TBD-1 Devastator torpedo planes prepare to take-off from the carrier during operations in the south Pacific area, 4 May 1942. Note the launching officer making arm signals in the lower left-center. Take-offs averaged one every thirty seconds. (NARA)

USS *Yorktown* (CV-5) anchored in a Haitian harbor, circa 1938-40. (USNHHC)

Having been hit by anti-aircraft fire, a burning Japanese aircraft, possibly a kamikaze, is pictured from USS *Randolph* (CV-15) during the American carrier raids on Japan, 13-14 May 1945. The picture is dated 14 May. (USNHHC)

Lieutenant Edward H. 'Butch' O'Hare, USN (left), and Lieutenant Commander John 'Jimmy' Thach (right) shaking hands in front of a Grumman F4F Wildcat fighter plane at an Oahu air base, circa April-May 1942. Both men were assigned to Fighting Squadron Three (VF-3), of which Thach was Commanding Officer. (USNHHC)

Lieutenant Edward H. 'Butch' O'Hare pictured beside an F4F Wildcat fighter, probably circa April-May 1942. USS *O'Hare* (DD-889) was named in his honor. (NARA)

A pair of Grumman F4F-3 Wildcat fighters of Fighting Squadron Three (VF-3) in flight near Naval Air Station Kaneohe, Oahu, Hawaii, on 10 April 1942. The aircraft are Bureau #3976 (marked F-1, and nearest the camera), flown by VF-3's Commanding Officer, Lieutenant Commander John S. Thach, and Bureau #3986, flown by Lieutenant Edward H. O'Hare. Both of these aircraft were lost while assigned to Fighting Squadron Two (VF-2) with USS *Lexington* (CV-2), during the Battle of Coral Sea in May 1942. (NARA)

A Japanese Zeke-type Kamikaze aircraft diving on the Cleveland-class light cruiser USS *Columbia* (CL-56) during the Lingayen Gulf operation, 6 January 1945. This plane, afire after hits from the ship's guns, crashed close aboard, showering *Columbia*'s superstructure with gasoline. (USNHHC)

A captured Japanese Mitsubishi A6M5 zero-sen photographed on 25 September 1944. The A6M5, an improved version of the earlier A6M2 and A6M3 variants, had a reduced wing span and exhaust stacks in place of the cowl flaps of the earlier models. During World War II the Zero was officially referred to by the Allied code name *Zeke*, but the name Zero had so caught the public mind that it was also widely used. It was Japanese practice to use the last digits of the year of adoption to identify airplane types; since the *Zeke* was first produced in 1940 (the year 2600 in the Japanese calendar), it was known as the zero-sen (zero fighter). This particular aircraft had been painted with US insignia, which have, in turn, been painted out before the photograph was taken; the white star shows conspicuously through the red paint. It seems to retain its original Japanese paint scheme; dark olive green on sides and upper surfaces, and on the entire cowling, with light gray underneath. (USNHHC)

A portrait of Admiral John S. Thach taken on 26 February 1965. (USNHHC)

Lieutenant Commander John S. Thach, commanding officer of Fighting Squadron Three (VF-3), pictured in the cockpit of an F4F Wildcat fighter, 10 April 1942. The Japanese flags on the fuselage denote 'kills' Thach made while flying from USS *Lexington* (CV-2) on 20 February 1942. (USNHHC)

USS *Bunker Hill* (CV-17) burning after being hit by a Kamikaze, off Okinawa, 11 May 1945. The photograph was taken from USS *Bataan* (CVL-29). (USNHHC)

had been launched several hours ago and none of them had reported sighting any US ships. It now seemed safe to rearm the planes being held in reserve. Still, Nagumo was disregarding a specific order from his commander-in-chief. This was a very, very serious thing for any naval officer in any Navy to do, but especially so for an officer of the rigidly disciplined Imperial Japanese Navy. Nagumo ordered that the anti-ship torpedoes and armor-piercing bombs on the reserve planes be replaced with high-explosive ordnance for attacking land-based targets. It was a hard, back-breaking job for the plane handlers, but Nagumo was determined to finish off the source of all of these attacks on his ships once and for all. The attacking planes, especially the big bombers, were obviously coming from the US base on Midway. The work of rearming the reserve planes went on for a little more than ten minutes. Then at 0728 a completely unexpected report from a search plane from the cruiser *Tone* made Admiral Nagumo's blood run cold and so shocked the usually aggressive Japanese admiral that he now became tentative and indecisive. The search plane's pilot reported spotting ten US 'surface ships' 250 miles north of Midway:

> Sighted what appears to be enemy composed of 10 (ships), bearing 10 degrees, distance 240 miles from Midway, on course 150 degrees, speed 20 knots.[116]

The US ships were in the perfect spot for the Americans to wait in ambush for the Japanese. That is exactly why weeks ago Admiral Nimitz had dubbed that same spot north of Midway as 'Point Luck'. Maddeningly, the search plane pilot did not say whether or not the enemy fleet included any aircraft carriers. If it did, Admiral Nagumo and the entire *Kido Butai* were in the most desperate kind of trouble imaginable. Then the flagship ordered the search plane pilot to describe the types of ships in the American force. Back came the following shocking reply:

> The enemy is accompanied by what appears to be a carrier in position to the rear of the others.[117]

Amazingly, Admiral Nagumo hesitated at this critical moment. He decided to wait for Lieutenant Tomonaga's planes to return from bombing Midway, rearm them, and then launch a 'grand-scale air attack' on the American fleet.[118] Critical time was being lost, something that Nagumo and all the sailors aboard the *Kido Butai* would never be able to get back. The air attacks by American land-based bombers from Midway kept on coming and coming. After Nagumo had changed his orders for the second time, the Japanese deck crews had the maddening job of hoisting nineteen 100lb Type 91 aerial torpedoes back onto the same planes that they had just removed them from. The heavy labor went on right through a series of unsuccessful attacks by semi-obsolete US Vindicator dive bombers and by modern B-17 Flying Fortress heavy bombers. The Zeros shot down almost all the old, fragile Vindicators. The B-17s flew at such a high altitude that there was almost no chance that they would actually hit a Japanese ship, and from miles up the US bomber pilots could not tell the difference between direct hits and near misses. The land-based attacks did no actual physical damage to the *Kido Butai*, but they apparently deeply damaged Admiral Nagumo's psyche and kept him in a near-continuous state of confusion.

When the high-flying US Army Air Force pilots got back to Oahu they claimed to have wrecked the enemy fleet and won the Battle of Midway all by themselves. No one in Hawaii could dispute their story, and the American press ran wild with front-page headlines telling the entire country about how Army Air Force B-17s had won the great battle.[119] In reality, not a single bomb from any of the Flying Fortresses had scored a hit on any of the Japanese ships.

In the hectic rush to ready their planes for an attack on the US fleet, the Japanese maintenance crews got sloppy. They carelessly began stacking torpedoes and bombs and laying gasoline hoses all over their decks.[120] This almost criminal negligence would never have been tolerated in peacetime. In the middle of a pitched battle, it was almost suicidal. Once more the Japanese were behaving like they thought that they were invincible. The four carriers of the *Kido Butai* were about as vulnerable to an air attack as they possibly could be, and thanks to the great skill of the pilots of Fighting Three, and to the sacrifice of Torpedo Squadron Three, there were now no Zeros overhead to protect them. The stage was now set for the most stunning reversal of fortune of World War Two.

Beginner's Mistakes

Hornet and *Enterprise* both turned into the wind and began launching planes at 0700 and 0706, respectively.[121] The planes in an early World War Two Navy air group would typically orbit over their carrier until they were all airborne. This system was called 'deferred departure'. Then the whole air group – fighters, dive bombers, and torpedo planes – would form up and head out together. They would all try to hit the enemy ships as one big unit. The Americans hoped that two such powerful air strikes from both *Hornet* and *Enterprise* would wreck the Japanese fleet in short order. Unfortunately, things did not work out quite the way they had planned. By early 1942 the Japanese were already past masters of the complex art of carrier warfare. They could launch an entire air group in just ten minutes. In those early days the less experienced Americans were getting on the job training right in the middle of a world war, and they were learning the hard way. Lieutenant Commander Wade McClusky, the *Enterprise* air group leader, had taken off early on flying a dive bomber. He had been circling over the carrier for about half an hour, wasting a lot of precious gas. To McClusky looking down, the people on the flight deck seemed to be moving in slow motion. Only the two squadrons of dive bombers had gotten airborne, and they too were using up a lot of gas. The plane handlers were apparently having trouble getting the ancient Devastator torpedo planes into the air. One old torpedo plane's engine would not turn over at all. Activity on the flight deck was agonizingly slow, and then it seemed to have ground to a halt. The ship's radar detected what was probably a Japanese search plane on the southern horizon.[122] None of *Enterprise*'s fighters or torpedo planes had even taken off yet. They were all still on board, but Admiral Spruance knew that he could wait no longer. Dozens of Japanese bombers and torpedo planes might appear overhead at any second. A sailor blinkered Spruance's order up to McClusky and the rest of the dive bombers: 'Proceed on your mission.' McClusky and two squadrons of dive bombers banked away from *Enterprise* and headed south-west. Unbelievably, no fighters or torpedo planes accompanied them. Still, McClusky was about to make some of the most critical tactical decisions of the Pacific War. According to Admiral Nimitz, McClusky's next moves decided the fate of the US forces at Midway.

Aboard *Hornet* things were even more disorganized. Captain Marc Mitscher was a very experienced naval aviator. In 1944–45 he proved himself a brilliant tactician when he commanded the enormous Fast Carrier Task Force in the Western Pacific. At Midway, he decided to launch the old, slow torpedo planes first. The torpedo planes would immediately head out towards the Japanese fleet. Mitscher planned to then launch the faster dive bombers and fighters. They could catch up with the torpedo planes enroute. This 'running rendezvous' would save both time and precious fuel. Such a complex system probably would have worked out well with a talented and experienced pilot like Mitscher leading the *Hornet*'s air group. Jimmie Thach and the veteran pilots aboard *Yorktown* used the same system to link up, and it worked like clockwork for them.[123] Unfortunately, Commander Stanhope Ring, the man who actually led *Hornet*'s air group at Midway, turned out to be a less than stellar leader. He was also a bit of an oddball. Ring was the only American naval officer that anyone ever saw who carried a British-style swagger stick. To this day, it is unclear on just what course or courses Ring thought he was leading the *Hornet*'s air group on.

Some of his pilots ran out of gas and had to ditch in the sea. Many were rescued. Others were never seen again. Some *Hornet* pilots ran low on gas, flew to the nearby base on Midway, and refueled there. None of the pilots flying with Ring actually made contact with the Japanese. All told, forty-two planes from *Hornet* were lost, and they did no damage at all to the Japanese.[124] So on the brand-new *Hornet*, full of brand-new pilots, Mitscher's decision to use a more complicated launching system caused wholesale confusion. This confusion, combined with some very questionable tactical leadership by Ring, ended in complete failure.

Like many of the pilots aboard *Hornet*, those in Torpedo Squadron 8 were pretty green. Ensign George 'Tex' Gay served as the squadron's navigator that day. He had never even taken off from an aircraft carrier carrying a live torpedo. Commander John Waldron, the squadron's intense, charismatic leader, was sure that he knew just where the Japanese fleet could be found. Waldron was absolutely certain that the enemy carriers had not sailed as far west as Captain Mitscher or Ring suspected. In this Waldron was correct. Waldron and Ring apparently engaged in a brief, heated verbal exchange over the radio despite the fact that they both were under strict orders to maintain radio silence.[125] Waldron thought that the Japanese would have changed course when their search planes first spotted the American fleet. Amazingly, Waldron broke formation and led his squadron on a course further south than the one that the rest of the *Hornet* air group had been following. One has to wonder if Waldron would have been court-martialed if he had not died a hero's death later that morning. The Japanese had indeed changed course, and their progress had been slowed down by constant, if ineffective, attacks by land-based torpedo planes and bombers from Midway. So Waldron led his squadron directly to the Japanese carriers. Torpedo 8 was the only *Hornet* squadron to actually attack the Japanese carriers that day. Unfortunately, Waldron was also leading his pilots and crewmen into what amounted to his own private war against the most powerful units of the Imperial Navy.

By flying on a very different course than the one flown by everybody else, Waldron practically guaranteed that his squadron of vulnerable torpedo planes would have no hope of getting any fighter support. Torpedo Squadron 8 would face the deadly Zeros alone.

At 0920 Waldron called out that he had spotted smoke on the horizon. Tex Gay was bringing up the tail end of Torpedo 8 so he had a ring-side view of everything that happened.[126] Suddenly three big enemy aircraft carriers materialized right in front of him. Waldron came back up on the radio and ordered an immediate attack. Then he wished his men 'good luck'. Dozens of Zeros came in firing from three or four different directions. Torpedo Squadron 8 was in mortal trouble right from the start. A torpedo plane at the front of the formation got hit right away. It caught fire and crashed. Commander Waldron's cockpit burst into flames. Gay saw Waldron stand up and try to step out onto a wing. Then his TBD slammed into the water. Commander Waldron was gone in a flash. A machine gun burst killed Gay's rear-seat gunner, Bob Huntington. Another torpedo plane blew up. Then all of the other TBDs were burning. One after another they all crashed. Soon Tex Gay was the only American pilot still flying. He launched his torpedo at a carrier, but did not see where it went. Gay ended up barreling right down the middle of the flight deck of one of the Japanese carriers. For those few seconds when he was directly over the carrier, nobody was shooting at him. Gay saw bombs, torpedoes and gasoline hoses strewn everywhere on the enemy flight deck.[127] The Japanese seemed to be refueling and rearming their planes. Once Gay swept past the carrier everyone started shooting at him again. A spent bullet hit his left arm and lodged just under the skin. He squeezed the slug out and popped it into his mouth. Then 20mm cannon fire hit his engine, but the TBD continued flying for a minute or so. Then Ensign Gay had to ditch, and he hit the water with a tremendous splash. Seawater began pouring into his cockpit. Gay desperately tried to force open the canopy, but it was jammed. He pushed and pushed but the thing would not budge. The water was rising up to his armpits. He was about to drown, so Gay just stood up and busted head-first right through the canopy glass.

About twenty minutes after George Gay was shot down, Torpedo Squadron 6 from *Enterprise* showed up. They tried to attack the Japanese flagship, *Akagi* but it was the same sad story. Zeros destroyed ten of Commander E.E. 'Gene' Lindsey's fourteen torpedo planes after a couple of passes.[128] Again, the Americans scored no hits. After the slaughter of the torpedo plane squadrons at Midway, the US Navy scrapped the semi-obsolete TBD.

Ensign Gay was the only member of Torpedo Squadron 8 to survive the morning's battle. Twenty-nine of the squadron's thirty airmen had died in three or four intensely violent minutes. Gay spent the rest of the day and the following night in his plane's little yellow life raft. Several times he got into the water and put a seat cushion over his head to hide from the lookouts when Japanese ships passed close by. A PBY search plane rescued him the next day.

Before that Ensign George 'Tex' Gay would have a grandstand, front-row view of the turning point of the Pacific War.

Chapter 6

'It Was Like Flying Inside a Beehive'

Because Admiral Fletcher wanted to recover his search planes first, *Yorktown* (Task Force 17) did not start launching its strike on the Japanese carriers until 1030.[129] Commander Lance 'Lem' Massey's dozen Devastator torpedo planes flew down near the water at 1,500ft. Lieutenant Commander Max Leslie's seventeen Dauntless dive bombers were stacked way up almost out of sight at 16,000ft. Lieutenant Commander John Thach positioned his tiny escort of six Wildcat fighters 1,000ft above the vulnerable torpedo planes. He guessed that the faster dive bombers would likely be able to get through to the enemy carriers on their own.

Thach's decision to protect the torpedo planes turned out to be the correct one. On this day making the right decisions would really count.

Minutes after the *Yorktown* planes took off, four huge explosions detonated directly beneath them down on the ocean's surface. Jimmie Thach almost jumped out of his seat, but he was tightly buckled in. Thach scanned the sky and saw that there were no Zeros lurking anywhere in sight. The nearest Japanese ships were probably over 100 miles away. So what the hell was going on? Up at 16,000ft Max Leslie was pounding on his plane's instrument panel in helpless fury. Defective arming switches had released the bombs from four of his dive bombers prematurely, including the bomb that was on Leslie's own plane. Leslie still had seventeen dive bombers in his squadron, but now only thirteen of his pilots had anything left to drop on the Japanese.

An hour later a sharp-eyed torpedo plane pilot spotted smudges of black smoke on the distant horizon. The *Yorktown* squadrons had found the Japanese fleet, but they had flown a bit too far east. One after another all thirty-five American planes banked gracefully right and headed towards the smoke.

Since before Pearl Harbor Jimmie Thach had worked tirelessly coaching his pilots on how he thought they should deal with Japan's superb pilots in their superior Mitsubishi Zero fighters. Unfortunately, Thach was now leading what amounted to a hastily organized 'composite squadron' thrown together at the last minute to defend Midway. Some of his new pilots had only a cursory notion of Thach's tactical ideas. Most of the highly talented veterans that Thach had commanded since the beginning of the war were on other assignments. Many had been transferred to *Lexington* in anticipation of the Battle of the Coral Sea. Butch O'Hare, Thach's best pilot, had just been to the White House to pick up his Medal of Honor.

Two squadrons of dive bombers from *Enterprise* had flown a similar course earlier that morning when visibility was worse. They must have just missed spotting the Japanese fleet, and had flown much too far to the south. Lieutenant Commander Wade McClusky guessed exactly what had happened and had the guts to turn two squadrons of dive bombers completely around. He changed his search plan entirely. A few minutes after making their turn, the *Enterprise* pilots came upon the lone Japanese destroyer *Arashi* (Storm). She was headed north-west at top speed. Every move that McClusky made that morning was brilliant, and his timing proved to be perfect. He guessed that the destroyer was racing to catch up with the enemy carrier force, so he turned his squadrons north-west.

All the US planes were operating under strict radio silence so they could not coordinate their movements. Still, McClusky's two squadrons were about to locate the unsuspecting Japanese and hit them at exactly the right moment. When McClusky's planes were just over the horizon, another seventeen dive bombers from *Yorktown* were preparing to dive on the Japanese fleet. Most critically, half of the forty or so Zeros defending the Japanese carriers were off tangling with Thach's six Wildcats, and for the first time Zeros were getting shot down left and right. The rest of the Zeros were trying to shoot up the old torpedo planes that Thach was escorting.

***

When Thach's Wildcats and the rest of *Yorktown*'s planes were only minutes from the Japanese carriers, most of the Zeros were already aloft, waiting. A few more enemy fighters were just taking off. Thach knew that his men were up against long odds. He knew that the American Wildcat was slower to accelerate and far less maneuverable than the Zero. Compared to the number of enemy fighters that they would probably be facing, his escort group of six Wildcats was ridiculously small. Thach had requested more fighters, but was turned down. Two of his pilots, Ensigns Ram Dibb and Dan Sheedy, were inexperienced rookies. All the Zero pilots were hardened combat veterans with an unbroken record of victory after victory under their belts.

When *Yorktown*'s strike group was still well out of anti-aircraft range, a Japanese cruiser began firing brilliant pyrotechnic shells.[130] One shell was crimson, the other bright orange. Both exploded far in front of the *Yorktown* formation. This turned out to be a surprisingly effective Japanese method of signaling their Zero fighters about incoming threats. Almost immediately, a Zero that none of the Americans ever saw shot down Ensign Edgar Bassett. Bassett's Wildcat just burst into flames and nosedived. Burning like a blowtorch, it spiraled down 3,000ft straight into the Pacific. Nobody saw Ed Bassett after that. Thach scanned the sky for more Zeros and spotted about twenty more up above and behind him. Each one dove down on his Wildcats firing short, controlled bursts as they went. The Zeros attacked the American fighters individually. So many Japanese fighters were up there that they almost seemed to be lining up for a chance to take a shot at the less maneuverable Wildcats. Each Zero dove in accelerating at terrific speed. Then each one pulled up and climbed out of range in the blink of an eye. Thach was impressed with the obvious skill of the Japanese pilots. They were flying air show-style stunts. He had expected to be outnumbered, but Thach was surprised that so many Zeros were concentrating on his small escort force. In reality, his attack had pulled all the Japanese fighters down to a very low altitude. They were now in no position to defend their carriers from a high-level dive bombing attack. Zero after Zero came screaming down, each one firing those short, controlled bursts.

Thach spotted another big formation of twenty Zeros streaming past his Wildcats. They started shooting up the old, slow TBD Devastator torpedo planes that he was trying to protect. Instantly, the torpedo plane pilots were up on the radio calling for fighter support. This new group of Zeros was slaughtering the helpless torpedo plane crews while Thach and his men had their hands full shooting it out with the first twenty Zeros. The Wildcat pilots were jinking like mad and firing burst after burst each time a Zero crossed their sights. Thach saw an old friend go down. A pair of Zeros made a perfectly timed, head-on run at Commander Lem Massey's Devastator and it exploded in a big fireball. Four or five more of the fragile old torpedo planes blew up. Bang! Bang! Bang! Bang! In less than a minute half the torpedo squadron was gone. It looked like all *Yorktown*'s fighters and torpedo planes were going to be shot down, but Jimmie Thach was going to take as many Zeros with him as he could.

Lieutenant Macomber had no wingman now that Ed Bassett was gone, so he became the favorite target for the Zeros. A Zero shot up Macomber's instrument panel, and only the thin armor plate on the back of his seat saved him from being chopped to pieces by 7.7mm machine gun slugs. His flying controls still functioned, so Macomber pulled in closer to Thach. Macomber dodged, twisted, and turned every time a Zero started shooting at him. Young Ensign Dibb was flying off Thach's right wing. He pulled in closer too. This bunched-up formation was the exact opposite of what Thach taught and what his experimental 'weaving' tactic required. Thach feared that no tactic would work against so many high-performance enemy fighters, and that all his Wildcats were about to be wiped out. He still tried to get Macomber to spread out. No response. Macomber's radio had been shot to pieces. With Dibb and Macomber following him closely, Thach started to maneuver. When the next Zero was fully committed to a high-speed firing pass, Thach rolled into a perfectly timed, hard right turn. Dibb and Macomber copied Thach's every move. The three Americans were now flying nearly perpendicular to the Zero's path. This limited the Japanese pilot to a difficult 'full deflection' shot. It forced him to quickly adjust his aim to give his target the proper lead. This was a hard adjustment for any pilot to make. It was especially difficult for Japanese pilots who had not been rigorously trained in the fine art of deflection shooting. Deflection shooting was a skill emphasized by the US Navy, but not by Imperial Japan. The Japanese pilot either got nervous or he was a very bad shot. He missed all three of the Wildcats. Another Zero pilot just completing his firing run pulled up too fast and stalled his wings. For two or three seconds he could not maneuver at all. He was helpless. Thach was on him in a flash and fired. The Zero blew up.

As the fight went on Thach was occasionally getting long shots at the Japanese as they pulled out of their dives, but this was nothing to write home about. Worse yet, the vulnerable torpedo planes that they were escorting were pulling ahead of Thach's outnumbered Wildcats. Soon they would have no protection from the Zeros at all. In the blink of an eye all the torpedo planes vanished under some low clouds. With Bassett lost and Macomber's radio out, Thach tried to find a combination that would work. He radioed his rookie wingman, Ram Dibb, to break out to the right. Dibb was one of a handful of new pilots who had learned Thach's new tactics. He was just itching for the chance to try them out. Dibb instantly pulled out about 300 yards. The two Wildcats were now flying parallel to each other and spread widely apart. They were in what

Thach originally called the 'beam defense' position. It was later known to all US Navy fighter pilots as the opening move of the legendary Thach Weave. The highest-scoring Japanese ace to survive the war had his own simple nickname for Thach's tactic. Saburo Sakai just called it the famous American 'double team'.[131] Now the US pilots would fight as a team. Now they would fight the deadly Zeros on even terms.

More and more Zeros dove in. One pilot came right after Dibb. He missed. Then the same Zero pilot climbed straight up. He swung into a wingover and looped back down for a second try. Dibb called for help: 'Skipper, there's a Zero on my tail!'[132] Thach saw what was happening. He got mad and for about twenty seconds Thach threw all his sophisticated tactical notions right out the window. He just lined up for a head-on shot at the Zero. It was risky thing to do. The two pilots were like two teenagers driving their jalopies straight at each other, playing 'chicken'. Thach later said he just lost his temper when the same Japanese pilot came back for another chance to get his rookie, 'too young to shave' wingman. The heavy F4F-4 Wildcat had six powerful 50-caliber machine guns and a bullet-resistant, Plexiglas windshield. It was the better plane to fly in this exact situation. Both pilots fired simultaneously. Thach's big 50-caliber slugs ripped into the Zero's engine. It exploded, and the Japanese pilot pulled up. Thach passed just feet under the burning Zero and got a false sense of intense heat. He held down his trigger, blasting away at the flaming Zero for as long as he could. Another Zero pilot streaked in directly behind Thach. He lined up for a perfect 'no-deflection' shot. Then Ensign Dibb came weaving in. A rookie no longer, he shot the Zero right off of Thach's tail.

About the time that Thach shot down his second Zero, Wade McClusky was leading his two squadrons of *Enterprise* dive bombers straight at the ships on the south-west side of the Japanese fleet. When he was about 35 miles out, McClusky could see all four Japanese carriers through his binoculars: the flagship *Akagi* (Red Castle), *Kaga* (an ancient Japanese province), *Soryu* (Blue Dragon), and *Hiryu* (Flying Dragon). All four of these carriers had taken part in the attack on Pearl

Harbor.[133] The ships were spread out over miles of ocean in a kind of circle formation. One was kicking up huge bow waves and making sharp turns. McClusky realized that it was trying to evade some unseen attack that was already taking place far below and miles away. This distant attack must have been the one made by Torpedo Squadron Three, the torpedo planes that Thach was escorting.

One thing amazed McClusky more than anything else – *nobody* was shooting at him. There were no Zeros around. There was no anti-aircraft fire coming his way. At this point nobody aboard the Japanese ships had the slightest inkling of the avalanche of bombs and machine gun fire that was about to rain down on them. With no time to lose, McClusky calmly broke radio silence and assigned targets. He and Lieutenant Earl Gallagher's dive bomber squadron Scouting Six would attack the nearest carrier. This ship was probably the huge *Kaga*. McClusky ordered Lieutenant Commander Dick Best's Bombing Six to strike the more distant carrier. It was almost certainly the Japanese fleet's flagship, *Akagi*.[134] About 30 miles away, over the carrier *Soryu*, Jimmie Thach's new weaving tactic was really starting to work. He shot down another Zero. It was Thach's third kill of the day. Next, Thach saw the five US torpedo planes that had survived the Zeros' onslaught. They were just beginning their final torpedo runs. They headed straight for the two closest enemy carriers. Worse yet for the Japanese, none of their lookouts spotted Max Leslie's seventeen dive bombers from *Yorktown* circling far overhead at 16,000ft.

Down near the ocean's surface, flying 'low cover' behind the torpedo planes, two of Thach's pilots, Machinist's Mate Tom Cheek and Ensign Dan Sheedy, fought their own war against the Zeros.[135] Cheek first saw a Zero make a firing pass at one of the lead torpedo planes. It missed. The Zero pilot climbed straight up, did a wingover and looped back down. He pulled gracefully right behind the formation of maddeningly slow Devastators. The Japanese flyer was trying to set up a shot at one of the torpedo planes at the tail end of the American squadron.

This gave Cheek the opening that he needed. He gunned his plane's engine and climbed up as fast as he could. Cheek's big fifties ripped into the Zero and caused it to belch flames just like the ones Thach had shot down. The burning Zero screamed straight past Cheek. It made no more turns or maneuvers of any kind, with what was likely a corpse at the controls. Cheek's Wildcat was already climbing close to the airframe's stall speed. The heavy recoil from his machine guns was just enough to cause his plane to slow down, lose lift and start to drop. Cheek shoved his stick forward and nosed down. He quickly got his fighter back under control. With his plane's throttle wide open, Cheek tried to get at two Zeros diving on the other side of the torpedo formation. His Wildcat was just coming out of a near stall. It was sluggish and moving way too slow. So Cheek fired off some tracers in front of the Zeros, hoping to give their pilots something to think about. Both enemy fighters gracefully pulled out of their dives. With dazzling speed they climbed straight up and out of range. The Zero's incredible climb rate amazed Cheek.

Cheek saw at least five more Zeros going after some Devastators far ahead of him. He was out of position to actually hit the first pair, so he used the same trick and fired tracers into their paths. Both Zero pilots pulled straight up into fantastic vertical climbs.[136] The next group of Japanese fighters succeeded in ripping into the Devastators. They shot down two or three of the old planes. Another Zero from the same group tried to roll in behind the torpedo planes for some easy kills. It pulled right in front of Cheek, directly behind what was left of the torpedo squadron. All the surviving rear seat gunners had a clear field of fire. Just before Cheek could open up, the combined fire from the rear seat men in the torpedo planes blew the Zero to pieces. Almost immediately 7.7mm machine gun slugs being fired from behind began ripping through Cheek's cockpit, wrecking most of his instruments. Cheek jinked and dodged for all he was worth. Like Macomber, he was saved by the light armor plate installed on the back of his seat. Next, the

Japanese pilot behind Cheek began firing his big 20mm cannon. This could tear right through the Wildcat's light armor. To Cheek's immense relief, the Japanese pilot missed what looked to be an easy shot. Cheek caught a quick glimpse of a couple of torpedo planes disappearing under low clouds far ahead, and he spotted more Zeros right above him. So he ducked into a nearby cloud.

When he emerged the torpedo planes were gone. One Zero was above him on his left. Five more were higher up on his right. There was also a strange 'spot' in the middle of Cheek's windshield, and it was growing fast. The detail-oriented Thach had wisely demanded that all cockpit glass be kept scrupulously clean. Cheek quickly realized that what looked like a spot on his windshield was actually a Zero coming straight at him. Cheek squeezed hard, much too hard on the trigger molded into his controls. His tracers smashed right into the oncoming Zero. The two fighters roared past each other, and again, Cheek turned his damaged fighter back into a cloud. He had lost all feeling in his right hand. It dropped limp into his lap. Cheek quickly regained some feeling in his fingers. He pulled out of the cloud, and the torpedo planes were nowhere to be seen. All the Zeros seemed to be gone too. They had apparently been recalled to their carriers. Tom Cheek turned north-west and began nursing his battered Wildcat back towards the American fleet.

Dan Sheedy was Cheek's wingman. He was having a devil of a time just keeping up with Cheek's flashy maneuvers. Sheedy hoped that Cheek would start a weave. That was something that he knew a little about. Sheedy had just been able to stay close to Cheek, and he had fired at the Zero that got on Cheek's tail. Sheedy just missed, so he may have startled the Japanese pilot and caused him to miss a fairly easy shot. So Sheedy may have saved Cheek from being ripped to shreds by the Zero's big cannon. Sheedy also eyeballed the Zero that had challenged Cheek with the head-on attack. That Zero exploded after the two fighters roared past each other. Another group of Zeros dove in on Sheedy's Wildcat. They thoroughly shot up his cockpit and damaged his landing gear. Shrapnel or bullets hit him in his a shoulder and in both ankles. Sheedy dove down almost to the water to get out of the line of fire. One of the Zeros dove after him. Again, a Zero and a Wildcat turned and faced each other head on. Both pilots fired simultaneously. Both seemed to miss. Sheedy turned back towards the Zero, and the enemy pilot did likewise. The Japanese pilot was still flying what appeared to be an undamaged fighter. Then he either misjudged his airspeed or his altitude. He missed his turn, dug his Zero's lower wing into the water, and cartwheeled to his death.[137] Sheedy was in severe pain. He had been hit in the shoulder and in both ankles. His Wildcat was smoking and there was blood everywhere inside the cockpit. With no other aircraft, friend or foe, in sight he turned for home. He headed back towards where he thought the American carriers would be. A raw rookie, Sheedy had no experience navigating out of sight of land on his own. He did remember that the sun had been behind his left shoulder on the flight out, so he kept it in front of him and to his right on the solo trip home.

Four thousand feet higher up Thach, Dibb and Macomber had been over the Japanese fleet fighting Zero after Zero for about fifteen minutes, maybe longer. Those fifteen minutes of continuous, non-stop, air-to-air combat felt like fifteen years of 'normal' flying. Thach later said that it had been like 'flying inside a beehive'.[138] As Thach and his men tangled with the Japanese fighters, he could see three of the four enemy carriers. The fourth carrier, *Hiryu*, was out of sight just over the horizon. Thach's old friend, Lem Massey, was dead. Massey's squadron of vulnerable torpedo planes had taken a terrible beating, and the Zeros had killed most of its crews. However, a small remnant was still flying, and bravely 'going for the carriers'. Thach thought he saw torpedo hits on two of the Japanese carriers, yet no Japanese sailor who survived Midway ever reported a successful torpedo attack by any American plane.

Thach and his men had shot down at least half a dozen of the deadly Zeros, probably more. Nobody had ever inflicted such losses on the 'invincible' Japanese fighter before. Yet Thach felt that he had failed in his primary mission – protecting the torpedo planes.

The nearly continuous attacks by the Japanese Zeros on Thach's Wildcats started to slow down. Then they stopped altogether. Suddenly most of the Zeros vanished. They must have been recalled to defend their carriers, but the recall order came too late. Far overhead, Jimmie Thach glimpsed something flashing in the sunlight. Next he saw a 'beautiful silver waterfall' as dozens and dozens of Dauntless dive bombers came hurtling down on the Japanese carriers, and now there were no Zeros in position to intercept them.[139] Thach had flown with these Navy bomber pilots for years, and knew that they were the best trained in the world. Now almost fifty of them were about to get an unimpeded, 'free shot' at many of the same ships that had attacked Pearl Harbor.

Ensign George 'Tex' Gay, the 'sole survivor' of Torpedo Squadron 8, had a ringside view of what happened next. The Japanese ships were so close to him that Gay was still in the water hiding under his black seat cushion. Then the Dauntless bombers dove in. It was the most accurate dive bombing attack that Ensign Gay had ever heard of. Every bomb seemed to be a direct hit. Gay saw no near misses at all. Explosion after explosions ripped the carriers apart. One carrier was so close to him that Gay felt each of the detonations in the pit of his stomach. In less than six minutes three huge Japanese aircraft carriers were burning uncontrollably from stem to stern. None of them would ever sail into Tokyo Bay again. The wrecked hulks of the burning enemy carriers slowly drifted away.[140] The rest of the Japanese fleet followed them. Gay finally felt that the Japanese were far enough away that he could safely inflate his yellow life raft.

Thach slowly circled what was left of the shattered Japanese fleet. He watched as the three great aircraft carriers burned furiously. One carrier was engulfed in strange blue and pink flames.[141] Huge columns of ugly black smoke towered thousands of feet above each one of them. All three were total wrecks.

Ensign Gay was rescued by a PBY amphibious search plane the following afternoon. Thach, Dibb, and Macomber all landed back on *Yorktown* without incident. Unfortunately, Tom Cheek was flying a Wildcat that had been shot up pretty badly. When he tried to land, his tail hook malfunctioned and missed catching the arresting wires. His plane went skidding uncontrollably down the flight deck. Cheek stood on his brakes and jammed the stick forward to avoid hitting the (crash) barrier and several other planes. His Wildcat cartwheeled over, slammed nose-first into the flight deck, and landed on its back. It trapped Cheek inside his cockpit. He just hung there motionless, upside down. A dozen sailors ran to what looked like was going to be a really grisly rescue. Then they heard somebody yelling, 'Get this thing to hell off me!'[142] Cheek walked away from the crash without so much as a scratch on him.

The Zeros had also thoroughly shot up Dan Sheedy's Wildcat. He landed on the first carrier that he saw, *Hornet.* When he touched down, his landing gear collapsed and all six of his 50-caliber machine guns started firing. Sheedy's guns killed five sailors working on the flight deck right in front of him. Sheedy's shoulder and ankle wounds hurt like hell, but they were not life threatening. Officially, he was cleared of any culpability for the accident. Still, Sheedy was never quite the same after watching his own guns cut down all of those sailors.

After landing on *Yorktown*, Thach hurried to Flag Plot, the control room, and gave his verbal report to Admiral Fletcher. Thach told Fletcher that the battle 'seemed to be going our way', and that he had seen three Japanese carriers burning.[143] Fletcher asked whether there was a fourth carrier out there that had not been hit. Thach could not say. He had only seen three. Wade McClusky had already reported that he had seen four Japanese carriers when he was approaching the Japanese fleet. However, McClusky had been wounded as he pulled out of his dive. In the confused rush to get him to *Enterprise*'s sick bay, this vital news was somehow missed.

Thach had just completed his verbal report when Fletcher had his question about a fourth Japanese carrier answered in a very direct but unwelcome way. The ship's radar screen suddenly sparkled to life. It was showing eighteen 'bogeys', and they were headed straight for *Yorktown.* The ship's klaxon began sounding. Hundreds of sailors were racing to their battle stations. So Fletcher's last question to Thach was answered. Yes, there definitely was at least one more Japanese flattop out there, and its planes were about to strike *Yorktown.*

Chapter 7

Six Minutes to Victory

The Battle of Midway is universally recognized as the turning point of World War Two in the Pacific. Prior to Midway the Japanese were almost unbeatable. Except for derailing Japan's plans to invade Australia at the Coral Sea, the Americans kept on losing battle after battle. Arguably, the exact moment when the tide turned permanently in favor of the United States occurred when Jimmie Thach looked up and saw scores of American dive bombers screaming down on the Japanese carriers, and there were no Zeros in position to intercept them. In the next six minutes the Japanese Navy lost half of its big fleet carriers. The Americans wrecked another big carrier later that afternoon. These great ships were the very heart and soul of the Imperial Navy's offensive striking power. After her fleet carriers were destroyed at Midway, Imperial Japan was always on the defensive right up until the last day of the war. The 'beautiful silver waterfall' that Thach saw turned out to be Max Leslie's squadron of seventeen Dauntless dive bombers from *Yorktown*. They attacked the nearest Japanese carrier, *Soryu*, and huge explosions and massive fires erupted all over the ship's flight deck. Thick columns of dirty black smoke boiled up thousands of feet into the air. In a matter of seconds *Soryu* was a total wreck. She was so obviously finished that the last four dive bomber pilots switched targets and attacked escort ships in the screen. Leslie and three of his pilots dove with no bombs at all, because the faulty arming switches had released their bombs prematurely. Still, he furiously machine gunned the Japanese carrier as he dove. When Leslie pulled out of his dive, he noticed big explosions going off on two other Japanese carriers about 10 miles away. Other Americans were certainly kicking the hell out of them.

Those 'Other Americans' turned out to be Wade McClusky, Dick Best, Earl Gallaher, and the rest of the two *other* dive bomber squadrons. When the *Enterprise* planes approached the two Japanese carriers nearest to them, Gallaher's squadron, Scouting Six, was ahead of Best's Bombing Six.[144] The normal dive bombing procedure would have been for Gallaher to attack the more distant carrier (*Akagi*), while Best would normally take the nearer one (*Kaga*). Best never heard McClusky's order reversing procedure and assigning *Akagi* to him, so all the *Enterprise* pilots were preparing to attack the *same* carrier, *Kaga*. This would have left the flagship, *Akagi*, unscathed. Fortunately, Best was a very quick thinker and was able to avoid what would have been a very major foul-up at the last second.[145]

Best had both divisions of Bombing Six spread out on either side of his plane as they neared *Kaga*. Best activated his dive brakes, the distinctive perforated 'flaps' that distinguish the Dauntless from other dive bombers. Then a dozen Dauntlesses from Scouting Six and the group commander himself, McClusky, dove right past him. They attacked the carrier that the startled Best thought was his target. Worse yet, many of Best's men dove with them. A tsunami of some twenty-five dive bombers crashed down on *Kaga*, most of the pilots scoring direct hits. Huge explosions and ferocious fires broke out all over the big carrier. Surprised and frustrated, Best stoically retracted his dive brakes. He led the five planes that he still had with him against the more distant carrier, the flagship *Akagi*. Best had often kidded that he was the 'best' dive bomber pilot in the Navy. He certainly was one of the best, but his corny joke was prophetic on this day, when it really counted. Best pushed over into what was about as steep a dive as can be made in a Dauntless. *Akagi* was just launching a Zero as he dove. Incredibly, there was no anti-aircraft fire at all, and the carrier made no evasive turns The Japanese had still not spotted them. Then Best yanked on his bomb release! His half-ton bomb struck amidships right next to the carrier's island. Two of his men got hits farther astern. Like the other Japanese carriers, the flagship erupted into a burning mass of smoke and flames.

The Americans had caught the Japanese at their most vulnerable. They were still refueling and rearming their planes for an attack on the American fleet. The wildly overconfident Japanese had recklessly strewn bombs and torpedoes and gasoline hoses all over their decks. When the American bombers struck, all that Japanese ordnance detonated. The Japanese themselves coined a phrase for the arrogant overconfidence that they displayed at the start of the war. They called it 'victory disease'. In six minutes the Americans destroyed three of the six aircraft carriers that had attacked Pearl Harbor. In six incredible minutes Japan went from winning the war in the Pacific, with a comfortable edge in naval airpower, to disastrous defeat. The Japanese lost two-thirds of their big fleet carriers at Midway. They also lost many of their highly skilled, front-line pilots. Maybe more importantly, they also lost many of their experienced mechanics, the men who had maintained their planes through six months of furious, non-stop combat. Imperial Japan never recovered from the disaster at Midway.

America was already building a huge fleet of dozens of powerful *Essex*-class carriers. These ships were much more numerous and of higher quality than anything that Japan's shipyards could produce. The Grumman Aircraft Corporation would soon churn out over 12,000 F6F Hellcat fighters, a type decidedly superior to the Zero. The Japanese replaced the pilots and mechanics lost at Midway with men of inferior skill and training. In contrast, the Americans invested vast sums in training tens of thousands of new pilots. As part of that, the Navy sent Jimmie Thach to Disney Studios in Burbank to produce and narrate a remarkable series of animated training films on fighter tactics. After Midway, the Americans went on the offensive in the Pacific.

That offensive ended three-and-a-half years later with Imperial Japan' surrendered in Tokyo Bay.

To give a brief example of the cool professionalism and calm, low-key mindset of the men who fought at Midway, a small part of Dick Best's official Action Report is quoted below. 'CV' is Navy parlance for an aircraft carrier, 'VS-6' is Scouting Squadron Six, while 'VB-6' is Best's own squadron, Bombing Six:

> The weather was clear and the visibility excellent. There were scattered cumulous clouds from 1,500 ft. to 2,500 ft. and the ceiling was unlimited … The Enterprise Air Group Commander designated by voice radio one CV target for himself and VS-6 and another CV target for VB-6. Commander Bombing Squadron Six understood his target to be the 'left hand' CV. He gave the attack signal, releasing his other two division leaders for individual division maneuvering and led his (first) division towards the 'left hand' CV. Almost at once he saw that VS-6 was diving on the 'left hand' CV and so he led his division against the 'right hand' CV which was of the 'KAGA' type. It was launching planes as the attack was made …[146]

Best thought that he had bombed *Kaga* or a sister ship. Subsequent investigation strongly suggests that he and his pilots destroyed the flagship, *Akagi*.

Defending *Yorktown*

Thach, Dibb, and Cheek were waiting for their planes to be rearmed and refueled when the first Japanese attack on *Yorktown* began.[147] While the air raid klaxon was sounding and the ship's crewmen were running to man their battle stations, Thach had his men head to the ready room and stay there. Right now their job was to prepare to take off at a moment's notice and keep out of the line of fire. Dick Crommelin's eight-plane division was overhead on combat air patrol, but they were getting low on gas, so Captain Buckmaster had every fighter on board warmed up and ready to go. The new section leaders were Art Brassfield, Bill Barnes, Bill Woollen and Scott McCuskey. They gunned their engines, raced down the flight deck, and climbed as fast as they could – throttles wide open! The radar showed that Japanese planes were a little over 30 miles out and climbing. The fact that the bogeys were climbing suggested that the attacking aircraft were dive bombers and not low-flying torpedo planes.

Lieutenant Michio Kobayashi led the incoming Japanese force. He was a veteran of the Pearl Harbor attack and an expert dive bomber pilot. Kobayashi commanded eighteen Val dive bombers and four Zero fighters. When he took off from *Hiryu*, Kobayashi had six Zeros with him. Two Zero pilots got their fighters badly damaged 'freelancing' a few minutes after taking off. All six of the foolhardy, super aggressive Zero pilots with him had peeled away from Kobayashi's formation to attack some American dive bombers that they spotted returning to the US fleet. The Japanese fighters apparently did no damage, but two of the Zeros got thoroughly shot up by the alert rear seat gunners in the Dauntlesses. Both pilots had to turn their damaged airplanes around and, rather shamefully, limp back to *Hiryu*.[148]

The American pilots defending *Yorktown* did not have time to organize themselves into regular sections and divisions, so the ensuing air battle turned into a series of violent, one-on-one gunfights. Each encounter was over in seconds. An exact description of events as they actually happened is now impossible to reconstruct. The following is what seems to have occurred: Lieutenant Kobayashi positioned his eighteen bombers in two V-shaped formations, and the four remaining Zeros followed. The trailing Zero pilots positioned themselves above the Val dive bombers. Woollen and Barnes attacked the Japanese from below. Both US pilots missed tough shots. They pulled up and tried high-side attacks, and each of them knocked down one enemy plane. Scott McCuskey hurtled right into the middle of one of Kobayashi's V-shaped formations. He nearly collided with two Vals. The Japanese planes scattered. McCuskey whipped around firing at point-blank range. Three of the bombers caught fire. Now events were speeding by at split-second speed. Art Brassfield spotted four bombers that may have been the ones scattered by McCuskey. He shot down three. Brassfield is officially credited with four kills because seconds later he shot down another dive bomber that was running for *Hiryu.* Mattson was Brassfield's wingman. He shot down one bomber. Ensign Harry Gibbs is credited with getting two 'probable' kills at about the same time.

The closest *Enterprise* fighters aloft were Roger Mehle's four-plane division from Fighting 6. As soon as he heard what was going on, Mehle requested permission to head for *Yorktown* to help out. At first his fighter director told Mehle to stay where he was; defending *Enterprise* was his job. Then Mehle got the okay. His pilots and some from *Hornet* raced over to help. When Mehle got near *Yorktown*, he lined up for an easy shot at one of Kobayashi's dive bombers but, maddeningly, his guns jammed. The rest of the *Enterprise* and *Hornet* fighters were too late. They had been too far away. The Vals were already diving on *Yorktown.* A division of fighters from *Hornet* did engage Kobayashi's force while it was returning to *Hiryu*, but *after* it had bombed *Yorktown.* These pilots shot down three Zeros and two dive bombers.[149] Fighting Three's combat air patrol pilots had done well. They had shot down ten or twelve enemy dive bombers in the space of a few wild minutes. Still, about half a dozen of the Vals got past them.

As the Japanese planes approached the American fleet all the anti-aircraft guns on *Yorktown* and her escorts opened fire. Kobayashi's pilots were highly skilled and very determined. Anti-aircraft fire cut one dive bomber in half directly over *Yorktown.* However, the dying pilot still managed to drop his bomb right in the middle of the carrier's flight deck. Another armor-piercing bomb hit near the forward elevator. It penetrated deep inside the ship. The explosion knocked out *Yorktown*'s propulsion system and started a couple of bad fires. Another Japanese pilot scored a third hit farther aft. The smoking *Yorktown* slowed down and then stopped moving altogether. The surviving Japanese pilots reported back to *Hiryu* that they had just left an American carrier burning. Aboard *Hiryu*, Admiral Yamaguchi was greatly relieved as he was sure that the Americans could only have one operational carrier left now. He thought that he was finally in a straight up carrier versus carrier fight. The overconfident Tamon Yamaguchi was supremely confident that he would always triumph over the faint-hearted Americans in any kind of even match.

In Fighting Three's ready room Jimmie Thach had been able to follow much of the action just by listening to the changing sounds of the anti-aircraft fire.[150] First, only the big, slow tempo, 5-inch dual-purpose guns were firing. This meant that the enemy planes were pretty far off. Then the smaller 40 and 20mm cannon joined in. The Japanese were getting closer. Finally, the light machine guns opened up. Now every gun on *Yorktown* was firing away, and the racket was deafening inside every compartment of the ship. Thach heard what sounded like four distant thuds. The thuds were not very loud, but two of them turned out to be hits by big armor-piercing bombs that exploded deep inside the ship. Those two bombs did enough damage to slow *Yorktown* and eventually to bring her to a dead stop. Admiral Fletcher could not command an entire fleet from a ship that could not move, so he and his staff transferred to the cruiser *Astoria*, and Admiral Spruance, aboard *Enterprise*, dispatched two cruisers and a pair of destroyers to help out.

Thach's main criticism of the American commanders at Midway was that they had divided their forces. This happened when Admiral Fletcher ordered *Enterprise* and *Hornet* forward to search out and attack the Japanese carriers while *Yorktown* remained behind to recover some search planes.[151] Thach saw this as the kind of fundamental tactical error that midshipmen studying at Annapolis are taught to avoid. Leaders who concentrate their forces typically do better than those who ignore the concept and split their forces. When discussing Fletcher's decision-making decades after Midway, then Admiral Thach called this idea one of the 'basic principles of warfare'.[152] Of course, Fletcher was trying to hit the Japanese before they could hit the US carriers. In this he succeeded brilliantly. Still, Thach always thought that the three US carriers should have been kept closer together. Then each carrier's air group could have been in position to help defend the others. Thach believed that if this had been done at Midway, the Americans would have had a much larger force of Wildcat fighters available and properly positioned nearby to successfully defend *Yorktown*.[153]

At 1.30 that afternoon Lieutenant Joichi Tomonaga took off from *Hiryu*. He would lead the second Japanese attack on *Yorktown*. Tomonaga had commanded the large, 108-plane strike on Midway that morning. After the tremendous American dive bombing attacks earlier that day, the *Kido Butai* did not have much firepower left to throw at the Americans. Now Tomonaga was reduced to leading a total force of just ten torpedo planes and six Zeros.[154]

Tomonaga was a bit over 6ft, very tall for a Japanese man in those days. He was handsome, tough, and a classic example of your hard-drinking samurai. During the morning raid on Midway, gunfire from a Marine fighter had hit his torpedo bomber's gas tank and it had started leaking. The mechanics had done a hasty patch job on the plane when he returned to *Hiryu*. Now Tomonaga was set to lead the critical second attack on *Yorktown*, and his gas tank was leaking again![155] Other Japanese pilots volunteered to take Tomonaga's plane. Tomonaga refused. This mission was certain to be a one-way trip for anyone taking off in a plane that was already leaking gas, but every torpedo plane that could fly was desperately needed now. Admiral Yamaguchi was grimly determined to hit back at the Americans and would put everything he had into this one last-ditch attack. So Joichi

Tomonaga proved himself to be as nonchalant about his own imminent death as all true samurai warriors were expected to be.

Then the worst possible news hit Admiral Yamaguchi and all of his men like a sharp knee right to the groin. A Japanese search plane reported spotting three American aircraft carriers, and all three seemed to be steaming along at a good clip. There was no smoke visible at all. Not one of them appeared to be on fire! In fact, not one of these US carriers seemed to have suffered any kind of damage at all! Admiral Yamaguchi was stunned sick. He had mistakenly thought that he was now in an even fight. Yamaguchi dragged himself to *Hiryu*'s bridge. Tomonaga's pilots quietly gathered together below on the flight deck to hear what their admiral had to say. They all understood how dire Japan's situation had become. Yamaguchi gave them a powerful, heartfelt speech, and told them all how critically important their mission was. The fate of the Japanese Empire literally depended on the performance of each and every one of them. Then Admiral Yamaguchi slowly climbed down from the bridge. He thankfully shook hands with Lieutenant Tomonaga and the rest of his pilots.

Tomonaga climbed into his command plane with the three red 'leader's feathers' painted on its tail. Then he roared off *Hiryu*'s flight deck for the last time. He headed east towards the American enemy and to what he knew would be his own certain death.

Yorktown had been dead in the water for about an hour. In that hour the ship's damage control parties had worked wonders. The great gashes in the flight deck had been patched. All the fires down below had been extinguished, and the engineers had installed auxiliary steam lines to the boilers. Incredibly, the badly damaged *Yorktown* was ready to get under way![156]

One critical difference between American and Japanese aircraft carriers during World War Two was in the important area of the damage control skill of their crews. American sailors were all highly trained damage control professionals, and US ships ran intense, realistic damage control drills all the time. The magnificent damage control work by *Yorktown*'s crew fooled the Japanese into thinking that the Americans still had three undamaged carriers near Midway when, in fact, they only had two. Now, the horribly wounded *Yorktown* appeared to be in fine shape. In fact, Captain Buckmaster could have easily sailed his carrier back to Pearl Harbor with no problems, but she would not be able to withstand even one more heavy attack.

The Japanese were 'offensive minded' to a startling degree. Training in such mundane matters as fighting gasoline and oil fires seems to have been given short shrift on many of their ships. The loss of the brand-new Japanese carrier *Taiho* and 1,600 members of her crew after a single torpedo hit at the Battle of the Philippine Sea strongly suggests that damage control was not a very high priority in the Imperial Navy.[157]

Yorktown's bridge called down and asked Thach if his fighters could take off if the carrier was traveling at 16 knots into the wind. Thach said that he thought that they could. Then *Yorktown* started moving! Lieutenant Tomonaga had divided his torpedo planes into two divisions. He would try to execute the same kind of 'anvil' attack that the Americans typically used. He wanted to hit *Yorktown* from both the starboard and port sides. Tomonaga's torpedo attack on *Yorktown* turned out to be the final Japanese air action of the Battle of Midway.

As the Japanese torpedo planes approached *Yorktown*, Scott McCuskey, Bill Woolen, Harry Gibbs and their wingmen were orbiting overhead on combat air patrol. Thach and his men were sprinting across the flight deck to their planes. McCuskey guessed that he was again dealing with dive bombers, so he climbed for altitude. As a result, he climbed much too high and completely missed Tomonaga's low-flying torpedo bombers. Realizing his mistake, McCuskey dove towards the sea. Woolen knocked down one torpedo plane, and a Zero shot down Ensign Gibbs. Down near the water, McCuskey tangled with another Zero. Unbelievably, he outmaneuvered the far more nimble Japanese fighter and shot it down! When Thach took off from the slow-moving *Yorktown.* His plane dropped down a lot closer to the water than he had expected, but the carrier was picking up speed. Ram Dibb took off next, and he had no trouble getting airborne at all.

Ensign Milton Tootle Jr came next. He was probably the last man to ever to take off from *Yorktown.* Tootle also flew one of the shortest and luckiest combat missions in aviation history.[158] Immediately after he got airborne, a Japanese torpedo plane flew right into his gunsight. Tootle fired a burst. The torpedo plane caught fire; nosed down, and crashed. Then a Zero came diving in and shot down Tootle's Wildcat. Almost immediately the destroyer *Anderson* charged in and its sailors pulled Tootle out of the water. Tootle did not have a scratch on him. Milton Tootle's entire mission from take-off, to shoot down, and rescue, had lasted about a minute.

Jimmie Thach had hardly raised his Wildcat's landing gear when he spotted a torpedo plane with three red 'leader's stripes' on its tail.[159] It was Lieutenant Tomonaga, and he was already in position to launch his torpedo at *Yorktown*'s starboard quarter. Thach rolled hard right and fired round after round into Tomonaga's command plane. The left wing crumpled and burned. Most of it fell off. Thach could see that there was nothing left of that wing but the structural ribbing. Somehow Tomonaga still managed to launch his torpedo and hit *Yorktown.*[160] It was an amazing, last-ditch, feat worthy of a true samurai. At the same time, two other torpedo planes were scoring hits on the carrier's port bow. *Yorktown*'s electrical circuits began to shut down, power was lost, and seawater began pouring into many of her compartments. The great ship started flooding. *Yorktown* quickly rolled and started listing badly. The sharp slope of the flight deck shut down air operations for good. As Thach flew towards *Enterprise* he thought that *Yorktown* was going to capsize right away.[161] Actually, the big carrier stayed afloat for several days, and some overly optimistic officers even had hopes of towing her back to Pearl Harbor.

Abandon Ship!

Jimmie Thach watched as Lieutenant Tomonaga's smoking torpedo plane plummeted into the sea. Tomonaga's left wing had burned off completely and was just a stub of structural framing by the time the plane hit the water. Then Thach spotted a Zero in the distance. He decided to go after it, but he had no wingman now, so he just hoped that the Japanese pilot would not spot him before he was close enough to open fire. As Thach closed in, the alert Zero pilot pulled up into a steep vertical climb. He flipped the Zero on its back and dove down behind Thach. This was the 'turning in' maneuver taught to all Zero pilots. It was the same tactic used against the Army pilot that Thach had talked to right after Pearl Harbor. Thach escaped into a nearby cloud and pulled up into a fast climb. Then he reversed course. When Thach emerged from the cloud, the Zero was gone.

Far below he saw a pathetic sight; *Yorktown* had rolled and was now listing about 25 degrees. Captain Buckmaster feared that his ship might suddenly capsize with two thousand men still on board, so he gave the gut-wrenching order: 'Abandon ship!'[162]

Twenty-year-old Stan 'Deacon' Linzey was a clarinet player in *Yorktown*'s band. The 'Deacon' was also an aspiring evangelical minister and would eventually become a full-fledged Navy chaplain. Linzey's present battle station was damage control on *Yorktown*'s third deck. His damage control party was working feverishly to stop some flooding just below the waterline, and Linzey was already plenty scared. He had seen first-hand what Japanese bombs could do to men working inside the steel compartments of an aircraft carrier. At the Coral Sea fight a big bomb had exploded in a compartment on the same deck where Linzey was stationed. It had ripped every man inside that compartment to shreds. Some men's bodies almost disintegrated when the terrific blast smashed them against the ship's steel bulkheads. Two Japanese torpedoes had just exploded on *Yorktown*'s port quarter. They hit well aft of Linzey's battle station, but they killed a dozen sailors and knocked out all of the lights on the third deck. No one will ever know exactly where Lieutenant Tomonaga's torpedo would have hit if Jimmie Thach had not shot him down. It may well have exploded right on top of Linzey's ten-man damage control party.

Water from a broken main was sloshing around Linzey's feet. The lights were out and it was pitch black everywhere on the third deck. Then *Yorktown* rolled and started to list badly. The starboard side of the deck lifted high up, and the port side slanted down towards the sea. Two sailors near Linzey turned on their blue emergency lanterns. They could see that the water-tight doors were now in one corner of the overhead (ceiling). One man with a lantern walked right up what had been the bulkhead. He opened a small emergency hatch and crawled up to the next deck. Every member of Linzey's party made the long, dark, slippery climb up to the open air of the hangar deck. The port quarter was underwater. Linzey saw that hundreds of life-jacketed sailors were already floating around on the ocean's surface. Hundreds more were stripping down to their skivvies. Some were lowering themselves 'hand over hand' down knotted ropes into the sea. Strangely, most of the sailors had neatly lined up their shoes along the deck as if they expected to return to the carrier later that day.

Linzey lowered himself down a rope into what turned out to be 6in of stinking, toxic muck. A thick coating of caustic bunker oil was floating on top of the salt water. The oil burned the men's eyes and throats, and it irritated any part of the skin that it touched. After spending about two hours treading water and gulping a nasty combination of oil and salt water, sailors from the destroyer *Balch* hauled a totally exhausted Linzey aboard.

When Jimmie Thach landed on *Enterprise*, Admiral Spruance wanted to hear his account of the morning battle. Thach told Spruance that he had seen three big enemy carriers fully engulfed in flames. All three were burning furiously and were total wrecks, damaged beyond any hope of repair. Thach never saw the fourth carrier. Yet after the air attacks on *Yorktown*, it was pretty obvious that there was at least one more Japanese carrier out there. Thach was still itching for a fight. He urgently recommended that Spruance take *Enterprise* and *Hornet* and go in hot pursuit after the Japanese.[163] It was a great temptation, yet Spruance was concerned that his carriers might run into a powerful force of Japanese battleships during the oncoming night. The American carriers had no battleships with them at all. Spruance still wanted to get that last Japanese carrier, but he also wanted to be close enough to Midway to protect it the following morning. So Spruance wisely decided not to take Thach's advice.

That evening Spruance headed the fleet east, away from the Japanese. He kept sailing east until midnight, then he turned south towards Midway. At dawn *Enterprise* and *Hornet* were again steaming west. Raymond Spruance had read Admiral Yamamoto's mind perfectly; a night battleship attack on the American carriers was exactly what he was hoping for. It was Yamamoto's last chance to snatch victory from the jaws of total defeat. By not falling into this, Yamamoto's last trap, Spruance had assured an historic American victory at Midway.

After hearing Thach's report, Spruance sent him to reorganize the fighter squadron aboard *Hornet.* The carrier's entire escort force of ten Wildcats had not returned from the morning battle as they had all run out of gas and ditched in the sea. Most of the pilots were rescued but two were lost. No planes from Torpedo Squadron 8 had returned either. Ensign 'Tex' Gay turned out to be the sole survivor of the dozens of flyers in Torpedo 8. Thach flew over to *Hornet* and took some *Yorktown* pilots with him.

After reorganizing *Hornet*'s fighters, Thach worked on his squadron's report on the battle. The outspoken Thach made it clear to the Navy leadership that the American Wildcat fighter was grossly inferior to the Japanese Zero.[164] His men had won only because they were better shots, and because they had fought as a team. Thach noted that his squadron had shot down an amazing thirty-two enemy planes during the course of the battle.[165] Admiral Nimitz' 'Graybook' logs show that extensive aerial searches the next morning found that all Japanese surface forces had completely withdrawn from the Midway area.[166]All the Japanese still afloat had simply cleared out. As events would show, there was at least one Japanese submarine still lurking nearby. Nevertheless, the Americans had achieved total and complete victory. The badly listing *Yorktown* was abandoned. People who saw the ship thought that she would capsize right away, but the tough old ship remained afloat until 7 June. Captain Buckmaster led a hand-picked repair party back on board. Then the Japanese submarine *I-168* stealthily approached the stricken carrier, evading the destroyers screening her. The sub then fired a full spread of torpedoes. One cut the destroyer *Hammann* in half, killing eighty men. Two torpedoes struck *Yorktown*, and Captain Buckmaster and his repair party left their ship for the last time. The mighty *Yorktown* finally started to go down.

Deacon Linzey recounted one of the saddest, most poignant events that occurred during the final evacuation of *Yorktown*.[167] Two critically wounded sailors, George Weise and Norman Pichette, were down in sick bay when Captain Buckmaster ordered the repair crews to leave the ship. The ship's medical personnel thought that both of the unconscious men were dying and that they were much too badly wounded to be moved. After the last boats had pulled away from *Yorktown*, Norman regained consciousness and awakened George. Pichette wrapped his bloody abdomen in a sheet. Then he painfully climbed up to a deck where there was a machine gun. He fired the machine gun as a signal to the rescue ships. Then Pichette passed out. The rescuers returned and were able to revive Norman for a short time. He was conscious just long enough to tell them about George down in sick bay. Then Norman Pichette died. George Weise recovered from his wounds, and he lived for many years after the war.

The Last Japanese Carrier

The search for the last Japanese carrier ended about the same time that the first torpedoes from Lieutenant Tomonaga's planes were ripping great gashes in the sides of *Yorktown.* The Americans had been sending out dozens of search planes for hours – mainly PBYs from Midway and dive bombers from the carriers. Everyone was looking for that fourth Japanese carrier. Everyone knew that at least one more enemy carrier had to be out there after the first dive bombing attack on *Yorktown.*

Lieutenant Sam Adams had completed the outward leg of his search and was about halfway home. Then Adams spotted the wakes of ten Japanese ships. They were far off and heading north: nine cruisers and destroyers. And, yes! They were escorting the carrier that everyone had been hunting all afternoon! It was *Hiryu.* Adams quickly radioed in what he was seeing. Suddenly a Zero came out of nowhere and made a firing pass at his Dauntless. The alert rear seat gunner quickly got off a short burst. Maybe he damaged the Zero pretty badly. Anyway, Adams managed to fly clear with no further trouble.

Everyone aboard *Enterprise* and *Hornet* scrambled to get all their dive bombers into the air as soon as possible. Lieutenant Earl Gallaher led a huge 'composite' squadron of two dozen Dauntlesses from *Enterprise.* They took off at 1530. *Hornet* launched sixteen dive bombers at 1603. No Wildcat fighters could go as the fighters had to stay behind to protect the American carriers. Still, sending forty Dauntless dive bombers to attack what was left of the Japanese fleet was almost overkill. The once mighty *Kido Butai* could now only muster six flyable Zeros.

Gallaher spotted the wakes of the Japanese ships at 1645. The sun was getting low in the west, but it was still broad daylight. Two dozen *Enterprise* bombers climbed higher and higher, way up to 19,000ft. The ships below seemed to be sailing along normally. They were making no evasive maneuvers. It looked like the Japanese were once again totally oblivious to the presence of US dive bombers approaching them. Then the half dozen Zeros still flying came slashing in from overhead. They quickly shot down three of the American dive bombers. One Zero pilot almost collided with Gallaher's plane. Defending their last flight deck, the Zero pilots flew fantastic stunts that seemed to defy the laws of aerodynamics. They fired at the diving Dauntlesses all the way down – something that was supposed to be impossible. One pilot turned his fighter into a 'falling leaf' to keep the diving Dauntlesses in his sights. The Zero pilots' epic performance apparently did have some effect. Several of the crack *Enterprise* pilots, including Gallaher, completely missed *Hiryu*. Their bombs flew wide of the mark and splashed harmlessly into the ocean. Still, it did not really matter. Dick Best and many more of the Dauntless pilots had yet to dive. Thousand pound bombs rained down on this, the last of the Japanese carriers, and detonated all over *Hiryu*. Uncontrollable fires raged everywhere. US reconnaissance photos taken later show that the forward half of *Hiryu*'s flight deck had been blasted into one enormous, steaming, crater.

Soryu sank at dusk that evening. A little later two internal explosions tore through the burning hulk of the giant *Kaga*. She slipped under the waves quietly. The flagship, *Akagi*, was abandoned later that night. The Japanese scuttled her just before dawn. A destroyer pumped several torpedoes into the still steaming wreck of *Hiryu* to keep her from falling into American hands. By daylight the following morning four of the great carriers of Japan's *Kido Butai* were simply gone. They had vanished without a trace, and almost all of the offensive firepower of the Imperial Japanese Navy had vanished with them.

Back at Pearl Harbor Admiral Nimitz could finally relax. The mortal threat to the Pacific Fleet had passed, and he had dealt with it brilliantly. Aboard *Enterprise*, Dick Best stopped worrying about his wife and baby living in Honolulu. Amazingly, Jimmie Thach soon found himself rubbing elbows with Hollywood's elite at a world famous movie studio. Two months after the Battle of Midway, the US First

Marine Division landed on Guadalcanal in the Solomon Islands. It was the beginning of a bloody American offensive that ended three years later with Imperial Japan's formal surrender in Tokyo Bay.

British Prime Minister Winston Churchill famously said that the Battle of El Alamein was not the 'beginning of end' of the war against the Nazis, but that it was 'the end of the beginning'. Precisely the same thing can be said about the Battle of Midway and the war in the Pacific.

Chapter 8

The Lost Zero of the Aleutians

The day before Lieutenant Tomonaga's planes bombed Midway, Zero fighters and Kate bombers from the carrier *Ryujo* attacked US bases in the frigid Aleutian Islands. They hit the base at Dutch Harbor again on 4 June. The raids were part of Japan's bizarre plan to invade the cold, sub-Arctic island chain. Most likely, the entire Aleutian fiasco was a concession by Admiral Yamamoto to appease the opponents of his Midway operation on the Imperial Navy's General Staff. The Japanese apparently hoped to draw the American fleet away from Midway by first attacking US bases in Alaska. Even if Joe Rochefort and his team of analysts had not broken the Japanese naval code and learned about Yamamoto's plan to attack Midway, the Americans were not likely to have fallen into such an obvious trap. Anyway, as Jimmie Thach could tell anyone who asked, the Aleutians were an extremely inhospitable place to operate in, and the entire island chain was just not that important. Several thousand Japanese troops did end up occupying Kiska and Attu, two remote, unimportant islands in the Aleutian chain.

However, the most strategically significant event of the entire Alaskan campaign occurred about twenty minutes before the second Japanese air raid on Dutch Harbor. Three Zeros shot down an American PBY Catalina patrol plane piloted by Navy Ensign Albert 'Bud' Mitchell. Several members of Mitchell's crew survived the initial attack, and were able to get into a small rubber life raft. Then the three Zeros returned and machine gunned the helpless men floating in the raft. All of the Americans were killed.[168] Petty Officer Tadayoshi Koga was one of the Zero pilots who shot up the raft but immediately after he must have realized that he was in desperate trouble. A single 50-caliber machine gun slug, apparently fired from Mitchell's PBY, had severed a hose inside Koga's engine. The Zero's Sakae engine was notoriously vulnerable to the heavy, 50-caliber machine gun rounds used by the Americans, and it began spewing out an ugly stream of oil and dirty black smoke.

Koga and his two companions turned towards treeless Akutan Island. The Japanese had designated Akutan as the place for any of their planes that were damaged while raiding Dutch Harbor to make emergency landings. A Japanese submarine would be waiting offshore to pick up any downed pilots. Koga spotted what looked like a green grassy meadow less than a mile from Akutan's shoreline. It looked like the perfect spot for an emergency landing. Petty Officer Koga lowered his landing gear and glided in for what should have been a fairly routine, forced landing. Unfortunately, Koga was not putting down on a grassy meadow as he apparently thought. He was landing in muskeg, a moss-covered bog. It is a common feature of the landscape in much of the sub-Arctic. The moss grows over mud and rotting vegetation, and is usually covered by a foot or two of ice cold water. The water never drains out of the muskeg because there is almost always a thick, impervious layer of permafrost beneath the bottom of the bog. Koga's landing gear apparently snapped off the moment his wheels plowed into the muck. The Zero flipped over on its back, and Petty Officer Koga was left hanging upside down in his flight harness.[169] His head was dangling half-submerged in the ice water. Hopefully, Koga died instantly from a broken neck or some other injury, otherwise, he must have had an incredibly excruciating death. The Americans eventually found him and buried him after a makeshift funeral service about 100 yards from where his Zero had crashed.

Akutan Island lies about 25 miles east of Dutch Harbor. It is really off the beaten path, so Koga's Zero lay in the bog unseen by anyone for about a month. One night a PBY piloted by Lieutenant William Thies on patrol out of Dutch Harbor was blown far off course by strong easterly winds and he flew directly over Akutan on his return flight. One of his gunners spotted Koga's downed Zero and the Navy rushed out crews to recover it. The plane was shipped to Jimmie Thach's old base, North Island Naval Air Station in San Diego, where it was repaired and put through an array of test flights.

Lieutenant Ed Sanders made twenty-four of the initial flights and found that at most speeds the Zero was extremely maneuverable. Of course, everybody already knew that, and American pilots had already begun fighting the Zero more intelligently. They had stopped trying to get into traditional turning dogfights with the far more maneuverable Japanese fighter, and had started using the Thach Weave when that was feasible. Yet, on that very first test flight Sanders had noticed that the Zero's ailerons responded very sluggishly at speeds over 200 knots. Rolls (turns) to the right were especially slow. Saunders also found flaws in the Sakae engine's float-style carburetor. It would sputter and the engine would lose power when Sanders put the Zero into a high-speed dive. All this was incredibly vital information for pilots already in combat in the Pacific. The Navy rushed the results of the test flights to the squadrons.

From Sanders' test flights US pilots now learned that they could break off contact with a Zero that was on their tail by putting their heavier Wildcats into high-speed dives and rolling right. The Zeros just could not keep up. The Americans might even be able to outmaneuver a Zero at very high speed, but nobody wanted to try that until fighters superior to the Zero were available.[170] The lessons learned from the flight tests of Koga's lost Zero did not win the war in the Pacific. They did not even shorten the war in any meaningful way. Still, they probably saved the lives of quite a few Navy and Marine Corps pilots who were going up against the Zero while flying inferior aircraft. Fortunately, the period when American pilots flew planes outclassed by the Zero came to an end in the fall of 1943.

Everyday Americans Go to War: The Story of the Grumman Hellcat and Rosie the Riveter

Imperial Japan's decision to attack the United States at Pearl Harbor was clearly a catastrophic blunder of historic proportions. It ensured Japan's total defeat, and it ensured an end to its dictatorial, monarchical system. Adolf Hitler's unthinking, almost off-the-cuff declaration of war against the US a few days later was at least as stupid. It literally turned out to be suicidal, both for Hitler personally, and for the Nazi regime. A brief look at just one part of the US aircraft manufacturing industry shows just how out of touch with reality the preening, evil men who ran the Axis states really were.

Something that the Axis leaders could not possibly have anticipated was how many Americans from all walks of life – most especially how tens of millions of American women – would drastically alter their lives and pitch in enthusiastically to help the war effort.

In 1942 Leroy Grumman was preparing to build a fighter that was more advanced than the Wildcat. He wanted to design a real 'Zero smasher', and that is just what his new airplane turned out to be. It was the outstanding, war-winning, F6F Hellcat.

After the Battle of Midway, Leon 'Jake' Swirlbul, the engineer who had helped Grumman start his aircraft company, traveled to Honolulu. Grumman and Swirlbul wanted to get recommendations from experienced fighter pilots. They wanted to know what features veteran Navy pilots thought should be built into their new fighter. Swirlbul met several leading American aces, including Jimmie Thach, Butch O'Hare, Jimmy Flatley from *Enterprise*, and Marion Carl of the Marines.[171] All of the pilots wanted a new fighter that was faster than the Zero. All of them wanted one that could outclimb the Zero. As O'Hare had famously said to FDR, they all wanted a fighter that could really 'go upstairs!' This meant that the new plane needed to have an engine much more powerful than the Pratt & Whitney R-1830 Twin Wasp in the Wildcat.

After the test flights of Petty Officer Koga's 'lost Zero' from the Aleutians, the Navy's technical people were also recommending a more powerful engine. Grumman eventually settled on the giant Pratt & Whitney R-2800 Double Wasp, which put out hundreds more horsepower than the 1830. It would make the new Hellcat noticeably faster than the Zero, and the big radial engine was designed to absorb an incredible amount of punishment and keep on running. Using the huge Double Wasp engine had the added benefit of putting a ton of metal directly in front of the pilot. This served as an addition to all the pilot-protecting armor that Leroy Grumman was planning to put into his new fighter. The Double Wasp powered the Chance Vought Corsair that would be flown successfully by 'Pappy' Boyington's Marine 'Black Sheep' squadron on Guadalcanal. It also powered the Air Force's P-47 Thunderbolt. The engine had an excellent two-stage supercharger that condensed the thin air at high altitude, so the Hellcat had a service ceiling approaching 40,000ft. Leroy Grumman was designing a fighter that could, in O'Hare's words, really 'go upstairs!'

Although most of the top pilots that Swirlbul spoke with seemed more than satisfied with all these major improvements, Jimmie Thach was not. The proposed new fighter looked to him like a faster, tougher version of the same old Wildcat. Thach thought of the F4F as an outmoded design, something out of the late 1930s. A Wildcat pilot had to do all sorts of jobs manually instead of just pressing a button or flipping a switch. For example, he had to hand-crank the landing gear up or down. This took a good deal of physical effort, and it could easily distract a pilot from far more important tasks, especially during tricky carrier landings. The Wildcat pilot also had to manually charge his guns. This meant pulling on cables that were physically attached to the guns. While the Browning machine guns were marvelous weapons, Wildcat pilots would sometimes jam them when using the cable charging system. This happened to Butch O'Hare's wingman, Duff Dufilho, on the day that O'Hare saved *Lexington* and won the Medal of

Honor. Manual back-ups for emergencies were okay, but Thach wanted Grumman to build a cutting-edge fighter where all the major systems were state of the art, in other words, hydraulic. Thach also suggested that a radio microphone be fitted inside the pilot's oxygen mask. It would replace the trouble-prone 'throat mike' that they had been using.

When the first Hellcat emerged from the Grumman factory in Bethpage, New York, it had all the extra features Thach had recommended. The Hellcat carried an enormous amount of hydraulic fluid, about 4 gallons. Hydraulics operated the wing flaps, the landing gear, the locking mechanism for the folding wings, the supercharger, and the cowl flaps (engine housing). Hydraulics charged the guns. Of course, the Hellcat, with a top speed of 400mph, was much faster – about 60mph faster – than the Zero in straight and level flight.[172] It could easily outclimb the Japanese fighter. It was also far, far faster in a dive. Everyone appreciated the many 'pilot protection' features that were built into the new fighter. Leroy Grumman, a former Navy pilot himself, had a simple philosophy about aircraft design. He drummed it into of his engineers: 'The pilot is more important than the airplane.'[173] There was armor everywhere inside the Hellcat. Grumman engineers designed a cockpit so tough that it would always be the last component on the Hellcat to fail.

The Hellcat turned out to be the real 'Zero smasher' that Grumman designed it to be. Hellcat pilots scored a total of 5,163 aerial kills during World War Two, with only 270 of the heavily armored Hellcats lost in combat. Against the Zero specifically, the kill ratio was a remarkable 13-1.

From the moment the first Japanese bomb dropped on Pearl Harbor, America was fully engaged in all-out war in a way that it had not been, at least since Appomattox. With millions of young American men going into the military, the Roosevelt Administration started a wildly successful public relations campaign aimed at US women. The PR campaign encouraged women to go into the workforce, especially into defense industries. Artist Norman Rockwell painted an iconic portrait of 'Rosie the Riveter' for the cover of the widely read *Saturday Evening Post* magazine. Rockwell portrayed a robust, red-headed 'Rosie' getting a sandwich out of her lunch box. She had a rivet gun on her lap and she was stepping on a copy of Adolf Hitler's book, *Mein Kampf.* A popular big band leader, Kay Kyser had a hit song about 'Rosie the Riveter', and well-known entertainment personalities jumped on the bandwagon. Millions of American women poured into the workforce as the entire country pitched in wholeheartedly to win the war.

After it had been awarded the Navy contract to build the Hellcat, no company needed a lot of Rosies more than Grumman. No company did more to recruit them, and no company did more to keep them happy. Jake Swirlbul, the man who had gone out to Hawaii to consult with Thach about the design of the new fighter, was Grumman's point man on what you might call 'Project Rosie'. When the wartime build-up first started, Grumman Aircraft mostly hired men with years of factory work experience. Many of them were World War One vets, but they were now too old to serve in the military. The US Navy only trained seven hundred new pilots in 1940, but it trained *twenty thousand* in 1943! It really was total war. Grumman suddenly needed a much larger skilled workforce to build all the planes that all those new pilots would be flying. That is where all the Rosies came in. They were not all lookalikes of the tough, thirty-something gal in Rockwell's portrait; some were grandmothers, some were middle aged. Others were very young women. Some were black, most were white. There were even a few women of Chinese descent. Virtually none of them had ever handled a power tool in their lives, and very few had even heard of a hydraulic press or seen a sheet metal saw. Yet they learned to do their strange new jobs astonishingly well. Most of them seemed to really enjoy helping the war effort. They were bright, they were enthusiastic, and they worked their hearts out. The normal work week at the Grumman plant at the beginning of the war was pretty long. People usually worked ten hour shifts, six days a week. Times were tough, so many people volunteered to work longer hours. Grumman employees often worked a couple of Sundays each month. The company's workforce grew from several hundred to over twenty thousand by V-J Day. Grumman built a brand-new plant just to produce the Hellcat, and dedicated, patriotic employees were inside that plant and hard at work even before the roof was finished. Most were women or older men. This was during the middle of the harsh Long Island winter. When production really ramped up in 1944, Grumman was delivering nearly 600 Hellcats a month to the Navy. Chance Vought was producing Corsairs, primarily for the Marines; Lockheed and Republic were building P-38 and P-47 fighters for the Army; and North American (today, part of Boeing) was building the incomparable P-51 Mustang. In stark contrast, Mitsubishi only built 145 Zeros in October 1944, thc company's best month.

The United States built more and better planes than either the Japanese or their German allies. America's massive production capacity, and a solidly unified American public, simply overwhelmed the Axis powers. The Marines and a relatively few Navy fighter pilots flew the Corsair, while Air Force pilots flew Lightnings, Thunderbolts and Mustangs. They all outperformed the Japanese during the final two years of the war. Still, the Grumman F6F Hellcat was unquestionably the plane, and the men who flew it, were unquestionably the pilots, who did the most to finally defeat the legendary Japanese Zero.

Jake Swirlbul, now the Grumman factory manager, went out of his way to help any employee with any kind of problem. His door was always open. Swirlbul opened a company nursery for women with children. He started company bowling leagues and a softball team. Swirlbul even brought in singers to entertain Grumman employees working during the long hours of the night shift. One of the biggest headaches for all civilians during World War Two had to do with automobiles. GM and Ford were busy making tanks and jeeps and even planes for the Army, Navy and Marines. The Government rationed rubber for tires. It rationed gasoline.

No civilian could buy a new automobile, so people were always having car problems. Swirlbul started something akin to an in-house, Grumman version of the Automobile Club. Any time a Grumman employee's car broke down, a mechanic in a green Grumman company tow truck came out and fixed the problem. Swirlbul's green tow trucks became a huge morale booster.

Grumman Wildcats fought at Midway and Guadalcanal. Grumman Hellcats and Avengers fought in the Central and Western Pacific – right up to the coasts of Japan. Nearly a thousand American airplanes, including 450 Grumman Hellcats and Avengers, flew overhead on 2 September 1945, the day that Imperial Japan formally surrendered aboard USS *Missouri* in Tokyo Bay.

Walt Disney Pitches in

When *Enterprise* and *Hornet* docked at Pearl Harbor it was hard for anyone to believe that the great battle was really over. The ominous threat that had hung over the Hawaiian Islands since 7 December was gone. The very real possibility that Imperial Japan might attack Oahu or even start landing troops on the West Coast was just gone. Like the four great aircraft carriers of the *Kido Butai*, that nightmare had simply vanished. Jimmie Thach received new orders. He learned that he was leaving the Pacific and would be heading back to the United States. Butch O'Hare and his wife, Rita, were weary of the nearly endless Navy publicity tours and war bond drives. He was tired of being the American public's favorite war hero. O'Hare happily returned to the Pacific. Shortly after Thach returned from Midway, O'Hare relieved him as skipper of Fighting Three. Unfortunately from O'Hare's perspective, the Navy stationed Fighting Three on Maui and began using it as an advanced training unit, not the front-line fighter squadron that it had been since the beginning of the war. So for a while O'Hare did nothing but train new pilots fresh out of Pensacola. There was no chance of returning to combat and he had plenty of unwanted spare time. A good athlete and a strong swimmer, O'Hare used the time to become an expert spear fisherman. He practically lived on the abundant aquatic life teeming in the ocean around Maui.

The US Navy frequently renumbered its squadrons, and Fighting Three became Fighting Six in July 1943. Shortly thereafter it became part of a brand-new administrative entity, Air Group Six. In late August O'Hare and his squadron finally found themselves back in a combat role. They were assigned to the new light carrier *Independence* (the *Evil I*), and they successfully raided enemy bases on Marcus and Wake Islands. Fighting Six was one of the first units to fly the new Hellcat fighter, which quickly proved to be superior to anything in the Japanese inventory. At Wake, O'Hare shot down at least one, and possibly two Zeros, plus a twin-engine Betty bomber.[174] O'Hare was not just a famous war hero widely admired by the public, he was a born leader. His pilots naturally took to his calm, low-key style of running things. O'Hare's most obvious character flaw was that he was never willing to let any of his men do something dangerous that he was not first willing to do himself. It was a fault that would cost O'Hare his life.

In October 1943, O'Hare was promoted to Air Group Commander and assigned to *Enterprise*. He was clearly one of the Navy's best pilots, and he had shown outstanding leadership skills. Still, he was pretty 'junior' to hold such an important post. Now he would not only command a squadron of fighters; he was responsible for the performance of every pilot and every plane aboard *Enterprise*, and O'Hare took his responsibilities very seriously. That November aircraft from *Enterprise* were pounding Japanese positions in the Gilbert Islands in the Central Pacific. The attacks were in preparation for Marine and Army amphibious assaults on Tarawa and Makin atolls. The three-day battle for Tarawa saw some of the bloodiest fighting of the entire war. Thanks to its powerful Hellcat and Corsair fighters, the

US Navy now had total control of the air over the Gilberts – at least during the daylight hours. Still, the Americans were having trouble stopping Japanese torpedo plane attacks on US ships that were being launched just after sunset. The American carriers needed to quickly develop a 'night fighter' capability. This was a difficult and dangerous assignment. Although O'Hare had dozens of top-notch pilots under his command, he decided to do the job of working out the best night fighter tactics himself. For about a week, O'Hare's so-called 'Black Panther' experimental operations went well. O'Hare would have a big, TBF torpedo plane carry heavy radar equipment aloft. The TBF crew would team up with a pair of Hellcat fighters, and direct the Hellcats towards incoming enemy torpedo planes. When a Hellcat pilot got close enough to a plane to see its blue exhaust flames, he would fire and usually hit the enemy plane.

On the night of 26 November, the Japanese launched a large number of torpedo plane attacks after sunset. O'Hare, another Hellcat pilot, and a TBF took off from *Enterprise*. Soon they thought they were closing in on a Japanese plane. Then something went wrong, but nobody knows for sure what really happened. A burst of machine gun fire came out of the darkness above them and O'Hare's plane was hit. *Enterprise*'s radar tracked his fighter as it plummeted thousands of feet down to the sea. Extensive searches found a little debris, but nothing more. For a time O'Hare was listed as missing in action. In reality, a great fighter pilot and a true American hero died that night.[175]

After the war, the *Chicago Tribune* launched a successful campaign to name the city's main airport after O'Hare. The city even erected an exhibit in Terminal Two dedicated to his wartime exploits. It featured a restored Grumman Wildcat fighter identical to the one that O'Hare flew at Rabaul on the day he shot down half a dozen Japanese bombers, singlehandedly saved *Lexington*, and won the Medal of Honor.

***

Jimmie Thach learned that he was getting a new job. It was an important one, and it was something that was almost tailor-made for him. Unlike a lot of highly talented people, Thach really loved to teach. He once said that if he had not joined the Navy he would probably have taken up elementary school teaching like his mom and dad. Thach's next assignment was to train thousands of new Navy and Marine Corps pilots, and teach them how to handle the kind of first-rate Japanese pilots that he had gone up against during the first months of the war.

Fortunately for the Americans the Imperial Navy's training system began to break down after the severe losses at Midway. The US Navy rotated its most successful combat veterans back to the United States so that they could train rookie pilots. In contrast, the Japanese kept their top aces in front-line units for extended tours. Many of Japan's best pilots were killed before they had a chance to pass along their hard-won fighting skills to less-experienced men. So in the last two and a half years of the war the quality of Japanese pilots was not nearly as high as it had been earlier.[176] The Americans flew better planes than the Japanese did in those last two years, and their pilots were much better trained. Additionally, US aircraft production was so great that the Japanese were almost always outnumbered. These factors explain the overwhelming, incredibly lopsided victories that American Navy pilots won in air battles later in the war. The aptly named 'Marianas Turkey Shoot' is the classic example of these one-sided engagements.

Thach left Hawaii and headed back to San Diego for a week's leave with Maddie and their new son, William. Thach discussed the problem of how to quickly train many thousands of new pilots with Jimmy Flatley. Flatley was a fighter ace himself, and the skipper of *Enterprise*'s 'Grim Reaper' squadron. Some form of training film was the obvious answer, yet in air-to-air combat fighters flew a lot faster and much farther apart than most people realized. A traditional training film showing actual pilots flying their planes would not give the new men an overall view of everything that was really happening, both inside and outside the cockpit. In air-to-air combat two, three or more different, but critical events can be occurring simultaneously. For example, when a pilot flying the Thach Weave (say, the 'leader') sees that his wingman is about to be attacked from behind, he instantly rolls (turns) towards his wingman. This alerts the wingman to the impending attack, and the wingman turns towards the leader, both to get out of the line of fire and to lead the attacker into the leader's gunsights. At the same time, the leader is setting up for what would likely be a very quick and fairly difficult shot at the incoming enemy plane. So with a traditional training film using actual pilots it would be hard to show the new men all of the many details that they needed to see. Yet training films of some sort were the only possible way to quickly teach so many new pilots what they needed to know before they faced the enemy.

Flatley came up with a brilliant solution: he suggested an animated film. Flatley thought that something along the lines of a Disney production might do the trick. Ironically, an animated, cartoon-like, training film might show new pilots more about how to stay alive and win in aerial combat than something that appeared to be lot more realistic. Flatley got the ball rolling, and called Walt Disney. Disney immediately volunteered his army of animation artists to help out the US Navy.[177]

Thach's next duty station was going to be at a huge new training facility in Jacksonville, Florida. The commander there was Rear Admiral A.B. Cook. Before he left San Diego for Jacksonville, Thach drove up to Burbank to meet Disney. It was just as Flatley had said; Disney was more than happy to help the war effort. The creator of Mickey Mouse and Donald Duck set aside an entire three-story studio building full of his best artists for Thach's training film project. They called it the 'Jacksonville Project'. Then Thach, his wife and baby son headed to Florida. He expected to spend a few days a month in Burbank writing scripts. The rest of his work would be in Jacksonville giving new pilots lectures on tactics and live fire demonstrations of aerial gunnery.

Early on Walt Disney developed some misgivings about the value of the animated films that they would be making. He was worried that grown men training for real life combat would not take his 'cartoons' seriously. After he read Thach's first script, Disney was also worried that he would never be able to find an announcer who could narrate the training films effectively. He needed someone knowledgeable enough to convey aloud the subtle points about fighter tactics that Thach was putting into his scripts. Disney need not have worried about his first concern. The training films turned out to be wildly popular with virtually all the Navy and Marine pilots who saw them. Years after the war men would frequently come up to Thach and thank him for saving their lives. They told him that the tactical knowledge that they gained by watching his animated training films had helped them survive air-to-air combat.

The problem of finding a good narrator was a different, more difficult matter. Disney and Thach auditioned dozens of actors and announcers who applied for the job but not one of them could put just the right emphasis on the subtle aspects of aerial combat that needed to be stressed. One day a frustrated Disney turned to Thach and told him that aside from writing the scripts he would also have to narrate them as well. This change dramatically increased the amount of time that Thach would have to spend in Southern California.

Thach, Disney and a small army of animators worked together feverishly for five hectic months. The training films had the studio's highest priority. They needed to finish them soon because huge numbers of new pilots needed to see them before shipping out to the Pacific. Many of Disney's animation artists became virtual experts on the tactics of fighter combat. They would talk enthusiastically to each other about aerial maneuvers using their hands to represent airplanes, just like fighter pilots did back on board the carriers. After five stress-filled months Thach and Walt Disney finally completed their work. Thach had written and narrated ten unusually detailed training films.

He had even played a small role in one of them, with those scenes apparently shot at Warner Brothers. Most of the films were about half an hour long.

At least two of the Thach-Disney-Navy training films are still available for viewing on YouTube: *Offensive Tactics Against Enemy Fighters*; and *World War II US Navy Fighter Tactics, Part Two: Attacking Fighters (with Jimmy Thach)*. It is intriguing to watch the films while listening to Thach's soft, 'southern' narration explaining the finer points of aerial combat. It is the exact same narration that thousands of US Navy and Marine Corps pilots heard many decades ago during World War Two.

In April 1944 Admiral John 'Slew' McCain flew down to Jacksonville from Washington DC to speak with Thach. McCain had commanded all Allied land-based aircraft in the South Pacific during the Guadalcanal campaign and had been chief of the Bureau of Aeronautics. Now he was the Navy's Deputy Chief of Staff. McCain only knew Thach by reputation, but he had heard that he was not a 'yes man'. So he offered him a job. It was a tough, challenging, and important job. Jimmie Thach was going back to the Pacific.

Chapter 9

Thach Goes Back to the War

When Admiral McCain took Thach aside at Jacksonville to offer him a job he also had to disclose some confidential information.[178] McCain told Thach that he was going to be leaving Washington, and that he would soon begin alternating command of the huge, incredibly powerful Fast Carrier Task Force with Admiral Marc Mitscher. The Task Force was easily the most powerful fleet that had ever put to sea, more than three times larger than Japan's *Kido Butai* that had attacked Midway. Of course, that *Kido Butai* no longer existed. It had been destroyed at Midway. American aircraft carriers were now steadily sweeping the Imperial Navy from the Pacific. The awesome power of the Fast Carrier Task Force was a tribute to the success of America's mobilization effort. The United States had harnessed its vast industrial potential and unified its entire population for a single task – winning the war. Admiral McCain wanted Thach to be his Operations Officer. His primary duty would be to plan and organize the Task Force's air strikes. Thach would oversee huge air strikes, sometimes involving a thousand planes at a time.

The Fast Carrier Task Force was made up of four smaller Task Groups. Each Task Group was usually made up of three or four carriers surrounded by a protective screen of battleships, cruisers, and destroyers. The carriers sailed close enough together so that their air groups could provide the other carriers with mutual defensive support. This was a lesson that the Americans had learned the hard way from the loss of *Yorktown* at Midway. The US Navy had also upgraded its weaponry tremendously. The new *Essex*-class carriers were superb ships. They were big, fast and had state-of-the-art damage control systems. Their quad-mounted Bofors 40mm anti-aircraft guns put out an incredible volume of fire. The super-secret proximity fuse dramatically increased the effectiveness of a single anti-aircraft shell. Gunners no longer had to score a direct hit on an enemy plane in order to inflict damage. They just needed to come close to the enemy plane. Then the proximity fuse would detonate and shrapnel would spray out from the exploding shell. One near miss was sometimes enough to severely damage or even destroy a Japanese plane. The old Devastator torpedo planes had been replaced by more modern TBF Avengers, while the Hellcat fighter was a vast improvement over the Wildcat. It flew faster. It climbed higher, and it was more heavily armored than the Wildcat. It also had a longer range. Thach took advantage of the Hellcat's greater range in developing one of his innovative defenses against the *kamikaze* suicide pilots.[179]

There were several big, complicated amphibious operations coming up: in the Philippines, the Mariana Islands, Iwo Jima and Okinawa. So command of the Fast Carriers would alternate back and forth between Mitscher and McCain. The purpose of alternating the commanders and their staffs was efficiency. While one admiral was executing an operation, the other admiral and his staff would be planning for the next one. So when Mitscher was preparing for assaults on Iwo Jima and Okinawa, McCain was executing the last phase of the Philippine campaign. When the time for planning the next operation came up the roles would reverse.

McCain wanted Thach to head out to the Pacific immediately after speaking with him at Jacksonville. The two men were almost like father and son right off the bat. McCain had Thach assigned to Admiral Mitscher's staff as an observer. McCain wanted Thach to note how operations were being handled and to look for any improvements that they might be able to make. McCain would follow him out to the Pacific in a few weeks. He had been working at a series of desk jobs in Washington DC since the end of the Guadalcanal campaign and had been far from the fighting. So he wisely planned to ease into his new job. He would first take charge of one of the smaller Task Groups while Admiral Mitscher remained in overall command. When he had gotten his bearings, McCain would then relieve Mitscher. There were few admirals around who were as thoughtful and unassuming as Slew McCain.

When Admiral Mitscher was in charge of the fast carriers they were designated Task Force 58 and were under the overall purview of Admiral Spruance's Fifth Fleet. When McCain was in command, they were called Task Force 38 and it was part of Admiral Halsey's Third Fleet. Admiral McCain was sixty-one years old when he commanded the Fast Carriers, Marc Mitscher was fifty-eight. Yet both men looked like they were almost eighty by the time the war ended. Stress and the intense responsibility of their commands had wrecked their health. McCain died a few days after Japan surrendered. Mitscher died two years later.

When Admiral McCain 'hired' Jimmie Thach as his Operations Officer he issued him the highest-priority travel documents. Thach quickly got out to the new US fleet anchorage at Majuro in the Marshall Islands. Thach was stunned by the immense concentration of naval power anchored in the 25-mile long lagoon. There were more aircraft carriers moored at Majuro than he had ever seen in one place in his life! Thach boarded Admiral Mitscher's flagship, the 'new' *Lexington*. He was just in time to 'observe' the Battle of the Philippine Sea, the largest aircraft carrier battle in history. US Navy pilots nicknamed the initial phase of this lopsided American victory the Great Marianas Turkey Shoot.[180] Admiral Mitscher was quite familiar with Thach when he came aboard his flagship at Majuro. Mitscher had commanded *Hornet* at Midway. Thach had flown to the *Hornet* and helped reorganize her Air Group after it had sustained severe losses on the first day of the battle.

So instead of being a mere observer, Mitscher made Thach a special assistant to his chief of staff, Arleigh Burke.

The Fast Carrier Task Force got under way and headed out to battle on the morning following Thach's arrival. The Philippine Sea fight turned out to be an historic, overwhelming American victory. Yet the night before the big battle was a time of intense frustration for Thach, Admiral Mitscher, and for Mitscher's entire, aviation-oriented staff. US Marines and Army troops landed on Saipan in the Mariana Islands on 15 June 1944. Their defense was absolutely critical to the Japanese as the Marianas are only 1,200 miles from the home islands of Japan. If the Americans captured them the Japanese homeland would be within range of the giant B-29 bombers that were being built by Boeing in Seattle. In fact, the two atomic attacks that ended World War Two were launched from the island of Tinian, just a stone's throw away from Saipan. So the Japanese simply had to hold the Marianas.

The Fast Carrier Task Force left Majuro to shield the amphibious forces assaulting Saipan from a possible counter-attack by the Imperial Navy. Admiral Raymond Spruance was in overall command of the invasion and all related forces. Admiral Soemu Toyoda was now the leader of the Combined Fleet. Toyoda decided that the time for the final, decisive battle (*Kantai Kessen*) against the Americans had come at last. He ordered his carrier commander, Admiral Jisaburo Ozawa, to strike the American fleet with everything he had. Ozawa was considered a competent tactician, but was nicknamed the 'gargoyle' since he was widely thought of as the ugliest man in the Imperial Navy. Considering the intense pounding that the Japanese had been taking for the last year and a half, Admiral Ozawa still had quite a powerful fleet at his disposal. He commanded five big fleet carriers; four light carriers; five battleships, and dozens of cruisers and destroyers. The Japanese also had a natural meteorological advantage in the easterly trade winds that dominate the Philippine Sea. World War Two aircraft carriers had to be steaming into the wind to launch their planes. There were no catapults to launch planes like there are on carriers today. The Japanese fleet was positioned several hundred miles south-west of the Marianas. So, at least in theory, the Japanese could engage in or break off battle more easily than the Americans. Additionally, Admiral Toyoda planned to ferry in hundreds of land-based planes from Japan itself. They would first land on nearby Japanese-held island bases and refuel. Toyoda planned to use these additional aircraft to attack the American carriers.

Admiral Ozawa's fleet rendezvoused and refueled in the Philippine Sea on 16 June. His flagship was the brand-new, heavily armored carrier *Taiho* (Great Phoenix). US submarines spotted the Japanese fleet, and US radio direction-finding experts definitively placed the enemy carriers 350 miles south-west of the Marianas. A cautious Admiral Spruance ordered the US carriers to stick close to Saipan. Spruance thought that the carriers needed to be close by to protect the American invasion troops. During that night, Admiral Mitscher requested permission to move away from Saipan and go after the Japanese carriers. Spruance said no. He believed that Mitscher's primary job was to stay close to Saipan and protect the American troops. While Spruance's thinking might seem perfectly reasonable to a non-aviator, Jimmie Thach, Admiral Mitscher, and all the aviators on Mitscher's staff disagreed strongly. They spent that entire night trying to think of a way to change Spruance's mind. The aviators believed that there was little chance that the Japanese fleet could somehow get around the American carriers without first being sighted by the scores of US search planes that would be scouring the Philippine Sea. They were certain that there was no realistic way for the enemy to attack the US invasion force before the fast carriers intervened. Of course, if the Japanese did manage to attack the landing force they could and do enormous damage and inflict heavy casualties on the American troops. Still, by keeping the US carriers tied so closely to Saipan, Admiral Spruance was practically guaranteeing that American carrier pilots would eventually have to fly very long-range missions to hit the Japanese fleet. Many of them would probably run out of gas and have to ditch in the sea. The stage was now set for the Great Marianas Turkey Shoot.

Early the following morning, US radar detected a large number of Admiral Toyoda's land-based planes taking off from the Japanese-held island of Guam, and Hellcats were dispatched to intercept them. They shot down thirty-five of the Japanese planes while, incredibly, only one Hellcat was lost. The fighting went on in the same startlingly lopsided way for the rest of the day. At ten o'clock American radar detected a group of sixty-eight more enemy planes heading for the Task Force. These Japanese pilots were very brave, but, obviously, they were not very well trained. Seventy miles out, the Japanese started to circle, apparently trying to reorganize and regroup. Dozens of Hellcats pounced on them from all sides, and the Americans shot down twenty-five more enemy planes. Again, the Americans only lost one Hellcat. David McCampbell, the US Navy's all-time highest scoring ace, reported that Japanese planes were falling "like leaves."

The surviving Japanese pilots stoically flew on towards the American fleet and sixteen more were shot down. Fantastic swirling contrails materialized all over the sky, visible to the thousands of sailors aboard the American ships. Half a dozen Japanese planes actually broke through to the American fleet and one bombed the battleship *South Dakota.* The explosion killed about a dozen men but did no material damage to the ship. None of the Japanese pilots got anywhere near their primary targets, the American carriers. Shortly after 11 a.m. another raid by over a hundred Japanese planes came in and about seventy were shot down before they reached the US fleet. Some of the survivors did manage to attack the American carriers, but they scored no hits. These pilots were raw beginners compared to skilled men who had attacked Pearl Harbor and fought at Midway. About ninety-five of these planes were eventually shot down.

Then radar detected a third wave of forty-seven planes coming in, of which seven were shot down. Uncharacteristically, some of these Japanese pilots turned tail and ran for home. A few got through to the American carriers, but again, they scored no hits. A smaller group of eighteen planes attacked the carrier *Bunker Hill.* They too scored no hits, and eight were shot down. Hellcat pilots shot down thirty more land-based planes trying to land on Guam. The 'Turkey Shoot' part of the Battle of the Philippine Sea was over.

The Japanese had suffered stunning loses. They had only killed a dozen American sailors and done minor damage to a single US battleship. Lieutenant Alexander Vraciu was the highest-scoring Hellcat pilot of the day, shooting down six bombers in one mission. Around noon, the American submarine *Cavalla* (SS-244) pumped three torpedoes into *Shokaku*, one of the carriers that had attacked Pearl Harbor. A torpedo hit her near a tank holding aviation gasoline, and almost immediately vicious fires were raging throughout the hangar deck. A plane on the flight deck exploded and ammunition and bombs began detonating everywhere. Then a huge explosion tore the ship apart, killing 1,200 men.[181] This was more than the number of Americans killed when *Arizona* exploded at Pearl Harbor. A short time later, the submarine *Albacore* (SS-218) fired six torpedoes at Admiral Ozawa's brand-new flagship, *Taiho.* An alert Japanese dive bomber pilot spotted the wakes and dove, *kamikaze*-style, into one of the torpedoes. Only one torpedo hit the carrier.[182] *Taiho* was supposed to be heavily armored, and at first the carrier did not seem to be badly damaged at all. The forward elevator was wrecked and some fuel lines were broken, but the ship sailed along pretty much normally. Unfortunately for the Japanese, a gas leak was apparently spreading fumes throughout the ship. The flagship blew up at 1400 hours and the enormous blast killed 1,600 sailors. Again, this was more than the number of American sailors killed when the Arizona exploded at

Pearl Harbor. The loss of *Taiho* is the classic example of lousy Japanese damage control.[183]

All through the next night Task Force 58 raced west in pursuit of the Japanese, who were already steaming west. In fact, what was left of Ozawa's fleet was running away from the Americans at full speed. Admiral Mitscher sent out search planes at dawn and all through the next day but they made no sightings. Finally, late that afternoon an *Enterprise* dive bomber spotted the enemy fleet. They were 275 miles away and still running fast. Any US planes sent to attack them now would be returning to the carriers after dark, and few of the American pilots had been qualified for night carrier landings. These are always pretty tricky, and Mitscher's pilots would be running low on fuel. Nevertheless, Mitscher immediately launched a full deck load of planes. The US pilots now paid the price for Spruance's decision to keep the carriers close to Saipan. The Americans spotted the Japanese fleet just as the sun was starting to set. They sank the carrier *Hiyo* (Hawk) and several oilers. They also badly damaged the carriers *Zuikaku*, *Junyo*, and *Chiyoda*. Then the US pilots turned around and began the long, dangerous flight back through the darkness. Admiral Mitscher earned the gratitude of every naval aviator that night.[184] He turned on all of his fleet's lights, ignoring the very real threat of night attacks by enemy submarines. He also gave his pilots permission to land on any carrier that they could reach. Some of them made it, some ran out of gas, and had to ditch in the sea. About three quarters of the men who ditched were eventually rescued.

The Battle of the Philippine Sea destroyed the power of Japan's carrier air force once and for all. Unfortunately, it did not destroy Japan's ability to mount a ferocious defense of the islands it still held. Jimmie Thach, Admiral McCain and the men of Task Force 38 were about to face what Admiral Nimitz called the biggest surprise of the Pacific War, the *kamikazes*.

The *Kamikazes*

Admiral McCain relieved Mitscher of command of the Fast Carrier Task Force on 30 October 1944. Task Force 58 was now magically transformed into Task Force 38, although both admirals commanded exactly the same ships. Hopefully, the name switch served to confuse the Japanese a bit. The invasion of the island of Leyte in the Philippines was under way and things were going terribly – for the Japanese. The US Sixth Army was making good progress on the ground and punishing airstrikes by Fifth Air Force bombers and Navy carrier planes were hitting the Japanese Army everywhere. The United States' new fighters, Hellcats, Corsairs, Thunderbolts and Lightnings, continued to prove that they were far superior to the Zero and its variants. The Americans now had complete control of the air.

Rear Admiral Takajiro Onishi, commander of the First Air Fleet in the Northern Philippines, sent out a call for help. He desperately needed more pilots – a lot of them. Japanese pilots based in the occupied provinces of China and from the homeland flooded into the Philippines. They were to be based at the eighty or so airstrips in the islands that were still in Japanese hands. When the replacements showed up, Admiral Onishi was not impressed by what he saw. Most of the new pilots were pretty inexperienced and unskilled. They could never stand up to the well-trained Americans and their powerful new fighters in any kind of normal air-to-air combat. Onishi had to come up with a new plan that might stop the onslaught,[185] and what he came up with was almost uniquely Japanese. It probably would never have been seriously considered in any other country, being brilliant but verging on the diabolical.

While there had been sporadic suicide attacks on US ships before, Onishi decided to formally set up and train entire units of pilots who had volunteered to make suicide attacks, most particularly on aircraft carriers. The concept was positively fiendish, but by 1945 it was seen by the Onishi and other influential Japanese as the only kind of tactic, short of abject surrender, that might save their homeland from destruction. Onishi's squadrons mounted thousands of suicide attacks during 1944 and 1945.

In most wars a few combatants sometimes charge the enemy under circumstances that will very likely get them killed. Here the attacks were of an entirely different nature. They were consciously suicidal and organized on a massive scale that had never been seen before – at least in modern times. Onishi formed his first official *kamikaze* or 'Special Attack Unit' during the American invasion of the Philippines. The term *kamikaze* means Divine Wind and it refers to two different typhoons that appeared at the last moment and destroyed two different Mongol fleets that were sent by Kublai Khan to invade Japan. The Mongols had already conquered China and it seemed certain that they would soon overrun Japan. However, after their second invasion fleet was destroyed by a typhoon, the Mongols never attacked Japan again. This apparently really did happen twice during the thirteenth century. Admiral Onishi hoped that his suicide pilots would do the same thing to the Americans that the original *kamikaze* winds had done to Kublai Khan's ships.

The typical *kamikaze* plane was just a normal fighter or bomber stuffed with a big load of explosives. The suicide pilots would dive at the most important American vessel that they could reach, so the *kamikazes* almost always tried to hit an American aircraft carrier. The Japanese also built aircraft specifically designed for the *kamikazes*. The rocket-powered Ohka (Cherry Blossom) or Baka bomb is the most well-known example of these craft.[186] Jimmie Thach inspected a Baka bomb shortly after the surrender ceremonies in Tokyo Bay. It looks modern even by today's standards, and was essentially a flying bullet with a human being at the controls. There is a replica of a Baka bomb on display at the Yasukuni Shrine in Tokyo. As Thach would say years later, 'The Japanese had developed a kind of guided missile, long before anyone else had real guided missiles.'[187] Yet this horrific weapon was not guided by a gyroscope, or by radio waves or by a computer. It was guided by human eyes, human hands, and by a flesh and blood human brain.

The typical *kamikaze* pilot seems to have been a deeply patriotic teenager with little real flying experience. So volunteers for the *kamikaze* corps were put through a short, seven-day indoctrination and training course. Since the average *kamikaze* was not a very experienced pilot, the first two days of training were devoted to just learning how to take off. Then there were two days of learning how to fly in formation. The last three days were devoted to practicing attacks on American warships. Admiral Onishi believed that the most successful attacks would be made when two *kamikazes* simultaneously went after the same American ship. One of his suicide pilots would approach a US ship at a low altitude, while the other would dive in from above.

Five of Onishi's pilots made the first *kamikaze* attack on 25 October 1944[188] during the hectic fighting at the Battle of Leyte Gulf. His five suicide planes sank the escort carrier *St Lo* and damaged three other carriers. In other words, the first five *kamikaze* pilots inflicted far more damage on the Americans than 400 Japanese planes did at the lopsided Battle of the Philippine Sea. Onishi's first *kamikazes* had scored a remarkable success. It is hard to be certain now but *kamikaze* attacks apparently sank thirty-four US ships and damaged 368 others. *Kamikazes* killed almost 5,000 US sailors, mostly off Okinawa.

Those first *kamikaze* attacks were made five days before Jimmie Thach became Operations Officer of Task Force 38. Four days later, the carrier *Intrepid* was hit by a *kamikaze*, but it suffered only light damage. *Kamikazes* struck the big fleet carrier *Franklin* and the light carrier *Belleau Wood* the next day. They severely damaged both ships and killed over 900 US sailors. So the new Operations Officer of Task Force 38 clearly had his work cut out for him from the start.

Thach began thinking about ways to solve the very unusual problem of stopping attacks by pilots who actually wanted to get killed. He thought that a multi-layered defense would probably work best. Such an approach would take a tremendous amount of intense training. It would also take all of Task Force 38's technological superiority, but Thach thought that it could be done. The *kamikazes* posed a threat to every American aircraft carrier in the Western Pacific, and it was a threat that had come out of nowhere. Admiral Nimitz later called the *kamikazes* the biggest surprise of the Pacific War. This was an extreme emergency as ships and men were being lost at a shocking rate.

Before Thach could put any of his ideas into action, Admiral Halsey issued an order that increased the number of fighters on board the US carriers from fifty-four to an incredible ninety-one. Halsey's bold move made implementing Thach's innovative defensive ideas a lot easier. Thach first initiated an extensive series of multi-carrier training exercises.[189] He jokingly dubbed them 'Moose traps', a name that came from a storyline in the then popular *Li'l Abner* cartoon strip. Moose trap drills were not only intended to train the American pilots who would be defending the carriers against *kamikazes*: Thach also used them as trial and error experiments to help him discover what tactics worked best.

Thach wrote a detailed memos to the captains in all four of the Task Groups. He explained his plan precisely and the purpose of the Moose trap exercises. He harkened back to his days as the second-string quarterback at Annapolis. Thach wrote about how good football coaches have their second string team run plays against their first string. The second string's plays are typically the same plays used by the team's toughest opponents. Good football teams practice the same plays over and over again. They practice relentlessly until their coach thinks that they have perfected a good defense against the opponent. Thach wanted the Task Force to do exactly the same thing in preparing its defenses against the *kamikazes*. Some Hellcat pilots would pretend to be *kamikazes*. They would use the same tactics that Onishi's suicide pilots used. The rest of the Hellcats would 'play defense', while Task Force 38 would practice the same 'plays' over and over again. They would keep on practicing them until Thach thought that they had found the most effective defense. The Moose trap exercises were huge, with planes from twelve or more carriers practicing simultaneously. Hundreds of planes would be aloft maneuvering at the same time. As he had hoped, Thach developed his most successful anti-*kamikaze* defenses while observing and analyzing the Moose trap experiments.

One of his new tactics called for the 'delousing' American planes returning to Task Force 38 after attacking Japanese targets.[190] Thach came up with this idea early on when the Task Force was attacking Japanese targets in the Philippines. It worked this way. The Americans had discovered that *kamikazes* would often try to locate their aircraft carriers by trailing US planes returning from strike missions. Thach's remedy for this was to station picket destroyers between the American carriers and the targets being attacked. A fighter director would be stationed aboard each picket destroyer. The fighter director on the destroyer would control his own group of eight Hellcat fighters orbiting overhead. American pilots returning from a strike mission were instructed to fly over a picket destroyer. Then they would then make a sharp turn or sometimes circle the vessel. This gave the Hellcat pilots orbiting overhead an excellent chance of seeing and shooting down any *kamikaze* trailing the American strike planes.

Thach's most well-known tactic for defeating the *kamikazes* was the 'three-strike-system'. It was also called the 'Big Blue Blanket'.[191] The goal here was not to shoot down *kamikazes*, but to keep them from ever getting off the ground in the first place. The three-strike-system relied in part on the fact that the Hellcat had a much longer range than the Wildcat. The system was a way of synchronizing US airstrikes so that at least some Hellcats would be circling over the enemy airfields thought to be holding *kamikazes* for as much of the day as possible.

Hopefully, any *kamikaze* pilot trying to take off with a pair of Hellcats overhead would have his plane shot to pieces while he was still taxiing down the runway.

Prior to adopting Thach's system, Navy carriers would typically launch half of their planes in a first strike. When the first strike planes were almost back home, the carriers would then launch the rest of their planes. This system clearly gave an enemy a certain amount of time between strikes to repair damaged runways and mount counter-strikes. With eighty Japanese-held airstrips scattered around the Philippines, Thach had no chance of stopping 100 per cent of the suicide attacks. He hoped to keep enough *kamikazes* grounded that the picket destroyers and the combat air patrols defending the American carriers could handle the rest.

The three-strike system worked this way. At first light all of the Task Force carriers would launch two-thirds of their planes. Over a thousand aircraft would attack multiple targets on the first strike. Many Hellcats were now being used as fighter-bombers and about half of them would be carrying 500lb bombs. The fighter-bombers would plaster the target and immediately return to the carriers. The remaining Hellcats would have used up less fuel because they carried no bombs. These planes would orbit the enemy airfield and machine gun anything that moved. When the Hellcats orbiting the target ran low on fuel, another strike group would just be reaching the target. The Americans kept up their non-stop attacks all through the day. Under Thach's system the carriers were either launching or recovering planes all the time.[192]

The three-strike-system put a tremendous amount of pressure on the pilots, on their planes, and on the deck crews, but it worked. The ability of the Japanese to get *kamikazes* or any other planes into the air deteriorated rapidly. On 3 January Task Force 38 attacked Formosa (now, Taiwan). The Americans destroyed 204 planes on the ground, with only twenty-seven getting airborne. The next day they caught eighty-two planes on the ground, and Hellcats shot down the only three that were able to get into the air. Task Force 38 returned to the Philippines on 6 January for two days of strikes. The US pilots destroyed 106 planes on the ground. Again, only three Japanese pilots were able to take off and no enemy planes came within miles of Task Force 38's carriers.

The Americans again changed the name of what was still the same fleet. When Mitscher commanded, the fleet was called the First Fast Carrier Task Force. When McCain was in charge it became the Second Fast Carrier Task Force. Admiral Mitscher never fully adopted Thach's three-strike-system, although his Operations Officer, fighter ace Jimmy Flatley, recommended that he do so. Mitscher relied more on heavy airstrikes against enemy airfields and on relentless gunnery training. Mitscher did adopt the innovative use of picket destroyers.

The greatest advantage that the Fast Carriers enjoyed over land-based aviation was their fantastic mobility. The Japanese could only guess where the next American carrier airstrike would come from. They had to conduct long tedious searches to try to locate the carriers and strike back. McCain and Thach were fortunate in the assignments that they received. They made full use of their great mobility advantage and they could easily attack from any direction they wanted. They launched massive airstrikes against enemy targets in the Philippines, on Formosa and, eventually, on the Japanese homeland itself. Admiral Mitscher was not always so lucky. Mitscher commanded the Fast Carriers during the invasion of Okinawa, where they were ordered to stay near the landing beaches to protect the troops. Mitscher lost the enormous advantage that mobility gave to the Americans. The great majority of the 5,000 American sailors killed by *kamikazes* died at Okinawa, many from terrible burns. The men's bodies were placed inside canvas shrouds and buried at sea. That terrible April, *kamikazes* sank twenty-four American ships. Mitscher's own flagship, *Bunker Hill*, was hit by two *kamikazes* and 346 men including half of Mitscher's staff were killed. The damage was so severe that Mitscher had to transfer to *Enterprise*. On 27 May 1945, McCain relieved Admiral Mitscher for the last time. Japanese resistance on Okinawa had already ended. The Fast Carriers were now turned loose to wreak havoc on the home islands of Japan itself.

Chapter 10

The End Game

On 10 July 1945 more than 800 planes from the Fast Carriers struck the Tokyo area hard. Very few Japanese pilots got airborne that day, but those that did were pretty skilled. They seemed to be much better pilots than the ones that the Americans had encountered in the Philippines. The Japanese had apparently reserved some of their more experienced pilots for the final defense of the homeland. Still, there were only a handful of them, and they were up against hundreds and hundreds of Hellcats and Avengers. The Americans actually faced very little effective aerial opposition.

The Fast Carriers were mobile again. They were on the offensive again. Giant B-29 bombers were also conducting great fire-bombing raids against Japanese cities, which were primarily constructed of wood. In one horrific fire raid, several square miles of central Tokyo burned to the ground and 80,000 Japanese civilians were killed. This was total war. The Americans attacked everywhere.

The US was preparing for Operation Olympic, the invasion of the southern Japanese island of Kyushu. The Japanese were planning to use three thousand *kamikazes* to stop the Olympic landings. The Japanese Army still had 3 million armed troops stationed in the homeland. Old men, women, and children all over Japan were preparing stoically to fight to the death. The US Army was ready to bring in millions of veteran troops from Europe, and the Russians were about to declare war on Japan. The world was on the verge of one of the greatest bloodbaths of all time. The type and nature of the Fast Carriers' most important targets had changed. The Japanese Navy had basically ceased to exist, so there was no point in hitting traditional targets like shipyards and Navy bases. The primary target was now Japanese aviation, particularly concentrations of *kamikazes*. A secondary, but important target was the Japanese transportation system.

Thach planned to 'throw' strikes into the northern island of Hokkaido. The Japanese were apparently gathering large numbers of rocket-powered *Baka* suicide planes there. Thach learned after the war that many of the *Baka* weapons that the Americans destroyed were slated to be used in a mass suicide attack on US bomber bases in the Mariana Islands. Planes from the Fast Carriers shot up railroad trains and sank ferries shuttling troops and supplies to southern Japan.

With the war in Europe over, a fleet of British aircraft carriers joined the Americans. These had armored decks, so they were far less vulnerable to *kamikaze* attacks than US ones. During the last two months of the war, the Fast Carriers paraded boldly up and down the coast of Japan. The Americans would 'throw' a thousand-plane strike whenever a lucrative target presented itself. The *kamikazes* badly damaged several picket destroyers, but they never hit another US carrier.[193] The 'three-strike system' worked like a charm. Jimmy Thach was awarded the Legion of Merit for developing it. That August Admiral Halsey was informed of the coming atomic attacks on southern Japan. Halsey apparently told McCain. The Fast Carriers moved north.

After the bombings of Hiroshima and Nagasaki, the Japanese government signaled its willingness to surrender. Admiral Halsey issued a ceasefire order to the entire Third Fleet on 15 August. The three-strike system was shut down. US aircraft orbiting over Japanese airfields were recalled. Then radar detected about a dozen incoming *kamikazes* heading for the Fast Carriers. Admiral McCain queried Halsey for instructions. Jimmie Thach could quote Halsey's classic response over thirty years later: 'There's always someone who doesn't get the word soon enough.' Then McCain asked Halsey whether they should shoot the *kamikazes* down. Halsey replied, 'Yes, but shoot them down in a friendly fashion!'[194]

Thach totaled up Task Force 38's 'score' for the period between 1 July and 15 August 1945. The Fast Carriers had destroyed 2,423 enemy aircraft in just forty-five days. Imperial Japan formally surrendered on 2 September 1945.

The Surrender

Captain Mitsuo Fuchida was the man who led the surprise attack on Pearl Harbor. In 1941, he was about as hard core a Japanese nationalist as you could find. Surprisingly, he was also deeply involved in arranging the Japanese side of the surrender ceremonies in Tokyo Bay. After the success of the attack on Pearl Harbor, Fuchida, like Admiral Yamamoto, became a renowned national hero. The Japanese public simply adored him. He was rewarded with a rare personal audience with Emperor Hirohito himself. Fuchida was also one of the luckiest men to ever serve in the Japanese or any other navy. He had been selected to lead the first air strike on Midway, but he developed an acute case of appendicitis and had to be operated on en route. Lieutenant Joichi Tomonaga replaced him. So Tomonaga, instead of Fuchida, ended up dying under Jimmie Thach's guns. Fuchida was badly wounded during the American dive-bombing attack that wrecked *Akagi*. He barely survived and spent the rest of the war as a revered national hero and an influential staff officer. Fuchida was in Hiroshima for staff meetings *the day before* the atomic attack.[195] Then he returned to Tokyo. All the officers that Fuchida had been meeting with were killed by the atomic bomb the next day.

As mentioned, Fuchida was as diehard a samurai warrior as you could find. He was so hard core that he sported a Hitler-style brush mustache. Other Imperial Navy pilots called him 'Hitler' behind his back. A thousand Japanese officers are said to have committed suicide on the day that Japan surrendered. Fuchida would certainly have been one of them, but he became convinced that the Emperor wanted the military to surrender. Indeed, Hirohito really did want to cooperate with the Americans. Otherwise, the Emperor of Japan would surely have been tried by the Allies and probably hanged as a war criminal. Fuchida obeyed at once, as always. He did everything that he could to comply with Hirohito's wishes. The rest of the Japanese army and navy did the same. Like Fuchida, they caused the Americans no problems and behaved extremely well. They did just what Emperor Hirohito wanted them to do.

A former American POW converted Fuchida to Christianity after the war. Fuchida was astounded by the idea that one should love one's enemies. He had never heard anything like that before. He had always been taught that an honorable Japanese man should hate his enemies. Astonishingly, the pilot who led the attack on Pearl Harbor became an evangelical minister.[196] He even preached at one of the Reverend Billy Graham's televised crusades.

The formal surrender ceremonies took place in Tokyo Bay aboard the battleship *Missouri*, Admiral William Halsey's flagship. One of Fuchida's duties had been to find an expert harbor pilot to guide *Missouri* and other US ships in because Tokyo Bay was crammed full of mines. General Douglas MacArthur, the Supreme Allied Commander, presided over the surrender ceremonies. Admiral Halsey specifically asked McCain to make sure that Jimmie Thach was one of the officers present at the ceremony. Thach was not a big fan of General MacArthur. Nevertheless, Thach greatly admired the way that MacArthur's old-fashioned, optimistic speech completely won over the Japanese that day:

> We are gathered here, representatives of the major warring powers, to conclude a solemn agreement whereby peace may be restored. The issues, involving divergent ideals and ideologies, have been determined on the battlefields of the world and hence are not for our discussion or debate. Nor is it for us here to

> meet, representing as we do a majority of the peoples of the earth, in a spirit of distrust, malice, or hatred. But rather it is for us, both victors and vanquished, to rise to that higher dignity which alone befits the sacred purposes we are about to serve, committing all of our peoples unreservedly to faithful compliance with the undertakings they are here formally to assume. It is my earnest hope and indeed the hope of all mankind that from this solemn occasion a better world shall emerge out of the blood and carnage of the past – a world founded upon faith and understanding – a world dedicated to the dignity of man and the fulfillment of his most cherished wish – for freedom, tolerance and justice.

After all the parties had signed the surrender document MacArthur quickly ended the ceremony: 'Let us pray that peace be now restored to the world, and that God will preserve it always. These proceedings are closed.'[197]

Next a huge formation of 450 US Navy carrier planes and hundreds of giant B-29 bombers roared over Tokyo. Nobody who heard the roar of those planes ever forgot it. Later that day Thach inspected some suicide *Baka* bombs that the Japanese had hidden in caves near Yokosuka and was impressed by their advanced design. He also found a picture taken during the attack on Pearl Harbor. Someone had torn it to shreds.

***

Three days later Jimmie Thach and Admiral McCain were flying back home to San Diego. Admiral McCain was slated to become Deputy Director of the Veterans Administration. Thach had orders for Pensacola, where he became the head of flight training. Both men had been given fifteen-day leaves. One afternoon McCain invited Thach and Maddie to visit him at his home in Coronado. After Thach and Maddie left, Admiral McCain had a heart attack and died.[198] Worn out by the fierce pressure of commanding the Fast Carriers, McCain had given his life for his country just as surely as if he had been killed by a *kamikaze*. Feeling like he had just lost a second father, Thach accompanied McCain's body back to Washington for burial at Arlington National Cemetery. Thach and Maddie had two more children, John and William. In June 1950, Thach took command of the small anti-submarine carrier USS *Sicily*. It was based in what was now his, as well as Maddie's home town, San Diego.

The huge Fast Carrier Task Force that had destroyed the Japanese Navy just five years earlier had been decommissioned and broken up. Scandalously, the US Navy had only one big carrier operating west of the Hawaiian Islands. That same June, communist North Korean troops invaded the Republic of Korea. They took the South Koreans and the small US contingent present by complete surprise. Supplied with large numbers of first-class Russian tanks, the communist forces overwhelmed the South Korean Army, and took Seoul, the capital. The communists pushed what was left of the South Korean armed forces and the US contingent into a small, defensive perimeter around the port of Pusan, at the very southern tip of the Korean peninsula.

Thach immediately sailed west, even though *Sicily* only carried anti-submarine planes. He quickly offloaded his anti-sub aircraft at Guam and picked up a Marine Corsair squadron in Japan. The Marine unit was the old 'Black Sheep' squadron that had earned a terrific reputation at Guadalcanal. Some of its pilots still had combat experience. A Marine brigade landed at Pusan and reinforced the besieged Americans and South Koreans. By early August the Black Sheep squadron was relentlessly pounding away at the North Korean troops. Against all expectations, the Pusan perimeter held. In September, the Black Sheep squadron was again hitting the North Koreans, this time near Inchon, where General MacArthur's surprise amphibious assault led to the recapture of Seoul. An incredible 3 million Korean civilians were killed during the war. After huge numbers of Chinese troops entered the war, Thach's pilots supported the First Marine Division during its epic winter break out from encirclement at the Chosin Reservoir.

A year after arriving in Korea, Thach was ordered to take *Sicily* back to regular anti-submarine duty. In 1955 Thach was promoted to Rear Admiral and became Deputy Chief of Staff for Air, the Navy's top aviation post, where he shepherded the development of the successful A-7 Corsair II light carrier bomber. In the 1960s Thach had several serious run-ins with then Secretary of Defense Robert S. McNamara. He adamantly opposed McNamara's attempts to procure a single variable-geometry plane to serve as a bomber for the Air Force and as a fighter for the Navy. McNamara's efforts ended up in an epic boondoggle called the TFX program. The Air Force bought about 500 of the planes, while the Navy deemed the type unfit for service aboard carriers. Instead, the Navy developed the F-14 Tomcat. The Air Force version of the TFX became the F-111, which was retired from service in the 1990s. It was not a terribly successful airplane. McNamara apparently had Thach 'kicked upstairs' to get him out of his hair and out of Washington DC. Thach was promoted to four-star rank. He was stationed in London, where he served as the Commander in Chief of US Navy forces in Europe during the 1960s, retiring in 1967. Thach died on 15 April 1981.

The Navy named the Oliver Hazard Perry-class guided missile frigate *Thach* (FFG-43) in his honor. He and Maddie are buried at Fort Rosecrans National Cemetery on Point Loma overlooking San Diego Bay. The spot is about 3 miles from the place where Jimmie Thach first met a very talented rookie fighter pilot named Butch O'Hare.

Appendices

The following two appendices are official squadron reports written right after the Battle of Midway. The first is Jimmie Thach's Combat Report, part of which ended up as an enclosure in *Hornet*'s Action Report even though his squadron as a unit was never aboard that carrier. This probably happened because Admiral Spruance ordered to Thach to fly to *Hornet* and reorganize her fighter squadron after *Yorktown* was sunk. This is almost certainly the reason that Fighting Squadron Three's important accomplishments at Midway have received such little recognition by historians. A complete copy of Thach's report was located for me by the wonderful volunteer staff at the Buehler Library of the National Naval Aviation Museum in Pensacola.

The second appendix is the action report written by Dick Best, who led a squadron of dive bombers from *Enterprise* (Bombing Six). Best probably did more damage to the *Kido Butai* than any other American pilot at Midway. Best and two of his pilots destroyed one Japanese carrier by themselves, probably the flagship, *Akagi*. Best also scored a direct hit on *Hiryu*. She was the last Japanese carrier wrecked by the Americans at Midway. For those unfamiliar with World War Two Navy lingo, VF is shorthand for a fighter plane or a fighter squadron; VB means dive bomber, and a VT is a torpedo plane. A CV is an aircraft carrier. 'BB means battleship, and a DD is a destroyer.

Appendix 1

Lieutenant Commander John Thach's 'Combat Report' on the Battle of Midway

June 12, 1942
From: Commander Fighting Squadron Three
To: Commanding Officer, USS. Yorktown
Subject: The Battle of Midway – Combat Report

1. NARRATIVE OF EVENTS – FIGHTING SQUADRON THREE: (a) At 1105, a division of six (6) F4F-4 airplanes led by LtCdr Thach, departed from the USS. YORKTOWN as escort for VT-3 in an attack on enemy carriers reported bearing 233 T., distance 141 miles. Prior to take-off, the leader was informed that the enemy carrier had changed course to 270 T., but that this change of course should be used with caution, as it was probably for the purpose of launching planes, and not a change in base course. VT-3 had departed fifteen minutes earlier, but the visibility was excellent, both above and below the broken clouds and they were joined by the fighters at 1130. At 1200, VT-3, flying just below the clouds changed course to 245 T. At 1210, three enemy carriers in formation about four miles apart, supported by heavy cruisers and destroyers were sighted heading south-east. Four VF took a position up-sun about 6,000 feet from VT-3, who were at this time flying at about 2,000 feet altitude just above large, scattered clouds. The remaining two VF were closer over the VT squadron. At 1220 two bursts of A.A., near our VF, directed a squadron of about twenty (20) type Zero fighters toward us. They were coming from above and immediately attacked the VF escort. VT-3 dropped into a cloud and

disappeared from view, headed toward the port bow of the leading enemy carrier. I saw three torpedo hits on the leading carrier and one or two torpedo hits on the second carrier. Several bomb hits and near misses were seen on the ships of the inner screen, but were not able to see any of the VT planes retiring. Each time an attempt was made to straighten out and look for VT planes, the Zero fighters would be able to press home an attack from astern and one of the F4F-4s would be heavily hit and fall out of the fight. One was seen going straight down, leaving a smoke trail. Soon there were only three F4F-4s remaining in this aerial battle, but we continued to fight as a team, shooting Japs off of each other's tail, and taking 'pot' shots at them as they recovered from an attack. Cloud cover was available below, but was not taken due, partially to the desire to stick together for mutual support, and in order to join the retirement and rendezvous of the VT. However, no VT could be located, and it is doubtful if we could have assisted them in any event, due to the continual attacks made upon us by the enemy fighters. Many Zero fighters were kept engaged throughout the torpedo and dive-bombing attacks. Later, as the fight continued, it appeared that our tactics were beginning to be successful – purely as a defensive measure, however. There were so many Japanese fighters always above us that they had to circle around and await their turn to come in for an attack. Most of them used the same form of attack. They would attempt to approach from above-rear at high speed, shoot and recover by climbing vertically until they were out of reach. As each attacker approached, a turn was commenced and when the enemy came within gun-range, the turn was increased sharply by each plane in the formation. This appeared to keep the Japs bullets astern of the cockpit and if the Jap flew on past after shooting (as they usually did), the leader could, by reversing his turn, get a shot at the enemy head-on, or as he was climbing in his recovery. The performance of the Zero fighter is so far superior to our own that the Japanese pilots did not bother to drop their 100-gallon belly tanks while dogfighting. These tanks were heavy, as evidenced by the large quantities of gasoline streaming out when they were hit. At about 1240, there were only two Japanese VF remaining in the vicinity, the others having been shot down or returned to their burning carriers. These two had no more inclination to fight. When we departed at about 1245, three (3) enemy carriers were burning. The leading carrier was afire from stem to stern, and was shooting bright red and pink flames higher than the length of the ship. The second carrier was flaming and the third was covered with a large column of smoke, but no flame could be seen. Apparently, these six fighters were the only VF to make contact with enemy fighters during the combined and near simultaneous attack of the three carrier air groups from the *Yorktown*, *Hornet* and *Enterprise.* The enemy carriers were apparently untouched when this group arrived and it is believed the three VF were the last of the carrier attack group to leave the vicinity of the enemy carriers.

Three of the pilots of the VF escort are not available to make reports. Based on reports of the other three pilots, five, and probably six, Zero fighters were shot down and an additional four damaged.

The loyalty, teamwork and courage displayed by the pilots supporting the leader of this division of fighters who fought continuously for a period of twenty minutes over the enemy fleet against a force overwhelmingly superior in numbers and aircraft performance, was nothing short of magnificent.

(b) At about 1345, two six plane divisions led by Lt. (jg) R.G. Crommelin and Lt. (jg) A.J. Brassfield were launched and vectored out on course 250 T. At about 1405, contact was made with an enemy formation of eighteen (18) dive-bombers protected by many Zero fighters. The exact number of fighters has not been definitely established, although the Japanese usually provide a fighter escort of 16 to 20 VF with their attack groups. The enemy dive-bombers and fighters were immediately attacked. This enemy dive-bombing attack was disrupted and practically broken up. It is believed that only four and possibly five dive-bombers were able to release their bombs at the target. Many of the enemy jettisoned their bombs and attempted to fight back. Each time our VF attacked the enemy VB, they in turn were exposed to attack by the escorting Zero fighters. The results indicate, however, that our VF pilots concentrated on the dive-bombers. In this engagement, ten (10) dive-bombers were shot down and seven (7) additional damaged or shot down. Two Zero fighters were shot down and three (3) additional VF damaged or shot down. The pilots who survived this engagement were landed on the Enterprise and Hornet.

(c) At about 1630, the Yorktown having gotten underway again and able to make 15 knots, launched two divisions of four (4) VF each led by LtCdr. J.S. Thach and Lt. (jg) W.N. Leonard. An enemy torpedo plane attack developed during this take-off. The enemy VT was in A.A. range and the carrier was firing when the last few VF rolled down the deck. These pilots had only time to turn off the bow and fire at the enemy planes through a heavy barrage of our own anti-aircraft fire. Several of our VF were hit by A.A. fire from vessels of the screen and two of them were possibly shot down by A.A. This VF patrol could not be gassed before take-off and some of the planes had as little as 30 gallons of gasoline. The Yorktown, having been stopped since the previous bombing attack, had no combat air patrol in the air at the time the attack developed. Evidently, the combat air patrol from the other ships made no contact with the enemy VT at any time. The known results of the attack on enemy planes, made by the eight VF of this squadron who were launched as the attack was coming in, are as follows: Six (6) enemy VT, shot down and two VT damaged or probably shot down. Two (2) enemy VF shot down and two additional VF damaged or shot down.

2. STATISTICS:

(a) Enemy Losses.

Combat reports have not been received from eight (8) pilots. The following is based on reports from the remaining pilots of this squadron.

Enemy planes SHOT DOWN: VF – 9
(verified)
VB – 10
VT –6
TOTAL – 25

(b) Own Losses.
Five (5) pilots are missing in action. One (1) pilot was wounded in action. Five (5) pilots left on Yorktown (assume are now in ships of T.F. 17). Six (6) planes were lost due to enemy action. One (1) plane, on Yorktown, will have to be stricken due to crash on deck. One (1) plane, on Enterprise, needs minor repair. One (1) plane, on Enterprise, needs major repair. Four (4) planes, left on Yorktown, require major repair due to enemy action. Fourteen (14) planes now operating.

3. LESSONS LEARNED:
(a) Pilots in action against Japanese VF must stick together and fight as a team or else they will not survive.

(b) The Japanese fighter pilots usually attack from above rear at high speed and recover by climbing vertically until they have lost some speed and then pull on through to complete a small loop or high wing-over which places them out of reach and in position to attack again. By reversing the turn sharply after each attack the leader may get a shot at the enemy while he is climbing away or head on in a scissors if the Jap turns to meet it.

(c) Two hundred and forty (240) rounds of ammunition per gun is not enough. We should have 500 but would be satisfied with 400. In the F4F-4 airplane it would be better to reduce the number of guns to four in order to increase the amount of rounds carried per gun.

(d) Any success our fighter pilots may have against the Japanese Zero fighter is not due to the performance of the airplane we fly but is the result of the comparatively poor marksmanship of the Japanese, stupid mistakes made by some of their pilots and superior team work of some of our pilots. The only way we can ever bring our guns to bear on the Zero fighter is to trick them into recovering in front of an F4F or shoot them when they are preoccupied in firing at one of our own planes. The F4F airplane is pitifully inferior in climb, maneuverability and speed. The writer has flown the F4F aircraft without armor and leak proof tanks. Removal of their vital protection does not increase performance of the F4F sufficiently to come anywhere near the performance of the Zero fighter. This serious deficiency not only prevents our fighters from carrying out an assigned mission but it has had a definite and alarming effect on the morale of most of our carrier based VF pilots. If we expect to keep our carriers afloat we must provide a VF airplane superior to the Japanese Zero in at least climb and speed, if not maneuverability.

(e) VF pilots must be expert with their fixed guns. They have such a short time to do their work that they cannot afford to make a run on an enemy plane and miss. Opportunity must be afforded VF squadrons to practice on a target sleeve both ashore and at sea. They should not be required to stand alerts when temporarily based ashore but should use all of their time perfecting VF tactics, team-work and practice on a sleeve.

(f) Fighter directing in general was far from satisfactory. Many interceptions were missed. If one fighter director is to control aircraft from two or more carriers the facilities aboard ship must be reorganized and expanded to fit the needs. Above all each carrier should actually practice interceptions at sea. The maintenance of radio silence while in the vicinity of a Fleet Base is certainly of less importance. We must be able to send fighters out in sufficient numbers to meet enemy attack groups at least forty miles away. A pilot cannot navigate on the way out to an interception. He must be required to fly a compass course only.

(g) The pilots of VF-42 who participated in the Coral Sea engagement and the Battle of Midway have undergone a long and strenuous period of war operations at sea without rest or relaxation. It became necessary to ground some of these pilots before return to port. They are all without exception suffering from combat fatigue which a few days rest will not cure. It is recommended that they be returned to the United States for a period of leave and then be used at advanced training centers or to fit out a new carrier group.

J. S. THACH

Appendix 2

Lieutenant Commander Richard H. 'Dick' Best's Action Report for Bombing Squadron Six

Action Report of Bombing Squadron Six

FVB-6/A16/nhn

Bombing Squadron Six,
June 10, 1942

CONFIDENTIAL

From:	Commander Bombing Squadron Six.
To:	Commanding Officer, USS. ENTERPRISE.
Via:	Commander ENTERPRISE Air Group.
Subject:	Report of Action, June 4–6, 1942.
Reference:	(a) US Navy Regulations, Art. 874, para. 6.
Enclosure:	(A) Bombing Squadron Six Tactical Organization of June 1, 1942.

Bombing Squadron Six participated in four separate attacks against Japanese naval forces during the period June 4 to June 6, 1942, and in one photographic flight over Japanese naval forces on June 6, 1942. On June 4, 1942, the squadron consisted of twenty-one pilots, eleven of whom had been in the squadron for more than nine months, three others since December 1941, and seven for about two months. There were eighteen SBD-2 and SBD-3 planes assigned and all were in commission. Action was expected. Following is a chronological account of the part Bombing Squadron Six played in the actions.

Thursday, forenoon and afternoon.

On Thursday, June 4, 1942, Bombing Squadron Six participated in an attack on a Japanese force consisting of four aircraft carriers, several battleships or heavy cruisers, and a number of destroyers, about 150 miles northwest of Midway Island. The attack group was led by the Enterprise Air Group Commander and consisted of thirty-two SBDs; fifteen from VB-6, loaded with one 1,000 lb bomb each, sixteen from VS-6, loaded with one 500 lb bomb and two 100 lb bombs each, and the EAGC plane loaded with one 500 lb bomb and two 100 lb bombs. The squadron tactical organization was as follows:

First Division

6-B-1	Lt. R.H. Best	MURRAY, J.F., ACRM(PA)
6-B-2	Lt(jg) E.J. Kroeger	HALTERMAN, G.W.,RM3c
6-B-3	Ensign F.T. Weber	HILBERT, E.L.,AOM3c
6-B-5	Lt(jg) W.E. Roberts	STEINMAN, W.B.,AMM1c
6-B-6	Ensign D.W. Halsey	JENKINS, J.W.,RM3c

Second Division

6-B-7	Lt. J.R. Penland	HEARD, H.F.,ARM2c
6-B-8	Ensign T.F. Schneider	HOLDEN, G.L.,ARM2c
6-B-9	Ensign E.A. Greene	MUNTEAN, S.A.,RM3c
6-B-11	Ensign T.W. Ramsay	DUNCAN, S.L., ARM2c
6-B-12	Ensign L.A. Hopkins	ANDERSON, E.R., RM3c

Third Division

6-B-13	Lt(jg) J.J. Van Buren	NELSON, H.W.,JR., ARM1c
6-B-14	Ensign N.F. Vandivier	KEANEY, L.E.J., Sea1c
6-B-15	Ensign G.H. Goldsmith	PATTERSON, J.W.,JR., ARM3c
6-B-16	Lt(jg) E.L. Anderson	MASON, S.J.,JR., ARM2c
6-B-18	Ensign B.S. Varian, jr.	YOUNG C.R., ARM3c

The attack group departed at 0930 and climbed to 20,000 ft. enroute to the objective. Shortly before reaching the objective several VB-6 pilots encountered difficulties with oxygen supply. The Squadron Commander noted the oxygen difficulties of his wing men. He removed his oxygen mask so that he would have the same reaction as other pilots and led the squadron to a position directly below the remainder of the attack force at an altitude of 15,000 ft.

At about 1205, the enemy fleet was sighted and was seen to consist of 4 CV, 4 BB or CA and 8 to 10 DD. The weather was clear and visibility excellent. There were scattered cumulus clouds from 1,500 ft. to 2,500 ft. and the ceiling was unlimited. The surface wind was 5 to 8 knots from the south-east. It was known that other attack groups including three squadrons of SBDs, three squadrons of TBDs and accompanying fighters were due to arrive at the same objective at about the same time as the group of which Bombing Squadron Six was a part. The Enterprise Air Group Commander designated by voice radio one CV target for himself and VS-6 and another CV target for VB-6. Commander Bombing Squadron Six understood his target to be the 'left hand' CV. He gave the attack signal, releasing his other two division leaders for individual division maneuvering and led his (first) division towards the 'left hand' CV. Almost at once he saw that VS-6 was diving on the 'left hand' CV and so led his division against the 'right hand' CV which was of the 'KAGA' type. It was launching planes as the attack was made. At least three 1,000 lb bomb hits were observed on that target and it became a mass of flame and smoke. The first section of the first division joined up immediately after pull-out from the dive. At that time they sighted own torpedo planes coming in under heavy attack from enemy fighters and AA fire. They also saw an attack by own dive bombers of a separate attack group on a third CV on which many hits were scored, the CV becoming enveloped in flames and smoke.

Shortly thereafter the first section was attacked by an enemy seaplane which was driven off by free gun fire. The first section then retired towards Midway for a short time, and when out of sight of the enemy fleet set course for parent ship and returned.

The second division leader delayed attack momentarily. He observed misses near the 'left hand' CV, and decided to dive on that target. While in his dive he observed several hits on that target, starting fires. He scored a direct hit in the middle of the carrier with his 1,000 lb bomb, and other 1,000 lb bomb hits were scored by planes following him. That CV appeared to suffer internal explosions in addition to bomb hits, and little of it was left visible in the midst of huge flames, and smoke. The third division apparently attacked the same target as did the second division. Only one pilot from that division returned.

The first three planes of the first division returned. Personnel of 6-B-5 were rescued, but are not available for compilation of this report. The pilot of 6-B-6 reported by radio that he must make a forced landing near the enemy fleet.

Only 6-B-12 of the second division returned. The division leader was attacked after pull-out from the dive by a 'zero' fighter and all his gasoline tanks badly punctured. He made a forced landing about thirty miles from the enemy fleet and together with his gunner was rescued twenty-eight hours later. The personnel of 6-B-8 were rescued but are not available for compilation of this report. The personnel of 6-B-9 got into their rubber boat after a forced landing about forty miles from own fleet, but there is no report of their having been rescued. The personnel of 6-B-11 got into their rubber boat after a forced landing about ten miles from own fleet, but search by a DD failed to find them.

Only 6-B-16 of the third division returned. 6-B-13 was in company with the second division leader until he was forced to land in the water, but has not been heard from since. 6-B-14 was sighted by another plane shortly after pull-out from the dive, and the later reported by radio that he was landing in the water, The personnel of 6-B-15 were rescued but are not available for compilation in this report. The personnel of 6-B-18 got into their rubber boat after a forced landing about fifty miles northeast of the enemy fleet.

Summarizing, five planes out of fifteen returned; the personnel of four other planes were rescued; the personnel of six planes are unaccounted for. One of the five planes which returned, 6-B-16, was so badly damaged by shrapnel and machine gun fire that it could not be flown on subsequent attacks.

The gunner of 6-B-16, MASON, Stuart James, Jr., 393 29 71, ARM2c, USN, was wounded in the face and in the legs by shrapnel, bullets, and plane fragments during pull-out from the dive and retirement from the enemy fleet. He continually manned his twin mount guns against enemy fighters until clear of them and later repaired the plane's damaged radio enabling the use of ZB in locating parent ship.

No fighter opposition was encountered prior to pull-outs from the dives. Apparently most of the AA fire was concentrated on the torpedo planes which were attacking at the same time. Most planes were attacked by fighters after pull-outs from dives.

The conduct of all pilots and gunners left nothing to be desired. All pilots remained in formation despite the obvious fact that carrying a 1,000 lb bomb for as long as they were carried entailed gasoline consumption that rendered possible return to own ships unlikely and despite oxygen supply difficulties which at least four pilots encountered. Dives were continued to a very low altitude in spite of danger from explosion of bombs dropped ahead of each plane. Hits resulted.

Thursday, afternoon and evening.

On Thursday afternoon and evening, June 4, 1942, Bombing Squadron Six participated in a second attack against Japanese surface ships. Only four of the seven VB-6 planes which remained after the first attack could be launched. Three of the four formed a section led by Commander Bombing Squadron Six; the fourth was assigned to a section of VB-3.

The attack group was led by Commander Scouting Squadron Six, and consisted of planes of VS-6, four planes of VB-6, each loaded with one 1,000 lb bomb, and fourteen planes of VB-3. VB-6 personnel on this flight consisted of:

6-B-1	Lt. R.H. Best	MURRAY, J.F., ACRM(PA)
6-B-2	Lt.(jg) E.J. Kroeger	HALTERMAN, G.W., RM3c
6-B-3	Ensign F.T. Weber	HILBERT, E.L., AOM3c
6-B-12	Ensign S.C. Hogan, jr.	BRAUN, E.K., Sealc

The objective was given as 1 CV, 2 BB, 3CA, and 4 DD at Lat. 31-40N, Long. 172-10 W.

The attack group departed at 1745 and climbed to 13,000 ft. while enroute to the objective. The objective was sighted at about 1845 to the north-west. It was seen to consist of 1 CV, 1 BB, 1 CA or Cl and 3 to 4 DD, the heavy ships separated by several miles and each accompanied by a destroyer. Three additional destroyers were sighted about thirty miles to the south-east, headed for the main enemy formation. Beyond these three destroyers to the south could be seen three large columns of smoke near the scene of the first engagement. The weather was the same as described for the first attack. The attack group climbed to 19,000ft. and circled to a position up-sun from the enemy. The attack was started at about 1905 with a high-speed run-in. At least four 'zero' fighters attacked before the push-over point was reached, and 6-B-3 was shot down. VS-6 dove first with the CV as a target. Misses were observed and Commander Bombing Squadron Six decided to dive on the CV also. The first section of VB-3 dove ahead of VB-6, also on the CV as a target. Two direct hits were observed. Then VB-6 dove scoring one direct hit. The CV was seen to be burning for two-thirds of its length from the stern forward. A direct hit was observed on a BB. Retirement was made at high speed and at low altitude. Advantage was also taken of broken cloud over at 2,000 to 3,000 ft.

Fairly heavy AA fire was encountered during the dive and after pull-out. 'Zero' fighters also attacked after pull-out.

At about 1920, 6-B-2 and 5-B-7, which were in company sighted and attacked a 'Kawanishi 95' seaplane and probably damaged it with fixed gun fire. It jettisoned its bombs and escaped.

At about 1940, Commander Bombing Squadron Six, who had retired initially to the westward, observed the enemy CV still burning, but moving with the fleet. Shortly thereafter he sighted an enemy low wing monoplane seaplane heading for the enemy fleet.

All VB-6 planes except 6-B-3 returned safely.

The pilots and gunners exhibited the same exemplary conduct as shown during the first attack of the day. All of the crews except that of 6-B-12 had flown on the first attack.

Friday, evening.

On Friday, June 5, 1942, the remaining six SBD planes of Bombing Squadron Six participated in an attack against a Japanese CL. The tactical organization consisted of:

6-B-4	Lt. L.A. Smith	CARUTHERS, H.H., AMM2c
6-B-2	Lt.(jg) E.J. Kroeger	HALTERMAN, G.W., RM3c
6-B-12	Ensign L.S. Hopkins	ANDERSON, E.R., RM3c
6-B-10	Lt. H.P. Lanham	GARAUDY, E.J.,ARM1c
6-B-1	Lt.(jg) E.L. Anderson	CHOCHALOUSEK, W.G., ARM1c
6-B-17	Ensign A.L. Rausch	JONES, H.L., AOM3c

The attack group was led by Lieutenant D.W. Shumway, VB-3 and consisted of a total of 32 SBDs from VB-3, VB-5, VB-6, and VS-6. All planes were armed with one 500lb bomb.

The objective was given as 1 CV (damaged), 2 BB, 3 CA and 4 DD which had been last reported at 1000 at Lat.30-00 N, Long.179-32 W, course 310° T., speed 1w knots.

Unusually heavy small calibre AA fire was encountered. Apparently large calibre guns were employed for AA also, using unfused projectiles, because many splashes but no shell bursts were seen.

All VB-6 planes returned safely.

Landing aboard was accomplished after dark. The pilots of 6-B-12 and 6-B-17 made their first night carrier landings. These pilots had had no night field carrier landing instruction. Each had made more than twenty or more day carrier landings.

Saturday, afternoon.

On Saturday, June 6, 1942, the remaining five SBD planes of Bombing Squadron Six participated in an attack against a Japanese force consisting of 1 CA, 1 CL and 2 DD. The tactical organization consisted of:

6-B-1	Lt. L.A. Smith	CARUTHERS, H.H., AMM2c
6-B-16	Lt(jg) E.L. Anderson	CHOCHALOUSEK, W.G., ARM1c
6-B-2	Ensign D.L. Ely	ARNOLD, G.H., Sea2c
6-B-10	Lt. H.P. Lanham	GARAUDY, E.J., ARM1c
6-B-17	Ensign H.W. Liffner	KIMBERLIN, M.L., AMM3c

The attack group was led by Lieut. Short, VS-5, and consisted of 31 SBDs from VB-3, VS-5, VB-6, VS-6; 3 TBDs from VT-6 and 12 F4F-4s from VF-6. All VB-6 planes carried 1,000 lb bombs as did most of the other SBDs.

The objective was given as 2 BB, 2 CA and several DD at Lat.29-33 N, Long.175-35 E, course 270° T., speed 15 Knots.

The attack group departed at 1315. The SBDs proceeded independently and climbed to about 19,000 ft. enroute to the objective. At 1400 1 CA, 1 CL and 2 DD were sighted. The SBDs continued thirty miles beyond this force searching for BBs. No other ships were sighted and a highspeed run-in was made on the force sighted at 1400 and attack delivered on it at about 1415. Most of the SBDs attacked the CA which was completely wrecked. Some individual pilots dove on the CL and at least one hit was observed.

All planes returned safely.

At 1750 a photographic flight was sent out to obtain pictures of damage to enemy ships in the above action. The flight was led by Lt (jg) E.J. Kroeger, A-V(N), USNR, VB-6, and in consisted of 3-B-10 and one SBD from VS-6. The photographer in 3-B-10 was Mr. A.D. Brick of Fox Movietone News.

Notes

1. Lundstrom, J., *The First Team, Pacific Naval Air Combat from Pearl Harbor to Midway* (US Naval Institute Press, 1984), p.356; Gayler, N.A.M., Stillwell, P.L., *Reminiscences of Admiral John Smith Thach* (US Naval Institute, 1977), pp.245–250.
2. Ibid., Lundstrom, pp.358–359.
3. Thach and Walt Disney produced a very clear, straightforward series of animated (cartoon-like) training films that were shown to new fighter pilots. *See*, for example, *Offensive Tactics Against Enemy Fighters.* It is narrated by Jimmie Thach himself. Remarkably, it is still available for viewing on YouTube.
4. Thach, *Reminiscences*, p.251.
5. Prange, G., *Miracle at Midway* (MJF Books, 2009).
6. *Jane's Fighting Aircraft of World War II* (Crescent, 1998), p.188.
7. Combat Report – Fighting Squadron Three, 12 June 1942. *See* Appendix 1. Action Reports – The Battle of Midway – (USS Hornet, Sea, Air and Space Museum, 2020), pp.255–257; *Reminiscences of Admiral John S. Thach* (US Naval Institute Press, 1977), pp.241–250.
8. Some contend that the pilots of the American Volunteer Group in China, the famed 'Flying Tigers', outfought Zeros during Japan's bloody invasion of that country. This may be so, but it seems unlikely. The Flying Tigers were outstanding pilots but they typically were up against the Imperial Army's Oscar. This fighter was built by Nakajima, and was very similar in appearance to Mitsubishi's Zero. *See* below.
9. In retrospect, the Battle of the Coral Sea is now seen as a long-term, strategic victory for the United States because it blunted Japan's advance towards Australia. In 1942, it was seen by the Japanese as a big win for

them because they inflicted more damage on the Americans than they had suffered. *See The Japanese Story of the Battle of Midway* (Office of Naval Intelligence, 1947), p.2. This translation is often referred to as the Nagumo Report.

10. The one exception is John Lundstrom's massively researched account of fighter combat during the early days of the Pacific War. *See* Lundstrom, J., *The First Team, Pacific Naval Air Combat from Pearl Harbor to Midway* (US Naval Institute Press, 1984). Lundstrom interviewed Admiral Thach, and corresponded with three of the four pilots who were with him the day that the Thach Weave was first used in combat.
11. Possibly, this glaring hole in the historical record of the Battle of Midway occurred because Thach's squadron report setting out the number of Japanese planes that Fighting Three shot down appears to have been initially filed as an enclosure to USS *Hornet*'s Action Report on Midway. This happened after Thach's carrier, *Yorktown*, was sunk. So the official, contemporaneous, first-hand account of the critical role that a handful of fighter pilots played in the great victory may have simply been overlooked by researchers for decades. *See Action Reports, The Battle of Midway* (USS Hornet, Sea, Air and Space Museum, 2020), pp.255–257.
12. Ewing, S., *Thach Weave: The Life of Jimmy Thach* (US Naval Institute, 2004).
13. In developing his anti-Kamikaze tactics, Thach literally compared them to successful football plays. *See* Thach, J., *Reminiscences*, p.391.
14. Ewing, S., *Thach Weave*, p.5.
15. Thach, *Reminiscences*, p.29.
16. Ibid., pp.44–46.
17. Ewing, S., *Thach Weave*, pp.7–8.
18. Thach, J., *Reminiscences*, pp.38–39.
19. This 1932 film portrayed Wallace Beery and Clark Gable as a pair of competing chief petty officers in early naval aviation.
20. Ewing, S., *Thach Weave*, pp.17–19.
21. Ibid., pp.19–26.
22. Thach, J., *Reminiscences*, p.79.

23. Ibid., p.87.
24. Ibid., p.79.
25. Ibid., pp.123–124.
26. Ibid., p.139.
27. Ewing, S., and Lundstrom, J., *Fateful Rendezvous, The Life of Butch O'Hare* (Bluejacket Books, 1997), p.59.
28. *Reminiscences of Admiral Noel A. Gayler* (Naval Institute Press, 2012), pp.92–93.
29. Ewing, S., and Lundstrom, J., *Fateful Rendezvous*, p.78.
30. Thach, J., *Reminiscences*, p.141.
31. Ibid., p.142.
32. Peattie, M., *Sunburst, The Rise of Japanese Naval Airpower* (Naval Institute Press, 2001), pp.18–20.
33. Horikoshi, J., *Eagles of Mitsubishi* (University of Washington Press, 1981), pp.4–7.
34. The final variant of the Zero produced by Mitsubishi had a top speed of 340mph and a sizzling climb rate of 3,020ft per minute. *Jane's Fighting Aircraft of World War II*, pp.187–188.
35. *See* Chang, I., *The Rape of Nanking* (Basic Books, 1997).
36. *Jane's*, pp.188, 190.
37. The actual average strength of the AVG was never more than sixty-two combat-ready pilots and fighters.
38. Thach, J., *Reminiscences*, pp.146–156.
39. Samson, J., *The Flying Tiger* (Lyons Press, 1987, 2005), p.76.
40. *See* Reminiscences (Oral History) of Captain Stephen Jurika (US Naval Institute Press, 1979).
41. Gayler, *Reminiscences*, p.85.
42. Horikoshi, J., *Eagles of Mitsubishi*, p.64.
43. Thach, J., *Reminiscences*, p.238.
44. Thach, J., *The Thach Weave is Born*, in Mason, J., ed., *The Pacific War Remembered* (Naval Institute Press, 2003), p.96, and Shaw, R., *Fighter Combat: Tactics and Maneuvering* (Naval Institute Press, 1985), p.211.
45. Sakai, S. *Samurai*, pp.216–217.
46. Ewing, S., Lundstrom J., *Fateful Rendezvous*, p.104.

47. Prange, G., *At Dawn We Slept* (Viking, 1981), p.406.
48. Ibid., pp.500–501.
49. Prange G., *God's Samurai* (Prange Enterprises Inc., 1990), p.35.
50. Prange G., pp.35–36; Fuchida, M., *For That One Day, The Memoirs of Mitsuo Fuchida*, (2011) translated by Shinsato, D., and Urabe, T., p.97.
51. Thach, J., *Reminiscences*, p.173.
52. *Reminiscences of Admiral Noel A. Gayler* (Naval Institute Press, 2012), p.96.
53. Ewing, S., and Lundstrom J., *Thach Weave*, pp.45–46.
54. Raymer, E., *Descent Into Darkness: Pearl Harbor, 1941 A Navy Diver's Memoir* (Naval Institute Press, 1996), pp.11–12.
55. Thach, J., *Oral History*, pp.173–174.
56. Raymer, E., *Descent Into Darkness*, pp.1–8.
57. Ibid., p.4.
58. Thach, J., *Reminiscences*, p.176.
59. Wukovits, J., *Pacific Alamo: The Battle for Wake Island* (New American Library, 2010), p.133.
60. Wukovits, J., *Pacific Alamo*, p.263.
61. Thach, J., *Reminiscences*, pp.178–179.
62. Parshall, J., and Tully, A., *Shattered Sword: The Untold Story of the Battle of Midway* (Potomac Books, 2005), pp.65–66.
63. Ewing, S., *Thach Weave*, p.50.
64. Thach, J., *Reminiscences*, pp.181–182.
65. Ibid., p.183.
66. Ibid., p.186.
67. Ibid., p.187.
68. Thach, J., *Reminiscences*, pp.193–194.
69. Ewing, S. and Lundstrom, J., *Fateful Rendezvous*, pp.129–134.
70. Ibid., p.129.
71. Thach, J., *Reminiscences*, pp.283–284.
72. *Fateful Rendezvous*, p.142.
73. Ibid.
74. Thach, J., *Reminiscences*, pp.202–204.

75. Ibid.
76. Ibid., p.206.
77. *Fateful Rendezvous*, p.150.
78. Ibid., p.154.
79. *Incredible Victory*, p.5.
80. Agawa, H., *The Reluctant Admiral, Yamamoto and the Imperial Navy* (Kodansha, 1979), p.11.
81. Ibid., p.73.
82. Okumiya, M., Horikoshi, J., Caidin M., *Zero* (Bantam, 1997), p.xviii.
83. Agawa, *The Reluctant Admiral*, pp.37–38.
84. Parshall, J. and Tully, A., *Shattered Sword: The Untold Story of the Battle of Midway* (Potomac Books, 2005), pp.65–66.
85. Agawa, *The Reluctant Admiral*, p.300.
86. Doolittle J., *I Could Never Be So Lucky Again* (Bantam, 1991), p.6.
87. Ibid., p.256.
88. Ibid., p.213.
89. Ibid., p.216.
90. Ibid., pp.220–221.
91. Ibid., p.195.
92. Ibid., p.226.
93. Ibid., p.254.
94. Lawson T., *Thirty Seconds Over Tokyo* (Pocket Books, 2002), p.69.
95. Carlson E., *Joe Rochefort's War* (Naval Institute Press, 2011), pp.20–21.
96. Ibid., pp.284–287.
97. Ibid., pp.333–335.
98. Ibid., pp.346–348.
99. Layton, E., *And I Was There* (Konecky & Konecky, 1985), p.434.
100. Ibid., p.468.
101. Carlson, E., *Joe Rochefort's War*, p.457.
102. *Incredible Victory*, p.30.
103. Ibid., p.33.
104. Thach, *Reminiscences*, pp.209–210.
105. Ibid., pp.210–211.
106. Ibid., pp.223–225.

107. *Incredible Victory*, p.59.
108. Ibid., pp.78–79.
109. Ibid., p.94.
110. Rochefort and his team did fail to predict that Yamamoto's 'Main Force' of battleships would be trailing hundreds of miles behind the Japanese carriers. While interesting, this 'failure' had no effect on the outcome of the battle.
111. Thach, *Reminiscences*, p.269.
112. Ibid., p.275.
113 Lord, *Incredible Victory*, p.98.
114. Nagumo Report, p.7.
115. Sixty-Ninth Bomb Squadron Report, Subject B-26 in Battle of Midway, 6 June 1942. pp.6–7.
116. Nagumo Report, p.7.
117. Ibid., p.7.
118. Ibid.
119. *See* L.C. Ramsey, Captain USN, Analysis of Army Attack.
120. Gay G., *Sole Survivor* (Naples Ad/Graphics Services, 1979), p.126.
121. Hornet, Report of Action, 4–6 June 1942, p.2; Enterprise, Report of Battle of Midway 4–6 June 1942, p.2.
122. Lord, W., *Incredible Victory*, p.140.
123. Thach, J., *Reminiscences*, p.254.
124. *Hornet*, Action Report, p.7.
125. Parshall, J., and Tully, A., *Shattered Sword* (Potomac Books, 2005), pp.206, 553 n. 5.
126. Gay, G., *Sole Survivor* (Naples Ads/Graphics Services, 1979), pp.119–126.
127. Ibid., p.126.
128. Enterprise, Report of Action, 13 June 1942, p.4.
129. Yorktown, Report of Action, 4 June 1942 and 6 June 1942, p.1.
130. Thach, J., *Reminiscences*, p.245.
131. Sakai, S., *Samurai!* (Ibooks, 1957), pp.216–217.
132. Thach, J., *Reminiscences*, p.247.
133. Thone, T., (ed.), *The Battle of Midway* (Naval Institute Press, 2013), pp.130, 134.

134. *See* Appendix 2.
135. Lundstrom J., *The First Team*, pp.356–360.
136. Ibid.
137. Ibid., p.359.
138. Thach, J., *Reminiscences.* p.247.
139. Ibid.,,., p.251.
140. Gay, G., *Sole Survivor*, p 131.
141. Ibid., p.253.
142. Lundstrom, J., *The First Team*, p.373.
143. Lord W., *Incredible Victory*, p.193.
144. *See* Appendix 2.
145. Ibid.
146. *See* Appendix 2.
147. Thach, J., *Reminiscences*, pp.266–267.
148. Lord, W., *Incredible Victory*, p.194.
149. *See* USS. Hornet, Report of Action, 4–6 June 1942, p.3.
150. Thach, J., *Reminiscences*, pp.266–267.
151. Ibid., p.275.
152. Ibid.
153. Ibid.
154. Nagumo Report, p.8.
155. Lundstrom, J., *The First Team*, p.393.
156. Thach, J., *Reminiscences*, p.267.
157. Y'Blood, W.T., *Red Sun Setting, The Battle of the Philippine Sea*, pp.128–130.
158. Thach, J., *Reminiscences*, pp.268–269.
159. Ibid., p.269.
160. *Id.*, p.270.
161. Ibid., p.271.
162. Linzey, S., *USS Yorktown at Midway* (Xulon Press, 1978), p.24.
163. Thach, J., *Reminiscences*, p.279.
164. *See* Appendix 2.
165. Ibid.
166. Nimitz, C., *Graybook Log, Vol. 1*, p.573.

167. Linzey, S., *USS Yorktown at Midway*, pp.123–124.
168. Rearden, J., *Cracking The Zero Mystery* (Stackpole Books, 1990), pp.71–74.
169. Ibid., p.76.
170. Admiral James Russell commanded a patrol squadron in the Aleutians when Koga's Zero was recovered. In his Oral History Russell states that Jimmie Thach flew against Koga's Zero when it was shipped to San Diego for flight testing. This story appears to be apocryphal since Thach never mentioned such flights when he was discussing the development of the Thach Weave in his Oral History. *See* Russell, J., Mason, J., ed., *The Pacific War Remembered* (Naval Institute Press, 2003), pp.108–111.
171. Ciminera, M., *The Aircraft Designers: A Grumman Historical Perspective* (American Institute of Aeronautics and Astronautics, 2013), p.23.
172. *Jane's Fighting Aircraft of World War Two* (Crescent Books, 1989), pp.188, 234.
173. Ciminera, M., pp.15–16.
174. Ewing, S., Lundstrom, J., *Fateful Rendezvous*, pp.212–214.
175. Ibid., pp.263–286.
176. *See New York Times*, 1 December 1942, p.2.
177. Thach, J., *Oral History*, pp.286–297.
178. Thach, J., *Reminiscences*, pp.310–311.
179. Ibid., pp.401–405.
180. Ibid., pp.319–320, pp.326–328.
181. Tillman, B., *Carrier Battle in the Philippine Sea* (Phalanx Press, 1994), p.19.
182. Ibid., p.18.
183. Y'Blood, W.T., *Red Sun Setting, The Battle of the Philippine Sea*, pp.128–130.
184. Ibid., p.328.
185. Inoguchi, R. and Nakajima, T., *The Divine Wind* (Bluejacket Books, 1958), pp.6–12.
186. Thach, J., *Reminiscences*, p.459.
187. Ibid., p.389.

188. Inoguchi, R., *The Divine Wind*, pp.57–59.
189. Ibid., pp.391–414.
190. Ibid., pp.392–93.
191. Ibid., pp.401–403.
192. Ibid., pp.404–405.
193. Thach, J., *Reminiscences*, p.396.
194. Ibid., p.476.
195. Prange, G., *God's Samurai* (Potomac Books, 1990), pp.148–149.
196. Ibid., p.241.
197. Naval History and Heritage Command website, www.history.navy.mil
198. Thach, J., *Reminiscences*, p.483.

Index